AWEN

The Quest of the Celtic Mysteries

Mike Harris

SKYLIGHT PRESS

This revised edition first published in Great Britain in 2011 by Skylight Press, 210 Brooklyn Road, Cheltenham, Glos GL51 8EA

Awen was originally published in 1999 by Melchior Press, California, USA.

Designed and typeset by Rebsie Fairholm
Illustrations by Mike Harris
Printed and bound in Great Britain by Lightning Source, Milton Keynes

www.skylightpress.co.uk

ISBN 978-1-908011-36-7

Contents

acknowledgements from first edition

First to the land and the tradition to which I am and will always be indebted. Then to those who have passed into it, who have given me so much ... all those so long ago who later came to be called names like Taliesin and Melangell and Myrddin. Also to those who passed that way in this age, Frederick Bligh Bond, Dion Fortune, Robert Graves and the Inklings. But especially to my mother who taught me how to love this wild place and to look within it to see the spiritual bond which holds humanity, creatures and angels so inevitably together.

I am indebted also to those who trained with, worked with and inspired me down the years, especially Basil Wilby, Wolfe van Brussel, Michael Waldron and Tony Duncan and most especially to Wendy Berg. I would also like to acknowledge the constant encouragement of fellow writer Sharon Le Fevre and the practical help of John Bird who so deftly handled negotiations between me and my computer and of course to Mark, for having the faith to ask me to produce the book in the first place.

Last, but by no means least, to my family – Jeanette, Phil, Kit and Jamie who so patiently kept the faith when I so frequently lost patience!

My love and gratitude to you all.

PREFACE TO REVISED EDITION

Since writing *Awen* in 1996, time has, as it must, changed things. I have lost contact with a few of those acknowledged previously, not least Tony Duncan, Michael Waldron and Sharon LeFevre through their untimely passing into what this book calls *Annwn*.

It's inevitable too that some of my views have changed in these intervening years. Archaeology and academe have made unprecedented assaults upon all things Celtic since I wrote this book, and long held views about Celtic Britain have been drastically revised. This has not affected *Awen* overmuch, because it's a book about magic and mythology rather than history, and the necessary historical revisions have been largely confined to Chapter One. With these revisions my earlier readers and my magical contemporaries assure me that *Awen* still serves as a good introductory first volume to the origins of the Celtic/Arthurian Mysteries. A further work, *Merlin's Chess,* expands the material in reconstructions and practical magical applications and goes into some detail about the practice of Gwyddbwyll, the magical chess game mentioned in the Triads and Mabinogion, and considers the implications of new archaeological findings like the Nebra star disk. *Merlin's Chess* is available from Ritemagic in CD format.

Since 1996 I have lectured and worked extensively in the Mysteries, both here and in the USA, promoting mainly Celtic magical themes. I have headed up a number of Groups and co-founded two "Avalonian" Mystery Schools, one of which, The Company of Avalon, I now lead and which provides supervised instruction in these things. I have also co-written a book about Polarity Magic,* which here and there further reaches behind the mythological themes that Awen outlines.

And, as Tolkien and his Hobbits would have it, "the road goes ever on."

---

* Wendy Berg and Mike Harris, *Polarity Magic, the Secret History of Western Religion*, Llewellyn, St Paul, Minnesota, USA.

Introduction

None hereafter shall return to his wonted duty, but Ariadne shall lie hidden, within the closed gateways of her seagirt headland.
– *Prophecy of Merlin* (Geoffrey of Monmouth, trans. Evans)

I think somehow that the principle of magic (when you say magic, people don't know the difference between magic and sorcery even), but anyhow the principle of magic will re-establish itself.
– *Robert Graves (interview with Malcolm Muggeridge, 1965)*

WHEN THE POET Robert Graves was exiled from his adopted home of Mallorca by the Spanish Civil War, he eventually came to Devon, which had in ancient times been part of the old Celtic kingdoms of the West. It was here, in 1944, in the village of Galmpton, at the turning point of a world war his generation had sworn would never happen again, that he drafted his "historic grammar of poetic myth" – the book that was to become *The White Goddess*. Perhaps unintentionally, this book, more than any other before or since, was responsible for defining that hitherto "closed gateway" where Ariadne, the Welsh Arianrhod, stands guard over what we now call "the Celtic Mysteries", or more properly, "the Brythonic Mysteries" – the Mysteries of Britain.

Mystery schools have existed since the beginning of time. They teach the secrets of the soul, not least its relationship to both the inner and outer universe, a universe invariably personified in the figure of the Great Mother, the Goddess. In Her, the origins of both human nature and all nature are vested. From her mythological cauldron rises what the Welsh initiate bards came to call *Awen*, inadequately translated as "inspiration", which enables the vision of the soul's relationship to these paradisal origins. It is these origins which poetry, art, music and magic seek to explore and explain. Such exploration entails radical changes in consciousness and the process that enables this is magic. Magic was defined by the late Dion

Fortune as the "making of changes in consciousness in conformity with will" and to sup Awen from the cauldron of the goddess is to undergo such a transformation and realise the relationship between inner and outer reality. Encapsulated in such a realisation, however, are the threads of both a personal and racial destiny and implicit in the weavings of destiny are the principles of sacrifice and sovereignty.

Sovereignty, rightly understood, has little to do with political ideology, but everything to do with roots. In the first instance, these roots are a realisation of the sacred relationship of a people to their land and to each other. This is the situation of the archetypal Adam and Eve in Eden, with the man's Adamic kingship empowered by the woman. Through her, he must wed his human nature to the all-nature, the Goddess, that she represents. Thus she is his queen and muse, the good earth and the all-nature that sustains and empowers him. Over and above this, their integrated, paradisal state is encapsulated within the Creator. This Creator is not necessarily the sage-like male God sketched by the patriarchal editors of Genesis to indicate close resemblance to Abraham and Moses. Neither, for us, may this Creator be only some super goddess figure. He – and She – may be all these things and more. At the heart of all sovereignty stands this archetypal three-fold relationship of the two fused together and held within the one. The ways of translating this archetypal relationship in order to come to an understanding of the human place in creation are as many as the creeds and philosophies that the human psyche may devise. Implicit in the living out of such creeds by both magical and mystical means is the principle of sacrifice.

Graves, like the bard Myrddin nearly fourteen hundred years earlier, had first-hand experience of how sovereignty was secured through sacrifice, of how the remote sages of a nation marked the parameters of sovereignty with the blood of young men. He was wounded during the First World War and, indeed, notice of his supposed death appeared in the British press. For some years later, living in Snowdonia with his first wife, he continued to suffer the effects of shell-shock. Myrddin too had wandered in the Celtic wilderness of Celyddon, half-mad after the Battle of Arfderydd. The price of Awen can be a high one, yet it may be that from such experiences of trauma, of psychological death, great bards (and poet laureates) are made.

Graves recognised the hand of the archeptypal *penkerdd* or "supreme bard" in the writings attributed to the Welsh bard Taliesin, who came to his bardic illumination after sipping the Awen from the forbidden cauldron of the goddess Ceridwen. In addition, he recognised what is known as *the single poetic theme*, which he defined as *"the test of the poet's vision ... the accuracy of his portrayal of the White Goddess."* He went on to quote his younger contemporary, the Welsh poet Alun Lewis, who wrote of *"The single poetic theme of life and death ... the question of what survives of the beloved."* According to Lewis, any poet worthy of the name could choose no other theme. Shortly after this, whilst serving with the South Wales Borderers in Burma, Lewis died. Witnesses say he was cleaning a Sten gun at the time. Poetry and magic are both disciplines of unreason, and suffer their own casualties.

Graves realised that the magical/poetic courtship of the White Goddess by her human bardic admirers inevitably invites psychological or actual death, but that this must be before the hapless bard can be reborn in illumination. He realised that the White Goddess is that lady who by virtue of her station in the Underworld, in the unconscious, as the Faery muse, the Jungian Anima, can be the nightmare, the white lady of madness and death. She is the initiatrix, and initiation and death are, at least in the language of metaphysics, interchangeable experiences. In spite of this, he was at pains to point out that he was never an occultist or a member of any mystery school. Even so, it may be said that he had first-hand experience of the trials of the Celtic initiate bards. After the horror of the trenches, the shell-shock and his realisation of the White Goddess, the transformative side-effects rippled on throughout Graves' life. His life-long romance with the Goddess comprised an unending and unhappy search for a flesh and blood muse, his goddess incarnate, who could, after trial and testing, fulfil the traditional role of the Celtic goddesses, which is to arm, illuminate and empower her sons.

He came to write *The White Goddess* at the turning point of the Second World War, when the British sovereignty, enshrined in the goddess figure of Britannia, so badly needed to arm and empower her sons and daughters. As the allied armies turned the course of the war, Graves suddenly found himself laying aside his planned work and almost obsessively juggling with Taliesin's poetic riddles of sacrifice and sovereignty. Meanwhile, other British bards were at work upon material that was set to arm the British folksoul. Sceptics will call this coincidence, the psychologist Jung would have called it *synchronicity,* and anybody who has experience of these matters knows that such synchronicities are commonplace as the appropriate impulses vibrate through the folksoul. These other "bards" or "mythographers," the famed Inklings J.R.R. Tolkien, C.S. Lewis and Charles Williams – intentionally set about composing mythopoeic material, as had the bards of old. Tolkien, like Graves, had known the horror of the trenches in the First World War and had been severely wounded. Lewis would soon enough come to know the agony of sacrifice in the realisation of his love for a woman with terminal cancer. Williams, being a member of an "operational" mystery school, and both a poet and magician, was more than aware of the role of the bard and the dynamics of the Inklings' mythopoeic undertaking.

That mythology should become the preoccupation of such men in such desperate times may be borne out by the realisation that those desperate times had themselves been borne out of the revival of ancient myth. Even now it sounds like the plot from some bizarre conspiracy novel, yet it cannot be denied that the Second World War was spawned from nothing more or less than Adolf Hitler's determination to live out a Teutonic myth. The power of mythology lived out by one man who was able to subsequently impose his vision upon the consciousness of a nation still seems unbelievable. And yet, intelligent and influential men, albeit with the SS runes upon their collars, met in the crypts of old Germanic castles and, in quasi-Templar rites, made Adolf Hitler their Baphomet.

The Inklings (and the "honorary Inkling" E.R. Eddison) meanwhile mythopoeically evoked patterns that lay deep in the magical recesses of the British folksoul. They fulfilled their bardic function in the most ancient and Druidic sense, hardly aware of how or why the tangled mythopoeic patterns their imaginations fell upon so precisely countered the perverted orderliness synthesised in Nazi dogma. Graves and the Inklings were, though separated only by the meagre distance between a Devon village and Oxford, oblivious to each other's parallel efforts. The Inklings performed their bardic duty, whilst Graves sought to define what that duty was. These dynamics of old magic, which may be found at the roots of the British folksoul, are mostly dormant until the sovereignty of Britain is threatened. Any threat to that sovereignty, that territorial sense of being, awakens that folksoul – jolting the bards to their visions, and (with no less dedication) grocers to their guns.

More than forty years later, during a smaller war in the Falklands, having passed through the grades of a mystery school, I was initiated into an esoteric fraternity. At that initiation I was enlisted into that same, peculiar, service to the Goddess. Accordingly, I was sworn to all those noble Onward Christian Soldier-type things where the battlefields of Europe and the playing fields of Eton (or even the unheard of public school I went to) supposedly draw together, in selfless spiritual endeavour. It goes without saying that the actuality of service in the Mysteries has as little to do with the pomp and circumstance of initiation as the reality of soldiering has to do with the Trooping of the Colour. Even so, it is perhaps no bad thing to evoke such naïveté into a world which celebrates its supposed toughness by indulging cynics rather than poets. Human beings need to reach beyond the confines of their little lives. They need to believe in magic.

The practice of white magic, which is the bread and butter activity of the Mysteries or of anybody who wants to build bridges between the 'within' of things and the mundane shape, touch and smell of things, is both an art and a technology. It seeks to set up that idyllic fusion between two modes of being and is therefore essentially about polarity. Ultimately however, magic when properly done tumbles over the edge of doing and falls into a way of becoming. When it does this it ceases to be magic and becomes mysticism, shifting its polarity focus from a dialogue with creation to a dialogue with the Creator. What was a working relationship with creation, soon becomes a very intimate relationship with *the One whom Creation is within.* This latter intimacy is what the single poetic theme must ultimately celebrate. Any other way of describing this consummation of the Soul with the One is probably presumptuous and futile.

When I came back from lecturing on these things in New Mexico in 1995, Mark Whitehead asked me to write this book. As I began to gather my material together, I wondered if Graves, and the handful of responsible commentators who took up the torch after him, hadn't already done the job. Walking the woods and moors around Cadair Idris, I was soon reminded that the Celtic Mysteries, and indeed any mystery system, is not an open and closed book but a living and evolving entity. It lives and changes like the landscape to which it, and the folksoul it serves, are welded.

I have been privileged for more than half my life to live among the woods, shores and mountains of Meirionydd (South Gwynedd) where the Mabinogi myths arose. What is described in these pages as "Celtic" must therefore for the most part be admitted to be "Welsh." The mysteries are experiential and my experience therefore comes from the land that I know – and that knows me! Indeed, I would venture to say that only whilst living and working magically within the appropriate landscape can one hope to really touch the mysteries of a place. The reality that traditional mystery systems are very much tied to a landscape, and describe the relationship of a tribe with its environment, may be understood simply from reading a Bible.

Of course the mysteries we describe as "Celtic" were not invented by the Celts. They were comparative latecomers to the British Isles and only adopted much of what they already found here (and recent research would seem to indicate that "Celtic Britain" had so become on its own terms, long before the historical Celtic influx following the Roman invasion of Gaul).

The traditional misconception that the Druids, the Celtic loremasters, built Stonehenge or any other great megalithic masterpieces, has now been pretty much erased from erstwhile popular conceptions of our early history. Most people now realise that the folk who began Stonehenge and Avebury were as far removed chronologically from Celtic Britain as the Iron Age Celts are from us (we are I suppose, the "cyber age Celts"!) That the Celts, even the Christianised Celts, subsequently sought to ensure the survival of a Neolithic and Bronze Age mystery system by encapsulating it in their own poetic mythography is, therefore, astonishing.

Finally, the inevitable caveat must be that, by the very nature of the material, there will be much in this book that cannot be "proved." Magic has its own kind of physics and poetic myth has its own kind of truth. All these things, not least magic, are differing ways of initiating and describing human experience. There have been books, and books about books, but the grist of these "mysteries" is best experienced out on the land, perhaps somewhere like the Ffordd Ddu in Meirionydd, standing among the old Bronze Age burials and standing stones, watching the sky fall and the sun plunge into the Celtic Sea. At such times the inexplicable unity between human nature and all nature may be known in a feeling summed up in that melancholic Welsh word *hiraeth* – a soul-felt yearning to return to innocence and paradise.

Mike Harris, Arthog, Wales, January 1999.

CHAPTER ONE

The People and the Land

I T BEGINS with the land ... for there is nowhere else where it can begin. A true mystery tradition is born from that most primal relationship, the intimacy between Mother Nature and her human children. This relationship, played out in Nature's ample lap, the landscape of the good Earth, is where what we call the *Celtic Mysteries* must be considered to begin.

Any true mystery system delineates the journey of a folksoul, that inner journey that a people must make to arrive at an understanding of who they are. The route that must be followed is set in starlight upon the body of the land and may, supposedly, only be read by the wise. The last inheritors of such wisdom in these Islands were the Celts, who finally embellished what they knew with many a philosophical, theological and metaphysical footnote. But the substance of these mysteries was never shaped to fit snugly to the intellect. The substance of these mysteries is about the bargains made by priestly poets with the hard faced landscape and the uneasy stars.

To understand the nature of those bargains one must understand what happens upon and within the Celtic landscape. We have to be aware of the friction of the people against their environment ... as tribes and ages come and go across the sacred land. It is almost as if this abrasion upon the landscape generates an electricity, a charge which flickers between the soul of a people and the soul of a place. This charge may still be felt in the lonely "Celtic" places of the north western Atlantic seaboard which mythology wedged between the north wind and the evening sky.

Our perspective will be for the most part Brythonic, that is, Welsh ... because this is where our own experience lies, and the mysteries are, above all, experiential. There can be no academic explanation for what the Welsh describe as *hiraeth* and *hwyl*. As to the Celtic Mysteries, they are only "Celtic" in the very restricting sense that this describes the latter stages of their evolution. People were making their bargains with the spirit of this land a long time before they adopted what we call a "Celtic" language and culture. When the Celts were still but a gleam in the eye of the god Gwydion, mainland Britain was occupied by some three quarters of a million people.

Paleolithic hunters and foragers had been coming and going to the area which was to become Britain for perhaps two hundred thousand years. These forays into the north of what was part of mainland Europe occurred during the interglacial periods, as the climate rewarmed and the ice retreated. Recognisable traces of early man in Wales have been found in cave shelters such as *Goats Hole* in the Gower Peninsula, where a skeleton of Cro Magnon man, some eighteen thousand years old, was discovered in 1823. The last of the Ice Ages came to an end some ten thousand years ago, and about seven thousand years ago changes in land and sea level caused the formation of the English Channel and North Sea, and Britain became an island. The image of the Otherworld island is central to all Celtic mythology and belief.

Only the Southern tip of Wales avoided the last of the Ice Ages, but as the ice eventually melted, folk ventured from their caves and roamed, hunting and gathering roots and berries, foraging and ambushing animals for food. Traces of these *Mesolithic* people have been found in *microliths,* the flint barbs of hunting and fishing equipment as well as antler and bone weapons and tools. Later it became apparent that herding was a more reliable way to secure nourishment than random hunting, until the herding nomads also realised how fertile the land herself can be. Farmers drifted into post glacial Britain from the European mainland and mixed with the indigenous tribes so that small tribal groups settled to raising animals and cultivating a primitive form of wheat crop. After a time hunting became relegated to a secondary food source, even if it retained primal importance for cultural reasons .

So, by late Neolithic times, some five thousand years ago, our ancestors had established a working relationship with the earth. The difference in outlook between these people and their Paleolithic ancestors, who had wandered the hills and forests as opportunist hunters, would have been profound. The people of late Neolithic times had become completely aware of the cycles of nature to the extent that they could anticipate, even regulate, their food supply. Each fertile, sheltered hollow of ice-scooped land had become a cauldron of continuing nourishment. They came to realise that the land in some way owned them and accordingly sustained them. She was their mother and without her indulgence they could not exist. They were no longer foragers and wanderers, the land had accepted them and rooted them in some particular place upon her splendid body. In realisation of a permanence and dependency upon a place, where She, the mother, sounded a particular note to which their souls were attuned, they built their barrows and henges. Five thousand years ago, the nomadic tribes of mainland Britain had, for the most part, found a home.

This meant that their attitude to their environment and the cycles that governed their lives were radically different from those of their nomadic ancestors. They entered into a rhythm with the land and the seasons, and whilst in some small measure their clearing and tending of crops and their husbandry of animals changed the land, the land in its turn changed them. Their lives became synchronised to the cycles of seasons and soil, cycles which were anticipated in the turning of the stars. They trusted to a place to sustain them and in time to take them back, deep beneath the rich peaty soil into the deep dark places under lakes and mountains where the stars also shone.

Among such folk, grafted to the land in small tribal units throughout Britain and Ireland, mystery traditions evolved. The mysteries which had been known to the hunters and cave dwellers, the mysteries which had come to know the spirit of the ravening mountain lion and the fleet of foot deer, became elaborated to focus the relationship between the tribe and the land herself. From this came the realisation that some sacred "father" of the tribe needed to consummate the tribal relationship with Mother Earth so that the tribe itself might be fertile and that the crops could grow. Such a consummation initially involved the tribal father literally entering the Mother Earth and his life essence being liberated to fertilise her. From this originated the practice often called *the cult of the Sacred King*. We call them "kings" now, but the ideas that the word expresses would of course have made little sense to them. These were the chosen mediators, the fathers of their tribe, and their emergence typifies the start of what we call the Bronze Age in Britain. In death they consummated their sacred marriages to the mother of the tribe … the good earth. In that absolute embrace they entered her – this was what their Neolithic ancestors had done by way of womb-like passage graves and barrows. But these were individuals who chose or were chosen, to die. For the most part their deaths were voluntary, for some things had to die so that others could in their turn be born. It was the way of things. By watching the crops and the seasons they knew this.

The British settlers of late Neolithic times had built their passage graves whilst the Pharaohs had built their pyramids. Both cultures seem to have recognised a spiritual process which involved entering the inner earth, the womb of the Mother, to know rebirth among the high bright stars. In this are the origins of initiatory practices which anticipate the fulfilment of human nature in the mother who is all nature. This is the grist of all initiatory mystery teaching as it began in these Islands, back among those forlorn barrows and frost cracked cromlechs that still litter the sacred earth of Britain and Ireland from five thousand years ago.

As their name implies, the Neo-lithic, the "New Stone" people, mastered the ability to quarry and work stone. So much can be seen from such feats of megalithic engineering in the Neolithic tombs of *Wayland's Smithy* and *West Kennet Barrow* in Southern England. In North Wales, less spectacular (but no less atmospheric) tombs can be found in the isolated *Carneddau Hengwm* tombs as well as the *Dyffryn Long Cairn* and *Capel Garmon* tombs. Later elaboration produced the magnificent *Bryn Celli Ddu* and *Barclodiad y Gawres* passage graves on Anglesey in the Irish *Boyne* tradition.

People who work with stone and get to know one rock from another soon notice the glint of metal in certain varieties. They look for ways of separating out the bright metal, and knowing that fire can crack stone they stumble upon ways of metal smelting. In this they realise that molten metal can be shaped in a mould and they develop a technology of casting. They realise, for example, that bronze, the alloy of tin and copper, is easier to form than just copper. Such realisations may have had their European origins in Iberia about four thousand years ago, but some recent opinion looks to an early indigenous metallurgy starting in Ireland and Wales in about 2,500 BC.

Archaeology calls the first of the metal-using folk *Beaker* people, from the beaker drinking vessels that are found in their tombs, along with bows and arrows and leaf shaped bronze daggers. Some Bronze Age priest, either from religious conviction or merely the delight of design, carved the outline of such a dagger on one of the stones of Stonehenge. In fact early casting techniques would have utilised carved stone moulds … thus the great Excalibur comes to be the sword drawn, in some versions of the legend, from the stone. In this we may also see a mythical metaphor of the progress from a stone to a metal technology.

Such a metaphor indeed worked out in the blending of the two races of people, who, as one culture, were to occupy these islands. So, whilst the Beaker folk emerged in Iberia in the West of Europe, another group, typified by their production of stone battle axes, even though they had a knowledge of metals, appear in the area of the present day Czech Republic. Both of these peoples seem to have subsequently met and fused in central Europe, and their fusion, like the blending of tin and copper, constitutes what we now know as one Bronze Age people.

History does not of course come and go in neat boxes and we can see a considerable overlap between Bronze Age and late Neolithic societies. The folk of the early and middle Bronze Age did, however, see the transition from settled and comparatively isolated agricultural societies to a much wider world. In time, agriculture uses up considerable amounts of land, and this, with population growth, leads to encroachment and confrontation. By the middle of the Bronze Age there was something of a population explosion and the population in Britain would have passed the million mark. As stock rearing also developed and (as in later Celtic times) cattle began to represent a "value", further incentives to raid neighbouring territories doubtless arose.

It is at this time, along with the new metal technologies, that we guess that a warrior aristocracy had its beginnings. Trade also opened up with the metal hungry civilisations around the Mediterranean who valued tin from Cornwall, gold from Ireland and both copper and gold from Wales. We can only guess at the technological sophistication of the Bronze Age copper miners in North Wales, working under Parys Mountain on Anglesey or 150 feet beneath the nearby Great Orme. Such feats would have been impossible without that same engineering skill which was simultaneously at work at Stonehenge. Both of these projects also involved sophisticated communication and transport. The copper from North Wales had to be combined with the tin from Cornwall to make Bronze. The so-called *bluestones*, which formed the most sacred part of Stonehenge, had to be moved from Pembrokeshire in south west Wales to Wiltshire in southern central England. So whilst the Egyptians were producing miracles of sacred, civil engineering, we should not assume that their British contemporaries were unable also to call upon a degree of technological knowledge when they needed to. Professor Thom's survey work at *Moel Ty Uchaf*, again in North Wales, which we shall visit later, showed how a small local stone circle just happened to be carefully laid out with pentagonal geometry nearly a thousand years before the Greeks were meant to have pioneered such feats.

The revolution of Neolithic times had been the abilities to make permanent settlements and produce and anticipate food supply, and also to harness enough corporate muscle and technique to undertake large earthworks and megalithic stone settings (*Stonehenge 1, Avebury 1, West Kennet Barrow, Wayland's Smithy*). The settings of these great megalithic sites not only indicates astronomical knowledge but also seems, as we shall discuss later, to indicate specialised knowledge about the earth's magnetic field. As the Bronze Age began to overlay these advances, however, the world rapidly became a much smaller place. The British Isles were settled extensively, not only by the indigenous population but by further immigrants.

Trade, travel and the development of warfare and raiding accelerated. If at this time we were to return to Stonehenge (some thousand or more years after its Neolithic inception) we would see that over the simple henge built by the Neolithic folk, great stones had been raised and secured in a very deliberate piece of architectural engineering. The logistics of getting the bluestones to their site would, as we've seen, indicate that the folk of Bronze Age Britain were used to operating somewhat beyond the confines of a tribal village and that some measure of hierarchal command was available to organise this.

The fact that this hierarchy was able to galvanise so much effort into one sacred objective at a site which, by then, had been in use for around a thousand years, may also indicate that the hierarchy was either a theocracy or at least a government in which priesthood had a dominant voice. We may assume (partly from looking at the Egyptian experience with its parallels of a long tradition of extraordinary sacred engineering and theocracy) that an initiatory based mystery religion had developed behind what came to be the governing hierarchy of Bronze Age Britain. It is clear that through the precious metal trade in general and the developing gold route (from Ireland and Wales through Europe towards the Balkans and Mediterranean) in particular, this hierarchy was anything but isolated from Middle Eastern ideas.

Whilst we shall attempt to show what foundations of spiritual belief and practice were laid at that time we must be cautious. As Owen Barfield pointed out, there is an inherent flaw in assuming that the thought processes of the ancients worked in the same way that ours do! Archaeology is, understandably, more comfortable with domestic relics or weapons than it is with "beliefs". That said, it is something of an irony that pretty much the only tangible points of contact that we have with our far ancestors are at the places where they expressed their beliefs in initiatory and funerary rites!

In a book which deals with the Mysteries, we cannot help but point out that there are of course faculties other than intellect which may be applied to these questions ... particularly in the study of initiatory systems. Trained intuition brought to bear at these old sites can, if sensibly applied, fill many gaps in our archaeological and anthropological knowledge. It is important to realise that the terms "scientific explanation" and "fact" are not exclusively interdependent, even though we have been conditioned to think that they are.

Whilst archaeology may be chary about what actually went on at such sites as Stonehenge, it is, however, less reticent about what went on in the world beyond those hallowed trilithons. When Stonehenge was started, folk were becoming used to being farmers rather than hunters. By the time it was suddenly, inexplicably, abandoned, a warrior aristocracy was in place and men whose ancestors had been nomadic hunters were developing skills and weaponry with which to efficiently hunt and kill each other. How this wheel of aggression and revenge, conquest and defence then began to turn and gather momentum becomes all too clear. We may suppose that the burgeoning new metal trade demanded new ore deposits from new areas, areas occupied by other tribes. New metals also meant new and better weapons and new weapons meant new conquests. The wheel was turning and the ability and inclination to progress tribal ambitions by military means became irresistible. Archaeological evidence shows that there was considerable upheaval in western Europe at this time.

Bronze Age evolution was its own worst enemy and eventually what had been a sophisticated and successful society began, like so many others, to fragment. The increasing sophistication of means by which men could slaughter each other was one thing. A deeper danger lay in the sophistication of Bronze Age agriculture. Since early Neolithic times, the land had been over-exploited and become much less fertile. This appears to have been coupled to climatic deterioration and a population explosion in the mid Bronze Age. These ingredients made for a hungry populace, who doubtless felt deserted by their traditional deities. From about 1,300 BC, religious and cultural institutions represented by the building and elaboration of stone circles and mortuary sites had pretty much ceased. Even "work in progress" on the great ritual monument at Stonehenge was abandoned, half finished, in about 1,350 BC. Such things point to the overthrow of a theocracy because of a perceived failure by mortal "sacred kings" and their priestly officials. The evolution of spear and sword in these twilight years of the Bronze Age are archaeologically obvious and the means for a disillusioned and angry population to express itself are thus shown to be all too available. When the ferment died down, many of the old sacred sites were ploughed over to raise much needed crops. There were no more elaborate tombs or stone circles and the population fragmented into tribal enclaves, which continued to compete for insufficient resources.

A fragmented tribal society consolidated over the next seven centuries in mainland Britain. It would have been a society which valued the skills of warriors and cattle raiders and as such was fertile ground for "the Celtic experience" of becoming a tribal people lead by local warrior aristocracies skilled in arms, horsemanship and the working of the new miracle metal ... iron. But unlike the later Romans or Normans these European Celts were never the bellicose representatives of a particular nation state. There was no "Celtic" nation, they didn't think of, or speak of, themselves as "Celts" because they were not in reality a people or a nation in the way which we would understand the term. They were a loose group of tribes who had shared language and culture. Old ideas of these continental Celts suddenly displacing over one million British people are absurd. This supposed series of invasions of the British Isles by continental Celts used to be identified by archaeologists as three immigrations ... Iron Age 'A', 'B' and 'C'. The first period was seen to have been one of primary settlement in about the sixth century BC, when the residues of the once sophisticated Bronze Age folk were supposedly subdued, enslaved and/or absorbed. This no longer appears to have been the case and it seems more likely that Britain adopted a "Celtic" language and culture in its own way and on its own terms. Likewise the previously supposed third century BC influx of Iron Age 'B', *La Tène* European Celtic culture, which now appears to have been adopted rather than imposed. Iron Age 'C' takes us almost into the parameters of the historical (as against prehistoric) period, when certainly European Celts came to Britain, not as invaders but as refugees, fleeing in the face of the Roman invasion of Gaul. Britain had adopted and developed a Celtic language and culture on its own terms, gradually rebuilding upon the crumbling foundations of a once powerful and cohesive Bronze Age culture and slowly re-establishing ancient links with the wider world. The climate had also began to improve. By about 500 BC mainland Britain had attained a sort of "Celtic equilibrium".

It is largely at this juncture that our assumptions about the Mysteries of Britain in general and the Celtic Mysteries in particular start to navigate some very muddy waters, and various confusions and misunderstandings arise. This is not helped by our supposedly Celtic "sources" some nine hundred years later, promulgating material that has precious little to do with (what we know of) Celtic Druidism but everything to do with (what we know of) the practices of Bronze Age and Neolithic mystery cults. As we shall later discuss, there was very much a continuity in the mystery traditions in these islands extending from those early Neolithic settlements and communal burials right through the Bronze Age and its turbulent demise and on through the pre-Roman, Romano Celtic and post-Roman periods. The folksoul of a people has a tremendous tenacity and is not so easily extinguished. The Celts themselves are a case in point … after two and a half thousand years and countless invasions and occupations, the Celts are still here, utterly distinctive in culture, belief and language … and politically very much alive and kicking!

Indications in late Romano Celtic and even early mediaeval times are that at least some of the beliefs of the Bronze Age people were still very much around, welded into a supposedly "Celtic" mystery system. The scope of these mysteries was (and is!) quite breathtaking, encompassing everything from primitive transformative cauldron myth on the one hand to the high mystical visions of the Holy Grail on the other. These are the foundations upon which so much that is integral to the British folksoul depends, from the legends of Arthur to the convictions expressed in Blake's poem which was to become, with Parry's music, the anthem "Jerusalem".

Even though the Celts inherited these mysteries and carried them through into the historical epoch, the pre-Christian Celts left no contemporary writings. As has been frequently pointed out, the development and retention of all philosophical, legal and metaphysical lore was vested in the Druids. These initiate bards held to an oral tradition in that they memorised information which could be recited to order, obviating any reason to write it down.

Only the invading Romans, some five or six hundred years after the first Celtic inclinations of the indigenous British, took the trouble to write any account of these Brythonic Celts. Sadly, their records betray the obvious bias towards an enemy and say nothing which is useful about the Celtic mystery tradition. Caesar and his cronies viewed the Celtic speaking peoples as an undifferentiated mass of barbarians, and slandered them in their propaganda. Ironically, by the standards not so much of the Romans but of the long forgotten Bronze Age, the continental Celts and their British imitators probably were barbarians.

The Greeks, who had met the Celts through trade rather than war, were a little more sympathetic and it is from them that we get the word "*Keltoi*" to identify the Celts as a group of tribes using a particular language.

The group of tribes which the Greeks identified as *Keltoi* had arisen in eastern Europe and expanded westwards to the Iberian peninsula and latterly northwards through Gaul and into Britain and Ireland. Initially their language was *Goidelic*, the language which became the basis of the Irish and Scots Gaelic languages, whereas the later development of replacing the Q sound with a P sound came to be adopted by the tribes of Brittany and thereafter mainland Britain. This became the Brythonic language from which Breton, Welsh and Cornish developed in their original forms. The Welsh language (which remains the strongest of the surviving Celtic languages) has moved from Brythonic to Late Brythonic to Old Welsh to Middle Welsh to Modern Welsh which now, needless to say, bears little resemblance to the Brythonic of the "original" British language.

The Druids

Because the Druids maintained an oral tradition and for the most part seem to have conducted their rites in groves of trees rather than stone built enclosures, it is hard to know exactly what tribal beliefs replaced those of their Bronze Age predecessors. Bronze Age and Neolithic tribes left remains, and remains can be made available for both physical and intuitive archaeology. Certainly we have late accounts of a garbled mythology from both Britain, Ireland and mainland Europe which give us a lot of material, but much of this has on the one hand later Judeo-Christian ingredients or, on the other hand, material which predates the Celtic impulse. The Taliesin material, for example, not least the *Preiddu Annwn* (Spoils of the Deep/Underworld … which we shall look at in detail later on), has traces of a cult seemingly based upon Bronze Age mortuary sites readily jumbled up with Judaic/Christian allusions and downright "too clever by half" jibes at the sixth century Christian bardic establishment. Other accounts of Druidic practice and belief are furnished by Roman commentators, whose natural bias and inept appraisal of comparative religion make their accounts all but worthless.

By the same token, remains from the Romano Celtic period in Romanised areas of Britain (such as the temple of *Nodens* at Lydney in Gloucestershire) betray a cocktail of Roman pantheism adapted for neo-Celtic use rather than Druidic belief and practice. We know from archaeological evidence that first century Roman military (not to mention 20th century British archaeological!) hysteria about "Celtic" mass sacrifice is largely unfounded. This isn't to say that Druidic rites didn't entail human sacrifice, but that it was probably the exception rather than the rule … certainly by the standards of the Colosseum at any rate! Furthermore (the finding of Lindow man in a Cheshire peat bog in the

1980s notwithstanding) the possibility would seem to be that where sacrifice did take place, it may to some extent have involved voluntary victims. The Taliesin bard leads us to believe that the *cult of the sacred king* albeit by metaphor and/or proxy, had in some senses survived from its ancient origins, along with the principles of *sovereignty* that it gave rise to, but this was not a Druidic innovation even if the pre-Christian Druids were involved in its continuance.

Other hallowed beliefs about the Druids, such as the mistletoe cut with the gold sickle, have also been shown to be probably false, simply because the widely travelled Roman commentators confused the customs of one of their vast array of occupied countries with another. More than this, they wrote primarily for the folks back home, who wanted to hear about deeds of derring do against wicked barbarians. The temptation to compose what is now pompously called "contra factual reportage" would have been overwhelming!

What cannot be confused however is the Druidic Celtic sense of place. Localities and tribes reflected local allegiance to particular gods and goddesses in their *onomastic* place names. Archaeological evidence also supports the way that sacred lakes, rivers and springs become a constant feature in evolving myth, right through into the Christian era. The physical evidence for this may be seen in the considerable quantities of valuable votive material found in many European and British rivers and lakes. On the traditional Druid stronghold of Anglesey, a very impressive hoard was found at *Llyn Cerrig Bach* when Valley airfield was being extended during the Second World War. The hoard included 138 assorted objects of wood, metal and stone which had been ritually deposited there throughout the last two hundred years of British/Celtic independence (before the Roman invasion of Anglesey). These included some very considerable items such as whole chariots (which probably had somewhat more esoteric significance at that time than as simple offerings for military success). As we shall later see, the Druids thought of such places as the entrance to the Otherworld of *Annwn* (the Deep) where their heroic ancestral gods and goddesses resided.

The arrangement of these gods and goddesses into a workable pantheon like the major Greek and Egyptian gods is, however, unsatisfactory. Whilst about fifty or so deities, out of many hundreds, appear to be universal, divine functions overlap and/or are much more difficult to define than the pantheons of classical mythology. This is hardly surprising in view of the character of Celtic society and the nature of religious practice. The Celts were not, as we have pointed out, a "nation". They were a loose knit conglomeration of tribes who only ceased to fight each other when some greater threat (like the Romans) loomed. Celtic history sadly indicates – right up to and since the assassination of Michael Collins in Ireland – that in some respects, Celtic parochialism and tribalism will always assert itself, frequently with tragic results. Consequently the majority of gods and goddesses were "local" spirits of place … the essence of tribal ancestors that had been absorbed into the immediate environment.

The only unifying force among the Celts were the Druids and the only stronghold of Druidism was Anglesey. Anglesey (*Mona*) alone represented the heart (or more properly the head!) of any notional, pre-Christian "Celtic folksoul".

When schoolchildren were taught history on a framework of crucial dates, everyone knew that the Roman legions set foot in Britain in 55 BC, then again in 54 BC. Julius Caesar was concerned that whilst any Celtic power in Gaul had been effectively crushed, Britain still remained a Celtic bastion which was too close for comfort and not least because many of the resentful refugee Belgic tribes had established themselves in Southern Britain. However, if Julius Caesar had intended his landing and skirmishing with these tribes to be the prelude to invasion and occupation proper, fate was to dictate otherwise. Julius was soon forced to turn his attention to domestic politics, but even so failed to be attentive enough to avoid the assassin's dagger. A lad called Octavian succeeded Julius. Octavian was later to become the divine Augustus (whose tax census was to place the birth of the Christ in a stable) but initially he was very much under the influence of Mark Anthony. As every film buff knows, Anthony's fatal interest was rather more in Cleopatra's Egypt than in Celtic Britain.

It was nearly a hundred years after the 54 BC foray that the Roman invasion and occupation of Britain eventually occurred. By this time, Pontius Pilate was twelve years or more past that fateful day when he had washed his hands, and the stuttering Claudius now wore the Imperial crown.

Whilst Julius Caesar's motive for invasion had been primarily to contain a Celtic threat, Claudius's motives were less bellicose. Ninety or more years after Julius Caesar, a number of the tribes in Southern Britain were well Romanised client states of the Empire. The Romanisation of Britain in Claudius's time was for the most part for economic reasons, but there were some nasty surprises. Whilst the Roman experience of the South coast tribes might have led them to believe that the Celts, as a whole, were now prepared to become part of the Pax Romana, the Northern and Western tribes soon left them in little doubt that this was not the case.

Even after alliances and counter alliances among the squabbling tribes and the defeat of the Celtic warlord Caractacus, the Celts of Wales, especially North West Wales, stoutly resisted occupation. Had they stayed in their barren hills, they may not have been such a concern to the Romans, but the fact that the hills were by no means barren, but rich in copper and gold, made them a military problem that could not be ignored. At the very heart of the problem was what we now call Druidism.

The Druids were not merely a pre-Christian Celtic priesthood. As we have noted, their role was somewhat wider than that. They held within their unwritten, bardic lore, the *memory* and the aspirations of a people. Everything that the British and Irish Celts had ever been or ever aspired to be, everything which was reflected in those local ancestral gods, goddesses and heroes was preserved and enshrined in the trained Druidic mind. It must have become obvious to the Romans that the equitable Romano-Celtic synthesis which they believed they had achieved in the Southern, civil zones of Britain, would be impossible elsewhere whilst the cancer of Druidism was allowed to thrive. Because of this, Anglesey, the heart of Druidism, had to be invaded. Not only was it the Druidic hub but (as in later ages) it was *Mona mam Cymru* ("Anglesey the mother of Wales") because its rich agricultural production could sustain the Snowdonia mountain tribes. It also happened to be the link with fabled Ireland, the source of the Celtic gold route, and we now know that a Roman invasion of Ireland was at least contemplated. So whilst Druidism was something of an indefinite target there were other factors which were worth Roman consideration. As far as the Druids went there were few temples to sack and no books to burn. The 'temples' and its 'scriptures' of Druidism were essentially the Druids themselves. In 63 AD the very capable Roman commander of the occupation forces, one Suetonius Paulinus marched up Watling Street towards Mona, to destroy those living temples.

Whilst other British tribes would for the most part have left the Welsh tribes, as such, to their fate, an attack upon the Anglesey, Mona, the spiritual hub of Celtic Britain, could not be ignored. This was very much in the character of the Celts. There was, as we've seen, little or no "national" cohesion, but true Celticism, true racial cohesion, did however exist at a deeper level. When Paulinus marched on Mona – *Mona mam Cymru*, mother of the Welsh, and indeed all the British tribes – a nerve at that deeper level, the folk soul of the British, was aroused. There is a Welsh world for this arousal, but it means what it means and there can be no exact translation in Anglo Saxon for *hwyl*.

Whilst Paulinus and his cohorts stood on the mainland side of the Menai Straits and received the stridency of the Mona Celts on the other, a

Celtic queen of southern Britain, called Boudicca, had scores of her own to settle. She was the widow of Prasugatus, King of the Iceni Celts, and on her husband's death the Romans had assumed that they could annex the Iceni tribal lands as a matter of course. Boudicca resisted and Rome shrugged off her resistance by flogging her. Her daughters, the princesses of the Iceni, were openly raped, as if to confirm Rome's chauvinistic sneer at such feminine precocity. The Rome of the Caesars and later the Rome of the Holy See were both to totally miscalculate Celtic motive, by being unable to grasp the matriarchal roots and feminine reverence in the Celtic psyche.

It may be that Boudicca's uprising, whilst Paulinus was preoccupied with the suppression of Anglesey, was merely opportune revenge. It is unlikely however that this was her only motive. As Paulinus marched towards the Menai Straits, a shiver would have been felt in the Celtic folk soul. Something would have to be done in some way to divert Paulinus's attention. Boudicca, popular symbol of Celtic pride, ground under the sandal of Imperial Rome, would have seemed destined to provide such a diversion.

The diversion that she provided was gruesomely spectacular, as she laid bloody waste to St Albans and Colchester. But it came too late. Having overcome initial Druid scare tactics on the shores of Anglesey, Paulinus proceeded to eliminate the Druid threat. In capturing Mona, which was as we have said, the granary, the sustaining mother for resistance in North Wales, he returned south. He halted at the centre of Britain, at the High Cross, where centuries later the Welsh nobleman Henry Tudor paused before riding across the meadows of nearby Bosworth field to take the British crown.

Paulinus waited and waited, cursing his missed rendezvous with the reinforcing second Legion from Gloucester, giving Boudicca time to continue her bloody diversion and burn and massacre Roman London. But Boudicca's diversion was soon to come to an end. At a site that the Celts were later to darkly call 'the place of the chariots', her huge army was crushed by the smaller but better disciplined Roman force. Boudicca's uprising, the last desperate rearguard action of the Celts, had failed to save the Druids. The blood of an army and of the largely civilian populations of three major cities was on her hands. Boudicca died by her own hand and the British Celtic dream awoke to a newer, darker world in the sixtieth year after the birth of a Christ that it had probably never heard of.

Nobody is quite sure when Britain did get to hear of Christianity. There is some speculation that the legion which had garrisoned Jerusalem during the last days of Christ subsequently turned up in North Wales, supposedly attached to the Chester (or *Deva*, as the Romans called it) garrison. This speculation runs nicely parallel with the legend that Longinus, the centurion who thrust the spear into the side of the crucified Christ, was later stationed in Britain. Be that as it may, there is little doubt that whilst the legions, or at least their Roman officers, were devotees of Mithras, they would in their communications with the Empire know of the troublesome Christ cult back home.

The British Celts would also have been aware of events in and around the Mediterranean. In addition to contact with their fellow Celts in mainland Europe, a lively trade brought Mediterranean shipping directly to the Western shores of Britain, and it is probably through this contact that the rumours of Christ first came to the demoralised Celtic ghettos of Brittany and Western Britain. It is this source which probably sowed the seed, not only of Celtic Christianity, but of the strange stream of esoteric Christian belief which later emerged in the Grail legends.

At the hub of these legends is the story of Joseph of Arimathea, prosperous Jewish merchant, (and later, major figure in the resurrection of Christ) coming to the West Country to trade for tin. There is an easy feasibility about this, but more to the point is that he could have brought the boy Jesus ben Joseph with him, then returned to Glastonbury some thirty years later with a cup containing the divine blood of that same boy who had walked so many years before in "England's green and pleasant land". The historical possibility *is* there, but the Church of Rome could never allow the chance of St Joseph of Arimathea having prior claim to St Peter and thus of the Holy See being subordinate to some misty heathen islands over the back fence of the civilised world. As time went on, the stubbornness of the early Celtic church, the Pelagian heresy, the influx of pagan Saxons and the heretical neo-gnosticism that was growing up around the Grail legends, made the possibilities of such a claim even more horrendous. The established church scoffed at the Glastonbury legend. Modern scholarship tends equally to scoff.

One factor which is frequently overlooked, however, is that had Joseph come to Glastonbury, he would not have been the first Jew to set foot in Romano Celtic Britain, and probably not the first Christianised Jew. It is known that there were Jewish communities in Roman Britain, and the martyrdom of a 'Christian' called Aaron at Caerleon suggests that *Minims* … Christianised Jews … were to be found not too distant from Glastonbury. Caerleon has other associations as the Roman fortress of Isca and as the place where Arthur was said to have been crowned at Pentecost. Here pieces of another puzzle may seem to fit, but for now we note that, in parallel to the Joseph of Arimathea/Glastonbury/Arthurian material, it is intriguing that Christianised Jews were in evidence where Mediterranean ships plied a busy trade around the mouth of the River Severn and Bridgwater Bay.

Whilst the hapless Aaron may not have been the one to bring Christ to the British, he and his fellow martyr Julian compete with St Alban for the doubtful honour of being the first British martyrs. It is agreed that the dates of these martyrdoms are 'early'. Nobody knows exactly how 'early'.

The Druids by no means faded at the coming of Christ. A legend from Ireland tells of how King Conchubar asked his Druid, Bucrach, why there was an extraordinary change in the heavenly bodies. The Druid is said to have replied that Jesus Christ, the Son of God, was at that moment being crucified by the Jews. Thus, as far as we know, Druidism had few qualms about the new Christ cult and many of the early 'saints' and Christian hermits appear to have been converted Druids. Further evidence of their anticipation may be seen in the almost overnight Christianisation of the old gods, giving them the opportunity to bask in the divine light, whilst being happily subordinate to it. Ironically the Celtic mythologies which are so much of a mishmash in the Druid era start to fall into place as they receive early Christianisation because Christianity adopted that useful habit of writing things down … albeit in Latin. But, beyond the Irish legend there is no contemporary "Druidic" record to the events in Palestine, and any immediate change in religious practice can only be culled from legends which were written down some hundreds of years later. The smoke of legend may, however, mark the flame of Christian revelation being fanned among the Celts more immediately after the death of Christ than is generally believed.

CHAPTER TWO

Merlin, Taliesin and the Bards

I T WAS NOT, as far as we know, until some six hundred years after the death of Christ that anything came to be written down in the native British tongue. There is only one known document in Brythonic and that is a faithful thirteenth century copy of the seventh century *Canu Aneirin.* The Canu, or song of, Aneirin consists of a collection of poems called *Y Gododdin* and four verse tales. These are fairly straightforward … the Gododdin for example is a *gwenwawd,* an elegy to the fallen at the Battle of Catraeth (Catterick) in about 600 AD. However, for all its historical feasibility, the *Canu* also contains perhaps the earliest mention of personages who stand at that uneasy juncture where history rubs shoulders with legend, for here we come across the earliest mentions of *Arthur, Merlin* and *Taliesin.*

On the power of these names, seemingly drawn from some primordial source, long before the coming of Christianity, and perhaps before the coming of the Celts themselves, a Brythonic mystery tradition is carried forward. It is from here that we can begin to get glimpses into what that tradition entailed. In doing so we may begin to unravel that complex knotwork and find our way both back to its roots and forward into its later elaboration.

In those later elaborations Geoffrey of Monmouth becomes a key figure at that juncture between the Celtic/Norman epoch and the Middle Ages proper. Later still, the tradition continues into Tudor times and onward to the Victorian age of romantic Celtic revival. When we finally come to this present time we see that all those archetypal Celtic bardic figures – *Arthur, Merlin and Taliesin* – are well represented through the art, theatre, films and literature of the present, and as their names resonate on through time, so do the mysteries that they represent. The names have thus become archetypal signatures so the student of the Mysteries will realise that these are much the same as *mystery names,* taken or awarded to reflect a spiritual function, aspiration or duty. In view of this, the derivation of names can reveal much about the archetypal character under consideration and the Mysteries that they represent.

Aneirin, the author of the original Brythonic writings, was a non-combatant (as his name implies) because he was a chaplain in holy orders. Because of this status he became the sole survivor, as a prisoner, from a force which was annihilated at the Battle of Catraeth in about 600 AD. His poem *Y Gododdin* is the elegy which he chanted in captivity for the souls of his fallen comrades after the battle. In this elegy he briefly mentions *Taliesin,* to point out that he, Aneirin, is not a warrior poet of the Taliesin school and that his liturgical incantations are, unlike those of a Taliesin, not the product of the traditional *awen* ... the Underworld inspiration of the Goddess, but (presumably) the product of the Holy Spirit. What Aneirin is doing is to make the point that even though he's a poet he is *not* an initiate/bard but a Christian priest. This is a point which will take on some importance later on.

Aneirin also mentions *Arthur,* when he compares the courage of one *Gwawrddur* to Arthur in the battle. There is also a brief mention of *"Mirdyn"* (*Myrddin/Merlin*) to draw a parallel between Aneirin's *gwenwawd*/elegy and the one that Myrddin said after (albeit some years after) the earlier battle of *Arfderydd* (at which Myrddin was almost certainly a combatant) in 573 AD.

Geoffrey's Merlin

After the *Canu Aneirin,* we come across *Myrddin* again in the tenth century *Armes Prydein,* which mentions his association with Taliesin. The *Armes Prydein* (Prophecies of Britain) are part of the later *Book of Taliesin.* Myrddin's mention in the Prophecies in association with Taliesin makes the opposite point that Aneirin was making in his mention of Taliesin. It tells us that he was considered to be part of a Taliesin cult, something that we shall expand upon later. Myrddin/Merlin is not, however, mentioned in Nennius's tenth century *Historia Britonum* ... even though Nennius mentions Aneirin and Taliesin. It is not until we get to Geoffrey of Monmouth's *History of the Kings of Britain* in 1136 that Merlin is featured as the lynchpin of Geoffrey's "history". Merlin's role was further acknowledged by Geoffrey appending his book with *The Prophecies of Merlin* and later producing his *Vita Merlini* ... the Life of Merlin.

Geoffrey's Merlin is the archetype of Celtic wisdom in the face of Saxon encroachment of the British Isles, and whilst Geoffrey was writing of a legendary time fused to an earlier historical period, his Welsh patriotic outpourings were coincidental with Owein Gwynedd's struggle against the English. Geoffrey, although a Welshman, was at this time part of the Anglo Norman establishment, and even though he was bishop elect of St Asaph he probably only ever viewed events from the comparative safety of Oxford! Geoffrey tells us that his essential source was a collection of ancient history/lore that was written in Brythonic, which he borrowed from Walter, Archdeacon of St Asaph. Whilst this source is no longer extant, we have no reason to believe that it wasn't available in Geoffrey's time – in fact the continued existence of material known to be available in mediaeval times is the exception rather than the rule. Whilst Geoffrey didn't write what modern academia could, in its wildest dreams, call "history", he does display a degree of historical integrity. He mentions other chroniclers like Nennius, Gildas and Bede. He also appears to draw on Bede's *De Natura Rerum* for his creation myth in the *Vita Merlini*. In some instances Geoffrey's history has actually, like his *Prophecies of Merlin*, been fulfilled in a sense. Some events which he cites, and which were presumed to be fictitious, have since been substantiated by archaeological discovery.

A dramatic example of this stemmed from Geoffrey's assertion that the Celtic Venedoti tribe had decapitated a Roman legion in London and thrown their severed heads into the stream of *Nantgallum*. In the later Saxon language this stream was called *Galobroc*, which later still became *Walbrook*. In the mid nineteenth century great numbers of skulls without skeletons were found in the bed of the Walbrook indicating that what had seemed to be a gruesome yet fictitious expression of Geoffrey's Celtic zeal was probably factual!

It is important however to understand how and why Geoffrey was writing. This is something which we must constantly bear in mind as we consider not only Merlin and Geoffrey, but other archetypal characters and what they are alleged to have written or had written about them. Geoffrey was writing in a particular *tradition,* a *bardic* tradition. He was not, nor ever intended to be, a "historian" as we would understand the term. He was continuing a bardic/poetic tradition which sought (and still seeks) to touch on the British folk soul, rather than the factual, chronological history of Britain. In writing this treatise on the Celtic/British folk soul for a Norman French audience, he employs Merlin as the guardian/caretaker of that folk soul.

Geoffrey used Merlin because he needed to find a flesh and blood character to fulfil this metaphysical, but no less real, archetypal role. To do this, he again employs his technique of what Professor Toby Griffen calls *"virtual history"*. This is a history structured upon a skeletal handful of fact to serve the writer's own agenda, which in this instance was a *bardic* agenda. So, like an espionage agent trying to find a real identity of some deceased person that he can borrow, Geoffrey finds a Celt in holy orders, like himself, who actually had existed and was actively involved in the historical period which he is describing. The factual character that he used to incarnate his wise, magical bard archetype was a Celtic poet (and later) monk called *Myrddin*.

Geoffrey would have been aware of the *Canu Aneirin*, in which, as we have said, Myrddin is mentioned. He would also have been aware of Taliesin who is mentioned in the same work, and to the link made between them in the *Armes Prydein*, where Myrddin is referred to as a prophet, or at least one who foretells the future. He would also have had access to works allegedly by Taliesin himself. Perhaps, as a number of commentators have pointed out, this is why he uses a tale very similar to Taliesin's dispute with Maelgwyn Gwynedd's bards in his tale of the youthful Merlin disputing with and confounding the bards of Vortigern. Other reasons for this 'overlap' will be considered in due course.

The documents which were to later become the *Black Book of Carmarthen*, which may have formed part of Geoffrey's source material, include a discourse between Myrddin and Taliesin. We may find that we have the sneaking feeling here that Geoffrey *knows* that we will check that a cleric called Myrddin did actually exist and that in checking we will find the association with Taliesin. Exactly *what* Taliesin stands for is something we shall examine shortly. That association would establish Merlin/Myrddin's magical credentials and make him enough of a wizard to perform such feats as the magical resetting of the "Giant's dance" at Stonehenge … another matter we shall consider later in detail!

The Myrddin of the *Black Book of Carmarthen* was a poet who like Aneirin seems to have been a cleric of the Celtic church. This, however appears to have been in his later life when he was based for a time at the monastery at Carmarthen – or *Caer Myrddin*. It is easy to evoke immediate mental pictures of tonsured, clean shaven monks filing into Vespers like good Benedictines should … but this was the fledgling Celtic church. Many of the monks were solitaries loosely belonging to a *clas* or centre of monastic authority who 'did their own thing'. In the early days of the church many still attended the old pre-Christian sacred wells and, Christianity notwithstanding, performed the duties implicit in bardic office of poet/priest (as Aneirin and Myrddin both were). A copyist in the later and, by then, much more formalised Augustinian/Norman monastery at Carmarthen sat down some six hundred years later, in about 1250, and produced an anthology subsequently known as the *Black Book of Carmarthen.* He was probably a Welshman among the predominantly Norman monks, who was heartened and inspired to find among the archives the writings of an earlier Welsh monk at the same monastery, our Celtic cleric Myrddin, whose poetry he enthusiastically included in his anthology, probably without realising quite what he had got hold of. But it is unlikely that he would have been the first to come across this material. As a Welshman in holy orders Geoffrey of Monmouth had probably had access to it just over a hundred years earlier. Maybe this is why the monk looked it out. His Norman superiors would have been familiar with Geoffrey's work!

The alteration of the name to *Merlin* rather than the original *Myrddin* is easily explained, in that whilst Geoffrey may have been writing in Latin, he was aware that his readership would be folk whose first language was Norman French. Geoffrey, who spoke Welsh, Latin and French, may have realised that he could not have his heroic wizard in possession of a name which could be seen by French readers as *Merdinius or Merdyn* "the one associated with excrement" … vide the modern French expletive *merde!* So he replaced the 'd' sound, or rather the original Welsh 'dd' sound (thhh) with the nearest suitable equivalent, the Welsh 'll'. These were probably the unheroic origins of our Anglo/Norman "Merlin"!

Myrddin

As to the original name Myrddin, this perhaps describes the poet/priest's role in life … the duties of his office, just as English names like Smith, Taylor, Baker and so on describe what somebody once actually *did* for a living. In this case the Brythonic equivalents of *Mor* meaning 'sea' or a mutation of the Welsh word *Dwr* meaning 'water' to *Myr,* may have been combined with *Din/Dyn,* meaning 'man'. This interpretation gives Merlin the title of "*Water Man*" which surprisingly confirms the likely attributes and activities of both the mythical Merlin and the actual Myrddin, both in Celtic religious observance and in British mystery lore.

The Celtic saints who performed "miracles" at their holy wells were but a hair's breadth from the Druids who performed magic at their sacred springs. When we look at some of the supposed saintly miracles which feature such feats as beheading followed by resuscitation, we know that we are closer to the cult of *Bran* than the creed of Christ ... John the Baptist notwithstanding! Taken in this context, Myrddin the monk of Carmarthen starts to show shades of the Merlin of legend that we generally prefer. Wells and springs were popular gateways to the Underworld of *Annwn* (the Deep), which enabled our Myrddin to stand in the Celtic imagination at the gates of the unseen. In the 'water' context Myrddin can be seen as one who performs baptism at a Holy Well, perhaps, just as *Siriol* did on the Druid isle of Anglesey at *Penmon*, where the well and the remains of a hut circle can still be seen. The "water man" title can also be seen in this baptismal context in the secondary names given to more celebrated Celtic saints like St David who had the epithet *Aquaticus*. This however may not be, in Myrddin's case, the only explanation of the name, as we shall see.

According to our earliest authority, who is Aneirin, Myrddin was at the Battle of Arfderydd where, suffering from what we would now call "combat fatigue", or Post Traumatic Stress Syndrome, he ran away to the wilds somewhat off his head. A bard of more recent times, the late Robert Graves, who went to the wilds of Wales suffering from what was called "shellshock" after the First World War, would have understood. Indeed anyone who has gone through an initiation regime will also understand. New Age optimism notwithstanding, the initiations of the mysteries can externalise in quite traumatic outer circumstances which leave their scars upon a life. This is not to give the pursuit of initiation into the Brythonic mysteries a melodramatic exclusivity. Less esoteric Celtic pursuits such as rock climbing or cave diving are potentially as, if not more, dangerous physically. Nonetheless we must understand that anyone who seriously seeks initiation into the mysteries is seeking radical changes in consciousness. It is no secret that for reasons which find their nearest academic summation in Carl Jung's *synchronicity,* such radicalism entails the risk of circumstances conspiring to produce the necessary jolt to consciousness.

It is, however, when normal consciousness is totally thrown out of gear by such conditions that the Muse strikes, and poetry and prophecy issue forth. In the twelfth century, *Giraldus Cambrensis* described how the inspired wandering bards, the *Awenddyion* (Awen = inspiration), went into various fits and contortions and *"are rendered beside themselves and become possessed as if by a spirit ..."* in the process of prophecy. Myrddin may even have attained his uncomplimentary title "water man" because of his slavering or wetting himself whilst thus possessed!

Whilst there is more to either Myrddin or Merlin than the spiritual crisis of a Celtic cleric and there is more to initiation and/or prophecy than a flirtation with psychosis, we realise that Myrddin in fact went through an experience at the battle of Arfderydd that would drive any man mad.

Myrddin, or whatever his name originally was, was a native of south west Wales, perhaps of Carmarthen itself, who ended up going north to seek his fortune ... or at least the patronage of somebody who had a fortune. As young men, both Myrddin and a poet/bard who called himself, or gave himself the title of, Taliesin, probably reckoned to make their living as praise poets under the richest patronage they could secure. Unfortunately when each of them tried to do this the remaining areas of western Britain which had a bardic culture, especially Wales and North West England, were plagued by dynastic wars as the last of the great Brythonic clans engaged in the traditional Celtic pastime of tribal feuding. Taliesin and Myrddin were however of differing generations and their much quoted "Conversation" about the experiences of this warfare related in the poem from the *Black Book of Carmarthen* makes it clear that they are each talking about different battles.

For the purposes of the comparable experience of tribal warfare in the latter half of the sixth century, (so called) Taliesin was the bard who went north in service of *Urien of Rheged*, whilst Myrddin was the bard who later went north in the service of *Gwenddolau*. There is, however, a connection between the two in that these separate battles were part of one war. The battle that Taliesin experienced in Wales between *Elgan* and *Maelgwyn Gwynedd* was part of an ongoing feud which later resulted in Myrddin's involvement in the battle of Arfderydd in Cumbria in 573. The feud was either between the clans of Dyfnwal and *Coel* or contending branches of the Coel dynasty itself. Myrddin went north to serve Gwenddolau because they both belonged to the same clan. In the battle however Gwenddolau was killed and Myrddin found himself on the wrong side and thus was, either directly or indirectly, instrumental in the death of his nephew, the son of his sister Gwendydd.

This is the tragedy which not unnaturally drove him to madness to become the wild man *Myrddin Wyllt*, hiding out in the forests of

Celyddon. He later returned to south Wales and supposedly took holy orders. Whether this was as the cleric who eventually became (by taking holy orders) able to say the long overdue poetic *gwenwawd* for his fallen comrades and thus finally find peace and/or to take on a more magical function then becomes a matter of conjecture.

Myrddin Wyllt ... in the wild wood

What we begin to see is that, like the skulls at the bottom of the Walbrook, Merlin was an historical entity, a flesh and blood Celt, a poet/priest who had been part of the ultimately tragic tribal intrigues and warfare which were later to enable much of the storyline of Arthurian legend. More than this he was a man who underwent the sort of trauma and subsequent psychic transformation which is a typical prerequisite of the magical or mystical experience which prompts poetic insight, initiation or religious conversion. One of many later mediaeval examples of this would be St Francis of Assisi, who in many respects doubtless resembled Myrddin Wyllt (wild Merlin*)* when he fled from the rich life of Assisi to live in the wild among the creatures.

In more modern times we can still see the particular trauma of war giving rise to the same imperative to leave civilisation to its sorry self and go to comparatively wild places to find solace in nature. The implication is that during this isolation the beginnings of a radical change in consciousness, often accompanied by poetical and/or spiritual insight, begins to make itself felt. We have already cited Robert Graves's coming to Harlech in Snowdonia after suffering shellshock in the First World War. Subsequently his war poetry was followed by more mythological themes and his later insights into the poetic muse, *The White Goddess,* based essentially upon Welsh mythology. J.R.R. Tolkien's remarkable mythopoeic faculties also seemed to follow on from the experience of being gravely wounded in the trenches in France and also have a Welsh flavour (not least in their Elven language). Tolkien spent much of his writing time in Arthog in Snowdonia, just below the mythically shrouded mountain of Cadair Idris. T.E. Lawrence, born in Tremadoc in Snowdonia, is another example. More recently one could cite the experiences of Laurens van der Post who, surviving the horrors of a Japanese Prison Camp, took himself off to live among the bushmen in the Kalahari Desert after the Second World War.

Merlin's flight into the wild to accommodate his trauma and radical change of consciousness following the battle of Arfderydd in 573, was never an isolated incident of human nature. There have been, and doubtless will still be, many a *Myrddin Wyllt*. Neither is this phenomenon exclusive to men. Legends abound of female saints who suffered the trauma of rape and/or torture and humiliation until a psychological turning point was reached when they fled to the wilds only to find that they experienced radical spiritual transformation. The Welsh Celtic saint *Melangell* is an outstanding example. In more recent years the gifted occultist and seer *Dion Fortune* told how she began her life-long magical journey following an experience where her first employer subjected her to deliberate and calculated psychological abuse to break her spirit. After the inevitable nervous breakdown she went to the country where she remained in a state of psychological limbo (a kind of mental wilderness) for some time until initiation into a mystery school induced a transformation of consciousness. The price of such radical transformations can, as we have demonstrated, be exceedingly high!

Myrddin's poetry asks us to picture him after the battle, hiding in an apple tree in the woods of Celyddon in remorse at slaying his kin and in fear of his life from King Rhydderch's henchman Gwasawg. *Celyddon,* which is generally thought to be a location in southern Scotland, was the name which later gave Charles Williams *Broceliande* for his poetic Arthurian writings. Williams was an initiate of a mystery school which was an offshoot of the esoterically much vaunted Hermetic Order of the Golden Dawn ... as well as being one of the three famed Inklings (together with C.S. Lewis and J.R.R. Tolkien). Thus as a poet/initiate himself, albeit of the early twentieth century, Williams perhaps had some insight into Myrddin's psychological state at the time. Such insight, intuitively or intentionally, made Williams use Broceliande/Celyddon as an allegory for the Collective Unconscious in which Merlin's own consciousness goes through its transformation. "Deep in the forest something stirred" would be an understatement of the psychotic upheavals going on in the undergrowth of Myrddin's own psyche. However we have some possible indications in his later poetry which hint at recollection and understanding of what was happening to him at the time, not in the bland phraseology of modern psychology, but in the richer terms of Celtic mythology.

The poem which is called *Oianau* or the "Oh's" of Myrddin, because each stanza begins with an *"Oian"* (Oh), is a development of his earlier poem *Afallennau* (Apple Trees*).* In this latter poem he continues to recount his Celyddon experiences and the pieces of prophecy which were beginning to emerge from his radically altered states of consciousness. Such altered states of consciousness are what a mythical Taliesin experiences at the hands of the goddess *Ceridwen* after tasting from her cauldron of *Awen* (inspiration). Ceridwen's cauldron and the forest of Celyddon are both, in our limiting psychological terminology, the Collective Unconscious (among other things) which Myrddin and "Taliesin" are thrust into. This is what gives them their overview of the nature of life, of time, space and events. In Taliesin's case this results, as we shall see in our next section, in a series of totem beast transformations followed by a series of poetic visions through time. In Myrddin's case it results, in Celyddon at least, in becoming like the wild creatures and the beginnings of specific prophecy. Myrddin's poetic recollection, whilst not describing personal totem transformations, does, however, include one major totem animal, a pig, the totem animal sacred to Ceridwen. Basically Myrddin and Taliesin are describing the same initiatory experience. Hints of this similarity of initiatory experience and subsequent confusion of name and function are acknowledged in the *Hanes Taliesin* when "Taliesin" says:

"Idno and Heinin called me Merlin
(but) At length every king shall call me Taliesin"

In further parallels of initiatory experience it may also be that the 'piglet' that Myrddin is so affectionately addressing in the *Oianau* is in fact his nickname for some flesh and blood representative or priestess of Ceridwen, the goddess at whose hands Taliesin received his initiation.

I have no proof of this except from the tone of the poem itself. I would, however, suggest that phrases such as *"Oh little piglet, sow in heat, my covering is threadbare"* and *"Oh little piglet … I would like to seek out the mountain of Maon and look at the stormy gaze of lovers"* and even *"Oh lively sow"* are not addressed to a tame porker, but are, on the other hand, a little over familiar to address the Goddess directly. Myrddin is playing mythopoeic games. That he is in some sense addressing the Underworld inspirational goddess Ceridwen before uttering each piece of prophecy is clear, but the phraseology is suggestive enough to make one believe that his leaps into altered consciousness are being assisted and empowered by a mediatory female power. This may have been a flesh and blood priestess or the Faery woman, who is the empowering intermediary of most mythopoeic Celtic material. She is the muse, because the wild wood of what we can choose to call either the Collective Unconscious or the Underworld of *Annwn* is her territory.

This 'woman' appears to have been *Gwendydd*, his supposed 'sister'. In the *Afallennau* poems he is out of favour with his sister (for being responsible for the death of her son) … *"Now Gwendydd doesn't love me, doesn't greet me"*. However in *Y Cyfoesi*, an alternative poetic narrative of his time in the forest of Celyddon from the *Red Book of Hergest*, he holds a dialogue with Gwendydd in a question and answer session of prophecy. This and the fact that her name has the Underworld prefix "Gwen" (see below) and that other traditions suggest her as his lover not his sister (or perhaps both!) tend to support the idea that she is some kind of priestess or Faery companion … a "sister" in esoteric endeavour. Furthermore the references in the original Welsh to Myrddin spending his time in the forest with "*gwyllon*", which Meirion Pennar translates as "wild things", looks suspiciously similar to "*gwyllion*", the traditional mountain Faeries of North Wales. There is also mention of a prophetic muse called *Chwyfleian* which Pennar translates as "*white phantom*" who may be the same Faery creature and whose name may also suggest a primitive form of *Guinevere!*

What our poetic monk from Carmarthen seems to be assembling around him, in various forms of disguise, are the prototypes of a number of ladies from later Arthurian legend, not least the prototype of Merlin's *Nimué*. In terms of psychology we can describe this feminine factor as Jung's Contra Sexual Image, but as we have said psychology falls painfully short in describing initiatory inner experience and the stages by which it receives empowerment. Mythopoeic imagery, as the poet Myrddin realised, fares a good deal better and Charles Williams again has his Taliesin witnessing Merlin and Nimué (who he calls *Brisen*) in Broceliande as priest and priestess working for the good of the soul of *Logres*, the inner, or Collective Unconscious, of Britain.

Whatever the later mythopoeic developments, however, we clearly have an original, historic Myrddin from the *Black Book of Carmarthen* who on close scrutiny is more than a cleric/poet who went through a bad time in some tribal battle. Whatever the embellishments of Geoffrey of Monmouth, Charles Williams or anybody else, we find a warrior bard in the Carmarthen texts, who subsequently became a bard in the same esoteric sense that (so called) Taliesin did. The altered states of consciousness, the prophecies, the totem sow, priestess of Ceridwen, and/or Faery woman, all point to somebody who, later Christian priesthood notwithstanding, was actively involved in a mystery tradition with all of its magical trappings. Further hints of this can be drawn from his poems in the *Black Book,* not least the *Afallennau* (Apple Trees) poem.

Myrddin's Afallennau and Avalon

It will be obvious at a glance that *Afallennau* is the source of *Avalon* in later Arthurian legend. Avalon is an inner place, a part of that inner wilderness represented by Celyddon. That it may also have once referred to an actual location on the physical landscape would have enhanced rather than detracted from its appeal. As we have pointed out, Celtic mythology was *onomastic*. The land itself was sacred and if the inner topography of the mythology could be matched up with the outer, physical landscape so much the better. Where the match between inner and outer was particularly appropriate, sacred places (like wells, lakes, springs and old burial mounds) acted as anchor points and stepping stones between the worlds.

Myrddin tells us that the apple trees that he *hides* in are in Celyddon. The *hiding* and *apples* symbolism prompts us to recall the *Mabinogi* story of *The Dream of Rhonabwy* where Owein and Arthur sit down to play a type of magical chess called *Gwyddbwyll,* which we shall consider in detail in a later chapter. The game is set up (as the excellent translation of Gwyn and Thomas Jones describes it) on "*a mantle of brocaded silk, and he spread the mantle in front of Arthur, and an apple of red gold at each of its corners*" and "*Gwen was the name of the mantle. And one of the properties of the mantle was that the man around whom it might be wrapped no one would see him*".

Here we have apples used to secure the means of invisibility and the name of the mantle *Gwen* ("white") is a sign that we are dealing with the Underworld of *Annwn*. Pretty much everyone and everything which comes from *Annwn* (including the sacred pigs) carries the adjective *wen/wynn/gwen/gwyn* ("white") in some form or another … A-wen, Cerid-wen, Gwen, Gwynhyfwr (Guinevere) etc. What Myrddin is doing is to poetically emphasise a journey into the invisible realms of Annwn/ Underworld. This is the world of the *Awen,* of poetic inspiration and paradisal ideal (what else could grow in a sixth century Celtic Christian Eden but an *apple* tree?!)

According to Graves's somewhat suspect *Tree Calendar/Alphabet/ Ogham* thesis, the wild apple was the noblest of seven "chief trees" and was Taliesin's symbol of poetic immortality. It was beneath the apple tree that the wild hind, the goddess of inspiration, the poetic muse *hid* herself. Graves also notes a poetic association in Irish with the phrasing of "hiding place of the wild hind" and "death sense" implying that the apple tree encounter with the goddess brings death and immortality and interestingly, in the context of Myrddin's lunacy, that such "death sense" is the sanity which is finally restored to the madman at the moment of his death ... or, we might add, initiation. In fact the red and white symbolism of *Annwn* (white) interacting with the mortal world (red) is obvious in the apple, with its inner bulk being of white-ish pulp and its outer surface red. In this we have the foundations of *Afal* (the welsh word for apple) – *lon* (Avalon).

The "white" Underworld of poetic inspiration, death and immortality was peopled in Celtic lore by the human ancestors, pre-human ancestors (the realm of Faery) and the Underworld powers ... notably the inspirational and transformative cauldron powers (which were attributed to both the giant god *Bran* and, as we have said, the goddess Ceridwen). As we shall see later on, Ceridwen's underworld cauldron was located on an island (traditionally in the middle of Llyn Tegid/Bala Lake in North Wales). This is the island to which the mythical Taliesin went to receive his initiation at the hands of Ceridwen in the *Hanes Taliesin* (story of Taliesin). Ceridwen's island is a prototype of Avalon. We can see this because the same cauldron that appears in the *Branwen Daughter of Llŷr* myth was brought from (the island of) Ireland and given to Bran (who unwisely gave it back to the Irish king!) One of the more remarkable properties of this cauldron was that it could bring slain warriors back to life. Thus the mortally wounded Arthur had to go to such an island, an *Afallon/Avalon*, as he says to Bedivere in Tennyson's *Morte d'Arthur*, to *"heal me of my grievous wound"*. It is interesting to follow through the association here of our Myrddin the "water man" as somebody who travels to an inner "island" ... an apple island of Avalon.

Where Avalon might have existed on the "outer" landscape becomes more of a problem. Popular Arthurian topography has placed it at that (equally legitimate) underworld location of Glastonbury, which would have been a series of islands on a lake and part of the Celtic kingdoms in the sixth century. Naturally for the sake of our Welsh bards, however: Taliesin, Myrddin and Aneirin, whose mythopoeic efforts laid, after all, the very foundations of Arthurian legend, one would rather see it within the wild country of north and west Wales. This is where it all began. This is the landscape of the *Mabinogi,* of the primitive cauldron myths from which the Grail sprang and where Arthur and his Celtic heroes were spawned before they grew into the romanticised pristine knights of the Middle Ages.

So, it would be easy enough to set that Underworld Isle of Apples back on Bala Lake where it all originated. Legend says that it was from this same lake that Excalibur was later drawn. At the end of the lake stands the old Roman cavalry fort of *Caer Gai*, the castle of Cei, who became the Sir Kay of later Arthurian legend, and early companion of the fostered boy king Arthur. Over the hills, wedged between Cadair Idris and the Aran ridge, is the hillside called Camlan, and just to the north a river, Afon Gamlan, both of which could so easily be the Camlan of that last battle of the Arthurian saga.

Less than four miles from where the Afon Gamlan joins the Mawddach at Ganllwyd is Caer March. In the elegaic *Grave poems* the poet reminds us that there is no grave known for Arthur, after this his supposed last battle, but in the preceding line does, however, tell us that there *is* a grave for March (and now it seems conveniently near by!)

After the battle, Bedwyr/Bedivere would have had only an hour or two's ride to return the sword to the lake from which it traditionally came and there, out on the lake, was Ceridwen's island of poetic apples, the original Avalon, with the cauldron which could restore and preserve the mortally wounded Arthur.

It all fits so easily to this Gwynedd landscape, bypassing the claims of the mediaeval Arthurian romancers and the Glastonbury monks and keeping things within the Welsh context of their source. There are problems with this of course, not least because Myrddin infers that the place of the apple trees is attached to the forest of Celyddon, which we know was located in the western lowlands of Scotland. At first glance he seems to hide here in an area of wild apple trees in the forest avoiding capture and death after the battle of Arfderydd, then, many years later (when the internecine feuds had died down) making his way back to Wales and eventually to Carmarthen. This obviates any geographical Avalon in either Wales or Somerset!

We do know that the island of Ceridwen's cauldron, our proto Avalon, was sited in the middle of Llyn Tegid … Bala Lake. The *Hanes Taliesin* goes so far as to name Ceridwen's husband as "*Tegid Foel*", and *Gwion Fach* … little Gwion, the lad who will become the legendary Taliesin, is from *Llanfair Caereinion* just across the Berwyn mountains. There is no mistaking the outer world location, the mythology insists upon it. But when we visit the lake, the island itself just isn't there! The lake is a deep glaciated ravine which was flooded in primordial time, plunging to considerable depth, a Welsh Loch Ness. There never was an island in the middle of it! As to the site of Arthur's grave being in Avalon, the Black Book confirms "*Anoeth bid bet y Arthur*" … "the grave of Arthur is a mystery". So there is no physical location for proto Avalon and no physical location for the resting place of Arthur with which it is associated.

The Death of Arthur

Camlan

The River Camlan at Ganllwyd, just a
few miles from Llanelltyd and in sight
of Cadair Idris. "Camlan" is reported
to have been the site of Arthur's last
battle, where he was mortally wounded.
An area called Caer March, dominated
by a tumulus, is about two miles away.
This may be the "grave of March"
referred to in the Graves Poems in the
Black Book of Carmarthen, below.

The Graves Poems from the Black Book of Carmarthen

**Bet y March, bet y Guythur, bet y Gugaun
Cledyfrut. Anoeth bid bet y Arthur.**

"A grave for March, a grave for Gwythyr, a grave for
Gwagan redsword. The grave of Arthur is a mystery."

Facsimile (right) of a long lost marker said to have been found by the
monks of Glastonbury Abbey, thus "proving" that a grave found there
was that of Arthur and Guinevere. The marker carried the inscription:

**Hic iacet Arthurus rex quondam rexque futurus.
(Here lies Arthur the once and future king.)**

The fact that the English king made the suggestion to the monks that the
grave was there, and, needing money, they miraculously found it shortly afterwards,
makes it almost certainly a piece of propaganda. It would have suited the king to
demonstrate to the unruly Welsh that their eternal mythical hero from centuries
gone by was just a dead man. The spurious grave marker would seem to give the
game away. If this was really the dead Arthur, he was obviously not "Rex futurus"!

Llyn Tegid (Bala Lake)

Bala Lake held the otherworld (and thus
invisible) island of Ceridwen where Taliesin
(a sometime companion of Arthur) received
his initiation/validation as a bard. It would
also seem to be the lake from which Arthur,
under much the same mythical provisions,
received Caledfwlch (Excalibur) from the

Lady of the Lake, and was thus the lake to which the sword was returned "from
whence it came" after the battle at Camlan. The River Camlan at Ganllwyd is no more
than twenty miles from the lake. The route would be the old Roman road which had
once led to the Roman cavalry post at Caer Gai. Cei, after whom it was named, was
"Sir Kay", the companion of Arthur from childhood.

We might think that Myrddin's apple riddles have lead us astray and that Avalon was a later, mediaeval invention concocted at Glastonbury to go along with its otherworldly legends and the Somerset monks' story for an English king that Arthur was buried there. Typically a Welsh "Avalon" would in any case be spelt "Afallon".

Here Professor Griffen provides a crumb of Celtic comfort. In his *Names from the Dawn of British Legend* (Llanerch 1994), he assures us that the correct *early* Welsh spelling of our elusive island would have been "Avalon" because the Double L ("ll") convention did not come into use until the tenth century. Prior to this it was pronounced in the current English way as "L". This shows that the idea of Avalon and indeed Myrddin's poetry are of a ripe old age, predating the Normans and the later improvisations of the Middle Ages. Our favourite improviser, Geoffrey, tells us that the sword Caliburn/Excalibur ... that came out of the lake (Llyn Tegid/Bala as we shall later see) "was forged in the Isle of Avalon". So if Geoffrey isn't on one of his more exotic flights of fancy in this we can say that the sword came "out of Bala Lake from Avalon".

That Avalon was thus a Faery/Underworld realm is confirmed in that the Lady of the Lake is a typical example of what Welsh folklore knows as a *Gwraig Annwn* ("a wife of the deep"), a beautiful Faery who inhabits lakes and wells.

The reason that we look for Avalon and never, like the grave of Arthur, find it, is therefore clear. Avalon is in the realm of Faery and the poetic/Edenic *afal* (apple) which gives it its name grows in this paradisal Celtic garden of the Hesperides and confers (as in the magical chess game of Gwyddbwyll) invisibility. Avalon may be approached and its portals identified on the physical landscape at Llyn Tegid, at Ynys Witrin (Glastonbury) or at Coed Celiddyon in Scotland, or any number of places, but as soon as any "waterman" crosses that Styx between incarnate and discarnate being and enters those portals he fades into the sacred landscape and is lost to view. What happened to Myrddin Wyllt in Celyddon is what happened to Thomas the Rhymer and to the mythical Taliesin and all those who have taken that fateful initiatory step into the mysteries of the land.

Again we see how what at first glance seems to be a nature poem of monastic Myrddin in his dotage is in fact laden with esoteric innuendo. This is the true mission of poetry, to facilitate a magic which compresses inner and normally incomprehensible mysteries into cartoon flashes of comprehension. In these seemingly simple verses Myrddin provided us with prophecy, with an account of the whole business of initiatory experience, as well as a multi-faceted mythical base for the magnificent edifice of the Arthurian legends, which were to follow.

The Scottish Merlin

Much has been made in recent years of a Merlin tradition in Scotland, particularly associated with Hart Fell. This is perfectly feasible in the light of Myrddin's experiences with the dynastic wars which, tragically, raged among the Celts themselves up and down most of the Western British Isles. We have already shown that Myrddin fled from the battle of Arfderydd which is near Longtown in Cumbria to Celyddon in the western lowlands of Scotland. A tradition of Myrddin Wyllt as *Llallogan*, which means "an outsider" or "strange man" equates with the Scottish wild man of the woods *Lailoken* who was associated with St Kentigern. The experiences of Myrddin as Llallogan may be culled from the poem *Y Cyfoesi* that we have already mentioned, which appears in the *Red Book of Hergest*. Certainly the later experiences of Thomas the Rhymer and, later still, Robert Kirk – of going into Faery and developing the gift of prophecy – continued a Myrddin/Underworld tradition in Scotland, which is so masterfully described in the books of R.J. Stewart (notably *The Underworld Initiation*).

The later Arthurian legends, which as we have seen, tend to pick out and highlight the salient points of earlier tradition, place one set of Arthurian characters in a Scottish setting. These are King *Lot of Lothian* and his wife *Morgause,* among whose children are *Gawain* and *Gareth.* Gawain was, however, known to the earlier Welsh mythographers as *Gwalchmai* (the Hawk of May). To what extent these characters were pure fiction or thumbnail sketches drawn from accounts of Myrddin, pseudo-Taliesin and Aneirin of the personalities involved in the northern clan wars, must be a matter of conjecture.

Merlin, Atlantis and the British Empire

Geoffrey's bardic "history" paved the way for one further aspect of Merlin which became adopted and adapted in more recent times. Geoffrey's history was not simply his "virtual" account of the struggles of the Celts against the Saxons. He sought to identify the birth of the Brythonic Celts and to give them a sense of origins and legitimacy. Whilst a good deal of the (pre-Geoffrey) Celtic mythological material has no doubt been lost since his time, there may still only have been, then as now, elusive fragments of myth to hint at "origins", with no precise mythological statement of Celtic beginnings in Britain. What Geoffrey failed to appreciate was that the Celts had arrived in small tribal units over a great period of time. They had not made a decisive arrival here as "a people" and their fragmented mythology of their origins reflected this. Geoffrey in wishing to tidy things up and emphasise the sense of one Celtic folk soul, soon set to work.

He made a Trojan called *Brutus* get a message from the oracle of Diana which would send him from the Mediterranean to northern Europe (Gaul) and thence to make landfall in an idyllic island which was only inhabited by a few giants. Here we have resonances of the Bran legend we are soon to examine and "The Island of the mighty". He called this new land Britain, after himself, and his companions were, he decided, no longer known as Trojans but as "Brythons."

To be fair, Geoffrey wasn't too far off the mark. From snatches of proto history and myth he had devised a construct of the drift of a group of peoples from southern central Europe who the Greeks had called *Keltoi,* from which our term *Celt* originates. Having got into northern Gaul they then crossed the Channel and made landfall in south West Britain.

Of course much the same scenario could have been applied to the earlier Beaker folk, but either way, for Geoffrey's purposes, it did the job.

However, racial memories of heroes and giants and journeys across the primordial seas were to touch more remote areas of the racial psyche than the incursions of Celtic or Bronze Age peoples into these islands. Geoffrey, the hijacker of historical themes, soon had his own ideas hijacked and embellished, and eventually even his history of Brythonic origins fell foul of the "improvers". The prize of these later hijackings was none other than his chief character, Merlin.

The eventual culprits were the Hermetic mystery lodges of nineteenth century Britain whose interest was a reflection of the Pre-Raphaelite obsession with Arthurian lore. The seers of these esoteric orders made credible links with the functions of the legendary Merlin and, seeing him as an archetypal *manu*, saw his hand in pre-human evolution. However, esoteric doctrines of the evolution of races who have inhabited the Earth sphere, whilst having an archetypal accuracy, are as careless of historical chronology as Geoffrey was when he got Merlin to build Stonehenge. Having said that, it is only fair to point out that in a study of bardism, and the mystery tradition which spawned it, we are more concerned with that *virtual* history which ferments in the cauldron of the Brythonic folksoul to create mythology than we are with either an *actual* or *factual* historical record.

The poetry and artistry of the Pre-Raphaelites, married to Victorian yearnings for esoteric explanations, soon recruited Merlin, realising that his association with water and his semi-divine origins (according to Geoffrey he was the result of a liaison between a princess and an otherworld being) qualified him for greater things than even Geoffrey had dreamed of. The ingredients were in place for an association which went back into the mists of prehistory where Merlin could walk with the likes of the biblical *Melchizadek* (Genesis, chapter 14), the Babylonian *Oannes* and the Atlantean *Narada*. These are the beings which the mystery schools sometimes call by the Theosophical term *manu*, to describe the great way-showers to humanity, whom initiate new epochs in the evolution of the planet.

St Paul used this theme to liken Christ to the great *manu* of Hebrew myth, *Melchizadek* of Genesis, who being *"without father, without mother, without descent, having neither beginning of days or end of life, but made like unto the son of God abideth a priest continually"*. Merlin legend can certainly go along with such a character. St Paul goes on (in his letter to the Hebrews) to assure his readers that *"About Melchizadek we shall have much to say"*, but either time or censorship seems to have prevented him from doing so. The mythopoeic writer J.R.R. Tolkien summed up this many faceted Merlin in his *Gandalf* character who appears in *The Hobbit, The Lord of the Rings, The Silmarillion* and accompanying books.

Gandalf is primarily presented as the grouchy old wizard who becomes the great mover behind matters of state. Like Myrddin Wyllt he also undergoes an initiation/transformation following a descent into (not just psychological) hell. It transpires that he is one of the *Istari*, wise, immortal beings of angelic origin sent from the paradisal, immortal lands over the Western sea to enter Middle Earth as priest/magicians to set things to rights.

Merlin was needed to produce this same multi-faceted character, which Tolkien was later to sense in Gandalf, as an archetype that had become resident in the British psyche. Tolkien's fellow mythopoeic writers, the "Inklings" C.S. Lewis and Charles Williams, also acknowledged this 'return' of Merlin in their own writings. The British mystery school tradition (of which Williams was an active member) had by then assimilated the realisation of this new homegrown *manu,* this new, universal Merlin, as the glue with which to bind a fragmented native mythology together, just as Geoffrey had done almost eight hundred years before.

This new Merlin, like Gandalf, had his origins from across the Western ocean. On the one hand he is the grumpy old "Druid" wizard who engineered the conception of Arthur, and the elevation of Arthur to kingship of all the Brythons, as well as the institution of the Round Table ideals (a post-Geoffrey innovation) of an equitable kingdom. On the other hand Merlin did this as an Atlantean manu, leaving the doomed islands in the Atlantic to graft its teaching to the evolution of the primitive British. It has to be said, in all fairness, that if we are to insist on any Merlin archetype evolving out of traumatic experience, then the Atlantean scenario of having one's homeland sink into the Atlantic depths in earthquake and volcanic fire would probably qualify!

In this latter Atlantean manifestation Merlin is said to have been given his mandate by the "previous" manu Narada, who brought in the original Atlantean epoch. In this esoteric myth Narada stands in for Merlin's traditional teacher *Blaise.* In that Merlin is of divine origin (albeit with an all too human temperament!) Narada is an extremely lofty being who is responsible for the pre-human races that have initial stewardship of the Earth. It is thus Narada who is credited with standing before the throne of the Most High God, respectfully reproofing his master and creator with that immortal phrase *"Said not the ancient ones before thee 'Make not man'"* ... a piece of hindsighted wisdom which the nice old man in the clouds must have reluctantly pondered both then and since! When humankind does, nonetheless, arrive in Earth, it is Merlin and his fellow manus who have to get stuck in and try and sort out the teething troubles. Despite initial success, yet as if to prove a point, the mythical initiatives of both Narada and Merlin fail (at least up until the time of writing!)

Atlantis fell on evil times and the misuse of magic unleashed the forces of its destruction. Merlin's Arthurian Britain finally collapsed in a battle where Arthur and his bastard son slew each other. In that same last battle, which seems to have been a thinly disguised rewrite of the futile internecine slaughter at Arfderydd, almost all the company of the Round Table, who embodied the ideals of a Brythonic paradisal plan, died.

At the historical time of Arfderydd, a golden age was ebbing away in futile and bloody Celtic feuding, Saxon incursion and the ever-tightening grip of the Church of Rome on native Celtic Christianity. Merlin, whether we see him as a Celtic war veteran or the great high priest who gauges the pulse of the Celtic folk soul, stands at the ebbing away of a Brythonic world. The Victorians, who had since re-conquered the known world, believed it was time to re instate that Brythonic/British ideal ... Merlin was in a sense required, they thought, to inaugurate some great Table Round which seemed to symbolise the British Empire, yet like the Arthurian, even the historical "Merlin", he ended up presiding over two bloody world wars and the fragmentation of that Empire. But he remains the essential archetype of wisdom and statesmanship in the British racial psyche and perhaps whilst he has seen a few battles lost, it may yet be that the war, the traumatic evolution of the British folksoul, can still be won.

Taliesin

Merlin, Taliesin and Aneirin left it a bit late to be Celts of renown, because by the time we first get a mention of them the Celtic era is almost over. Whilst we have dealt with a semi-historical Merlin/Myrddin and a definitely historical Aneirin, Taliesin remains something of an enigma. Close examination of the many poems attributed to him, in the *Peniarth 2* manuscript collection called *The Book of Taliesin*, which contains the previously cited *Armes Prydein (Prophecy of Britain)*, shows a wide range of stylistic and structural technique. Whilst such matters may appear trifling at first glance, they do in fact enable us to come to some fairly major conclusions.

Welsh bardic poetry was probably faithful in oral transmission but sporadic in its written record. It was designed to be recited and heard rather than read. However the written record, even when later copies are studied, betrays the intended pronunciation and metric structure of a piece. Because of bardic conservatism in poetic convention, held to particular rules of composition at particular times, and because the different languages in use (Brythonic, Old Welsh, Middle Welsh) demanded different orthography, meter and pronunciation, we are able to date poems fairly accurately. This can even be the case where we are dealing (as we inevitably are) with later copies of originals, because as long as the underlying structure can be gleaned, the language and style can be detected. Modern scholarship detecting such devices as *mesotomy* (a split syllable technique only used in Old Welsh and extensively apparent in the *Armes Prydein*) is even sophisticated enough *usually* to be able to detect any cheating. In other words if a poet in the Middle Welsh period was trying to write a piece in pseudo Old Welsh or the much earlier Brythonic style, this would be apparent.

The cult of Taliesin

The conclusions supported by such detective work on the *Book of Taliesin* have indicated that there was certainly more than one poet calling himself Taliesin. Unless Taliesin had lived for about five centuries, and during that time had been able to adapt to a wide range of composition styles in several linguistic variations, there must have been quite a few of "him". However this in no way invalidates the range of poetry that claims his authorship; indeed rather than detracting from the work of one individual it exemplifies a whole tradition! Taliesin represents an esoteric bardic cult which certain initiate poets seem to have represented over a long period of time. Whilst our written sources only date from the late Brythonic period of the *Canu Aneirin* (in which Taliesin is mentioned) in about 600 AD, the cult may have been a good deal older. Some of the lore expounded in Taliesin poetry seems, as we shall see, to have more to do with the mystery cults of the late Bronze Age than with the Celts, whilst other items show a sound grasp of Middle Eastern metaphysics and Christian esotericism. These are matters which we shall be considering at some length later in this book.

The Taliesin "trademark" continues to appear well into the thirteenth century and the fact that copies (and even copies of copies) of poems were continuously made, indicates that some esoteric sect of the bardic community continued to believe in at least the authority of the name. The tone of the poems varies enormously, from the unashamedly esoteric *Hanes Taliesin* and *Preiddu Annwn* on the one hand to the almost boot-licking praise poem *Ni'th oes Cystedlydd* ("You are the best") addressed to the poet's employer *Urien of Rheged*. This dichotomy has persuaded some commentators to suggest an historically verifiable Taliesin the praise-singer, employed by the historic personages of Urien of Rheged and *Cynan* in the sixth century, who was succeeded by a string of "Johnny come latelys" peddling dubious esoteric material in his name.

The problem seems to be the all too natural use of "him" and "his" attached to grasped historical straws. Once we get used to the idea that Taliesin was never a personal name, but rather an initiatory title given to members of a bardic cult or tradition, then we can see that perhaps Urien's bard was a member of this cult, or wanted others to think that he was. It is not inconceivable that an initiate bard who was entitled to use the name Taliesin had a mundane "day job" as a court poet! That such men placed themselves at times in positions where they could apply subtle influence has frequently been the case. For a ruler to be able to boast that he had a "Taliesin" as his bard may also have been the Dark Age equivalent of some self-important person claiming that he has a seventh dan black belt as his bodyguard!

I am persuaded that Geoffrey of Monmouth was well aware of this situation in Wales and wanted to use his Merlin figure to fulfil this "Taliesin" role. His references to Taliesin were intended to make the connection, but to make the point stick for his non-Welsh audience he used the model of an historically existing person who was a member of that cult (Myrddin) rather than the mythological Taliesin. Had Taliesin been a historically known figure, Geoffrey would not have given Myrddin the time of day! Hence, as we did earlier in this chapter, we return to the assertion in the *Hanes Taliesin*:

*"Idno and Heinin called me Merlin ...
(but) At length every king shall call me Taliesin"*

Whether an individual *Taliesin* existed right at the beginning, perhaps way back in the Bronze Age, is of little consequence. Yet it is to Taliesin, or rather to a whole flock of "Taliesins", that we owe many tracts of what is obviously mystery teaching. These have been hailed in recent years as the grist of the Celtic Mysteries ... even the *shamanic* Celtic mysteries ... but as we examine them we shall be asking just how "Celtic" they or their originators were.

The *Hanes Taliesin,* which describes how Taliesin originated, is a late piece of writing from the thirteenth century. Poets had been calling themselves Taliesin long before this, as we have seen, and indeed the earlier claims on the name were frequently attached to more sober material in the conventional court bard style. The reason for this is plain. At the height of their powers mystery cults have always tended to keep their public face comparatively expressionless. Nobody in the earlier days was giving the game away. The name was there but that was as much as they were telling. As the centuries went by, however, men broke ranks and spoke, sometimes for the most altruistic reasons. As the cult began to fade along with the whole bardic structure, there may well have been a fear that its knowledge would be lost to posterity. We certainly get a sense of this situation in "Taliesin's" delivery of the *Preiddeu Annwn* (discussed later) and we can perhaps see something of this too in Geoffrey of Monmouth's motives. This has certainly been the case with modern esoteric organisations. Israel Regardie's publication of the rituals and training papers of The Hermetic Order of the Golden Dawn in its sunset years seems to have been motivated along such lines.

In the *Hanes Taliesin* somebody has finally decided, one would hope from altruistic motive, to set down the core mythology of the cult, which embodies its initiatory procedures and philosophy. After Geoffrey of Monmouth's disclosures they probably thought that it didn't anyway matter that much any more. Geoffrey, who was probably an initiate of this Taliesin bardic system in its later, fading years, had published the *Prophecies* and provided, in Merlin, a king's bard who was as magically capable as the archetypal Taliesin. He has Merlin employing the Taliesin shape shifting techniques to get Uther Pendragon to mate with Ygraine so Arthur may be born. He also tells how Merlin, whilst only a youth, throws down the gauntlet to Vortigern's ignorant bards, to show how a real initiate, a real bard, stacked up against the modern pretenders at the de-mythologised Christian courts of petty rulers of a dwindling Welsh nation. This was a theme echoed by some other Taliesin initiate in his story of "Taliesin" challenging the bards of Maelgwyn Gwynedd. The complaint from this "old school" of esoteric bardism is clear … everywhere petty rulers in a fading Celtic world were employing bards who didn't know what real bardship was all about … so no wonder the English were having the Welsh for breakfast!

The later fantastic literature attributed to Taliesin and the magical abilities of Geoffrey's Merlin are, I would contend, a case of a magical bardic cult "coming out of the closet". This in itself had the desired effect of producing something of a Celtic revival at the time! We should however note the way that such "wisdom literature" was presented. Britain had by this time become a country whose Christianity was very much under the austere heel of Rome. The magic presented is therefore a mythology set in a Christian context. Geoffrey makes a point of being pro-Roman; Roman heroes are folded into his work and into the later Mabinogi material and Arthur is presented as a *dux bellorum* after the Roman model, and a Christian *dux bellorum* at that, fighting against the pagan Saxons. When the Taliesin initiate sets out to give a thinly disguised account of a magical journey to the underworld in the *Preiddeu Annwn* he is careful to open his poem with a disclaimer of any pagan intent. He begins the poem with the rather disjointing lines (Nash's translation) *"Praise to the Lord, the supreme ruler of the heavens, who hath extended his dominion to the shore of the world"* then, having put this safety device of orthodoxy in place, proceeds to take his audience plunging into the pre-Christian precincts of Annwn.

Such guarded disclosures of esoteric information were not confined to Wales; indeed the disclosure of esoteric secrets, usually stemming from a desperate bid for preservation of the knowledge, is a universal phenomenon. We see the same thing happening down the centuries with English folklore, as what were once esoteric ceremonies become folk dances and what were once secret lore become children's tales and folksongs. So here, albeit in English and almost, but not quite, as taught to every child in every Welsh speaking school, is the grist of the *Hanes Taliesin*.

hanes Taliesin

Somewhere beyond time as we now reckon it, the goddess Ceridwen lived on an island in the centre of Bala Lake with her husband Tegid Foel (for the lake is called *Tegid* in Welsh). Ceridwen and Tegid had two children, a daughter of exquisite beauty and a son of profound ugliness. The daughter was called *Creirwy* ("dear one") and the ugly son *Morfran* or sometimes *Afagddu* (the "darkest"). Tegid their father was a cruel man and one legend says that because of Tegid's cruelty, the lake spilled over one night and drowned everyone … at least everyone except a young harper who had been led away by the omen of a bird. We shall meet the young harper again soon, and his name in this tale may be Gwion. Later myth remembered Morfran as Mordred, yet his name is associated with the words *mor* (sea) and *Fran* (Bran).

In the time beyond time, when the mists that rose over the lake were the vapours from Ceridwen's cauldron, it was the gathering time, the time when the year slipped into winter and the cauldron of inspiration needed to be made ready. Ceridwen gathered mysterious herbs, that would simmer as potent dreams in the winter cauldron that was also the womb of rebirth. For this was the great cauldron that the raven god Bran had brought from Ireland, that other 'secret island' across the water. And in the cauldron of Bran the dead were brought to life again. More than this the cauldron would, Ceridwen hoped, give *awen* ... inspiration and wisdom to her son Afagddu to compensate for his ugliness.

So patiently Ceridwen gathered her herbs, whilst the evening sun hid itself further in the north and the winter moved closer. But whilst she was out gathering, there was nobody who would stir her cauldron. At length, she chose a young lad from over the Berwyn mountains in Llanfair Caereinion, called *Gwion*. So whilst Ceridwen gathered, Gwion stirred the heady, otherworld brew. Then one day towards the winter solstice, as Gwion stirred, three drops of the brew spattered onto his finger. The lad winced, then licked the drops off. Suddenly, little Gwion ap Gwreang from Llanfair Caereinion found that he could see across time. Past and future were laid before him. He looked into the near future, then looked again, realising that when Ceridwen had finished her gathering, she meant to kill him.

Not unnaturally he fled, hoping to leave the island in the lake and head for home. Ceridwen sensed what had happened and was after him, no longer the maternal herbalist, but a vampirous screaming hag. Then Gwion changed. He wasn't sure how he had changed, but something in the brew gave him the ability to transform. He became a hare; but Ceridwen, mistress of the cauldron of transformation, knew all about that and became a greyhound. Gwion became a fish, Ceridwen became an otter. Then Gwion changed to a bird and with a sinking feeling of the inevitable, he saw Ceridwen change into a hawk. Below him he saw a threshing floor at a farmstead and quickly fluttered down to earth and became a grain of corn. He thought that such a transformation might make him hard to detect, but Ceridwen swooped down nearby and became a hen. She clucked about pecking at the ground for a while. Then she had him, and he was swallowed up.

Having digested the grain that was Gwion, Ceridwen changed back to her normal self, but that was hardly the end of the matter. Within a short space of time she realised that she was pregnant, in fact pregnant with Gwion.

In due course Gwion was born, and despite herself, Ceridwen couldn't kill the beautiful child that lay against her ample breast. She had an uncanny feeling about the fate of this one, so she let fate take a hand. She put the child in a leather bag and took him to the sea, setting him adrift like Moses. The bag floated out into what is now Cardigan Bay and was gone.

It was May Eve, the season of Beltane, and a prince named *Elphin* had come to a weir in the Dovey estuary to net salmon. The salmon he was after was of course the traditional salmon of knowledge, but he netted another knowledge-bearing creature instead. Elphin retrieved the bag, opened it and found the child Gwion. The child said that he was a bard who had been in the bag for forty years and that his name was *Taliesin* which means "radiant brow". In fact the name is more appropriately translated as "Rainbow Brow", for whilst the Welsh word for rainbow is *enfys,* the rainbow is the *Caer Ceridwen* and therefore sacred to the goddess who initiated Taliesin. The child with the radiant/rainbow brow soon grew and became the great bard of the Celtic mysteries, the arch adept of his race. He first showed his bardic prowess in the court of Elphin's uncle Maelgwyn Gwynedd at Deganwy, to obtain the release of Elphin from prison. In a battle of poetic riddles Maelgwyn's court bards were defeated and Elphin was freed. The fame of Taliesin grew from this exploit to others until finally his fame soared into popular Welsh folklore to parallel that of Geoffrey's earlier Merlin.

As with the other mythologies we can for the most part trace the myth onto the landscape; in fact we can see it woven from the very elements of manifest nature.

Gwion had left Llanfair Caereinion as Gwion; then sipping from the cauldron of destiny on the mysterious island of the goddess, he had changed. But that was not enough. He had to go through, or be chased through, a fivefold transformation. He had transformed through three elements, even as a 'Taliesin' poem described the initiate being 'whirled around' between three elements. Firstly, the Gwion of the original story had changed from a boy to an animal that ran on the EARTH, thence to a fish in the element of WATER and thence to a bird, in the element of AIR. All these 'creature changes' by both Gwion and Ceridwen have 'totem' associations. On the fourth transformation he became a grain of wheat, the very symbol of life and cyclic growth, and in his fifth transformation a foetus implanted in the womb of the goddess. The fact that this transformation and consumption by the goddess, the real grist of the initiation process, takes place upon a threshing floor is also not without significance. It will be recalled that the Jerusalem temple, of which the Christianised bards of this time would of course have been aware, had been founded upon *the threshing floor of Ornan (or Araunah) the Jebusite.* The fact that the most holy place, the centre of the world, was therefore a rock platform upon which grain was threshed ... and subsequently used as a sacred offering ... would not have been lost upon the poet.

From the (next) 'cauldron' of Ceridwen's womb, and after a partial rebirth as 'son of the goddess' Gwion was consigned to the greater womb of the ocean. Both the cauldron and womb symbolism are preserved here in that the initiate is immersed in the universal amniotic fluid from which creation arose. He is then propelled on the currents of destiny as a star is carried along by the tides of deep space. From that ocean he was reborn again as Taliesin, bard of Prince Elphin.

There is no allegory here: to the initiate of the Celtic mysteries the winter island of Ceridwen, the cauldron, the elemental initiations, the 'entombment' in the womb of the underworld goddess, then the feeling of being helplessly set adrift before being found, would be all too real. We have looked at the reality of initiation in the grim experience of Myrddin, which can be set to the landscape, the outer garment of the goddess whose priest he became under the aegis of the Taliesin cult. The core mythology of the cult, set out in part in the *Hanes Taliesin,* may also be aligned to the landscape and certainly in part to that same landscape which includes an island of Avalon and a Camlan not too far away, as we have already discussed.

Che Goddess, the Bards and the Land

We have also discussed the fact that whilst the island of Ceridwen, our proto Avalon, does not physically exist, and never did, the lake surrounding it, Llyn Tegid, most certainly does. As we shall see, this lake became the focus of a number of mythological themes. The mountains which surround the lake and the whole area of the upper Dee Valley around Corwen and Bala were a geographical focus from which this mythological web extended. To the south west the Roman road runs parallel to the long ridge of the Berwyn and the Aran, until the Aran briefly dips before rearing up again into the great bastions of the Faery fortress of *Cadair Idris,* chair of the great star mage *Idris,* whom we shall meet later. Cadair Idris was also the site of Taliesin's further adventures in the high *Cadair* (chair*).* To the north is the other Roman road that was to become sacred to *Elen of the Roads,* which skirts *Tomen y Mur,* the onomastic site of the *Llew and Blodeuwedd* legend. The Trawsfynydd moors fall away from here, down into the vale of Maentwrog, another legendary location, then roll northward and westward again to the place where *Gwydion* defeated *Pryderi* and inland to *Dinas Emrys* where Merlin took on the bards of Vortigern.

The myths were about *sovereignty,* the relationship of man to the goddess and thus the land and so the bards crafted the myths to fit the landscape. The area around Llyn Tegid is a complex of Bronze Age, Iron Age, Roman and Dark Age sites. Even in the *Hanes,* which is essentially an inner, Underworld adventure, we can see the goddess and her initiate active in the landscape.

When the goddess called him, "little Gwion" (or the initiates who made the pilgrimage in his stead) went due north following her sacred star. He passed the old Caer in the area called *Ffynon Arthur* and kept going north, over the *Cefn Bran*, named after the great Underworld god of the cauldron, then over the Tanat valley and on up into the mountains of *Llanrhaeadr Ym Mochnant. Moch* is the Welsh for pigs, the creatures sacred to Ceridwen. Once he was up on the high open plateau the walking was safer and easier, but he turned slightly west to avoid going down the steep sides of the Rhaeadr valley and soon picked up the old trackway which connects the Bronze Age burial cairns that run from Cwm Rhiwiau up along the Berwyn ridge before dropping away from the burial site called *Bwrdd Arthur* (Arthur's Table) and the cairn of *Cadair Branwen* (the chair of Branwen, Bran's goddess/priestess sister whom we shall meet later). He then made his way down the hillside by the track which leads to the burial complex and circle of *Moel Ty Uchaf* (a site we shall consider in detail). Below him was the valley of the Dee shimmering in the autumn sunlight. He made his way down following the stream and came out on the floor of the valley by the old mound at *Caer Y Bont* and followed the Dee westwards to its source ... the myth-laden *Llyn Tegid.* On the lake he was drawn into the "Avalon" precincts of Ceridwen's inner realm of Annwn where he went through the transformation/shape shifting procedures, until finally he was absorbed into her very being. Then Ceridwen gave him rebirth into the outer world again but bound him in a leather bag, so that he was concealed from the world's gaze and unable to immediately make known the experience that he had gone through. The bards would have visualised her taking the bag and striking south west, down the valley, past the old Roman Cavalry fort at *Caer Gai* (which was later to become the castle of the Arthurian "Sir Kay") and on down the Roman road which heads towards Cadair Idris and the sea. She carried her burden westwards, past Brithdir and the mouth of the pass that leads to Camlan. Then on below the towering Cadair, the "uneasy chair above Caer Sidi" as one Taliesin initiate tells us, adding how he had had the sensation of being whirled around in a kind of vortex. This is the place where legend says that if anyone spends the night there he will awake as a bard or a madman ... or a corpse ... and even now corpses come off Cadair Idris!

Below Cadair Idris runs the old Bronze Age trackway, marked with standing stones and burials called the *Ffordd Ddu*, the dark road. This is the route that Ceridwen would have taken in last stage of her journey, with the leather bag, to the sea. The track would have brought her down to Cae Ddu where she would have thrown it into the surf and the currents would have taken it away round the headland and down to the Dovey estuary, where some time later Elphin would have caught it at his weir at a place understandably since called *Tre Taliesin*. There he was named at the season of Beltane, a Celtic Moses, mighty in magic so that all true bards were thereafter initiates in his name. Perhaps even a bard called *Gruffydd ap Arthur*, whom we may know better as Geoffrey of Monmouth.

CHAPTER THREE

The Search for Arthur

WHILST THE ORIGINS of King Arthur are, to say the least, uncertain, we must look initially for him in early Welsh myth, and proto history. This will not be the Arthur that we grew up with, and that is really the problem with King Arthur ... we *think* we know him!

The Arthur we grew up with, surrounded by his knights in late mediaeval plate armour charging across the Californian landscape of bad 1950s movies (not to mention the Gwynedd landscape of bad 1990s movies!) derived, with a great dollop of Hollywood re-modelling, from the British Victorian Arthur of Tennyson and the Pre-Raphaelite poets and painters. They in turn took their Arthur from mediaeval romance, and mediaeval romance had cultivated an Arthur who was only nominally Brythonic.

The problem with trying to seek out King Arthur is therefore that we have been so habituated to "having him around" that even historians assume that he must have existed, in spite of the very flimsy evidence which gives only passing mention to him before Geoffrey of Monmouth and the other mediaeval romancers got their teeth into him. As we have seen with Taliesin, such evidence – a poetic aside here and there – does not prove that a single individual of that particular name existed in a particular time frame.

Che arthur of history

As we mentioned in our last chapter, *Arthur* makes his first fleeting appearance in the old Celtic setting of our native Brythonic tongue along with Myrddin and Taliesin, in the poem called *Y Gododdin*, part of the *Canu Aneirin* … our earliest and only surviving Brythonic document. The mention is, however, hardly "factual". Aneirin simply remarks:

"Caer ceni bei ef Arthur
Rug ciuin uerthi ig disur
ig cynnor guernor Guaurdur."

Which may be approximately translated as *"Though he was no Arthur, among the mighty in battle, Gwawrddur, at the front, was insurmountable."* Unfortunately such an aside may be directly comparable with somebody saying "He was no Adonis, but women still seemed to find him attractive". Such would not be proof for Adonis's historical existence! Could any mortal man be as good looking as Adonis? Could any mortal warrior, even Gwawrddur, who could not, it seems, be bettered, be as good a warrior as Arthur? Whilst the Arthurian reference appears to be part of the original composition and not the addition of some later Arthurian romancer, Aneirin, alas, still can't show us that factual door, where legend steps through into history.

It is academically assumed that Arthur was a Romano Celtic cavalry commander of the sixth century, whose military professionalism … a gift for hit and run tactics … and undoubted courage, held back the encroaching Saxons. But these are only assumptions, and the irony remains that whilst we have no historical record of a Celtic *King* Arthur, he remains, in spite of all the monarchs that we *know* that we *have* had down the ages, the most written about and the most admired.

The first mention of Arthur's role in what appear to be historical events occurs in Nennius's *Historia Brittonum*. Nennius mentions Arthur, but not as a king, merely as a war leader – *dux bellorum* is the specific Roman rank which he gives him. It is from this first mention that scholars take their picture of Arthur, a warrior from a Romanised family, and thus familiar with the disciplined and professional methods which had typified the Imperial army. This is not the Arthur of either old Celtic – or modern Californian – myth! This is the Arthur of *legend*. Like the majority of historians, Nennius tended to be a collator, rather than a *witness,* making his compilation at the monastery of Bangor in about 800 AD. He freely admits in his bad Latin that *"I have brought together all that I found … from the annals of the Romans, writings of the holy fathers **and the traditions of our old men."***

This frank and telling last phrase, admitting to the inclusion of folklore, trawled from fireside chats some three hundred years after the supposed dates of the events being described, cannot by any stretch of the imagination allow Nennius to be considered a 'factual' historian in the modern sense. This is not to decry his efforts in any way. The folk that we cite as early British 'historians' would have been confounded by our concept of factual 'history'. Their purpose was not to clinically record events but rather to give a 'flavour' of their own or ancestral times and grind any particular axes that they had along the way. Indeed some historians still use this approach!

One commentator who had an axe to grind in a big way was *St Gildas*. Gildas is a bitter disappointment to modern scholars in search of that door where myth and legend can emerge dressed in fact, because Gildas is the only known commentator from what is presumed to be the time of an *Arthur*. It is assumed that Gildas, a monk who was commenting upon the state of Britain in about 540 AD, would have mentioned Arthur in his *De Excidio Britanniae* (The Ruin of Britain). The reason for this is that Gildas mentions the battle of Camlan in which later commentators say that Arthur was killed. The Easter Annals (written much later) cite the battle to have taken place in 539 AD, and Gildas, talking about it, confirms the approximate date but doesn't mention Arthur. Moreover, Gildas certainly isn't shy to name names, albeit most of them in derogatory terms. He launches into a series of condemnations of Welsh notables of the mid sixth century with the spleen of an Old Testament prophet (a persona which he proudly cultivated!) As we shall shortly see, Gildas seems to have taken his Christian calling as a sign from God to conduct a crusade of anti-regal invective which would have made even John the Baptist wince!

Gildas's mission was to make it clear that the "Ruin of Britain" at the hands of the encroaching Saxon savages was due to the ungodly behaviour of the British population in general, and its rulers in particular. Here and there he does, however, give praise ... typically to anyone who might reinstate the old Pax Romana. He praises Ambrosius Aurelianus, a Romanised leader in post Roman Britain, for example. He even makes it clear that Ambrosius was not a king but a military leader after the old Roman model, the very *dux bellorum* that Nennius later makes Arthur out to be. In fact judging by the dates of reputed Arthurian battles, Ambrosius would have been a little before Gildas's time whereas the assumed historical Arthur would have been pretty much a contemporary. Gildas also talks about the battle of Badon Hill, which was reputed by Nennius and tradition to be Arthur's greatest victory. But nowhere at all does Gildas actually mention Arthur!

There are a number of conclusions which have been drawn from this. The one that runs: Arthur was involved in some squabble with Gildas's family, so Gildas, out of pique, excised all mention of Arthur from his record … is highly unlikely. If this were the case, Gildas might not have mentioned Arthur as the victor of Badon Hill, but he would have got some satisfaction from mentioning Arthur's defeat and death at Camlan. In fact Gildas shows us that anyone who got his back up could be only too sure of a mention in what has come to be called his "complaining book". Another conclusion that has, more naturally, been drawn, is that Arthur was a pseudonym for somebody else who is more directly mentioned in the records … but who? Whilst it is not the brief of this book to sift all the assumptions, suffice it to say that Ambrosius has been found wanting on a number of counts, as has Maelgwyn Gwynedd, whom we shall meet shortly. The Breton *Riothamus* can fit the legend but not the history and then there is the Welsh prince *Cynglas,* who is also found wanting … but not before we have considered some curious puns which Gildas makes about him.

aRthuR, the Bear and the stars

Cynglas is interesting in that Gildas goes out of his way to be especially insulting about him. It was traditional to give heroic animal names to certain leaders and warriors. Gildas, however, uses this device as a vehicle for his most vehement insults. In Cynglas's case he uses the bear image in what we might call a *contra Arthurian* way. Gildas doesn't want this image of a bear to evoke ideas of strength and endurance as one would expect; in Cynglas's case it is the image of a lumbering, rough and inept creature, rolling in its own muck. This would be of little or no consequence except, as we have noted, the name Arthur is seen to derive from the Welsh word *Arth,* which means "Bear"!

Gildas's insult doesn't however simply call Cynglas "a filthy, rough bear". He asks "*Why have you been rolling in the muck of your past misdemeanours since your adolescence … you bear, you ruler (rider?) of many, and charioteer of the bear's stronghold, despiser of the Almighty and tyrant of his people? Cynglas, meaning in the Roman tongue … yellow butcher.*"

This last bit is nonsense of course. The name *Cynglas* means nothing like "yellow butcher", it translates from the Welsh as "blue dog". But Gildas, like the old bards he would have so despised, was nonetheless adept at using sarcasm and pun to vitriolic effect. His 'dog' has changed from a noble hound to scavenging, ravening hyena. The refined colour of royalty, blue, has also transformed to the colour of urine! But the word play is more interesting earlier in the passage. It is perhaps here that we get our first, albeit fleeting, glimpse of the mythical Arthur of ancient star lore and the Arthur which (the cult of) Taliesin knew.

Gildas mentions a bear, a bear's stronghold and a charioteer. These are the heavenly constellations of *Ursa Minor* (the Little Bear), *Draco* (the Dragon) and *Auriga* (Chariot driver). Auriga in Greek myth represented Erecthonius, the son of Vulcan, who was born deformed, but having invented the four horse chariot, was rewarded with a constellation in the night sky! Since by Cynglas's time horsemen had long replaced charioteers in warfare, the inference is that Cynglas is not only deformed but an outdated and inept warrior as well! The major star in Auriga, Capella, also happens to be of a yellow hue ... but that may be assuming greater subtlety to Gildas's insult than even Gildas would have been aware of. The overall inference is however clear – Cynglas is being assigned to an ancient Celtic past that the Romanophile Gildas doesn't approve of!

Ursa Minor, the Little Bear (as opposed to Ursa Major, the famous Plough or Great Bear), is the smaller, fainter but more mythologically important of the two 'bear' constellations because it holds the Pole Star, Polaris, which marks the axial point towards which the Earth tilts ... the north celestial pole. This stellar axis symbolism was what, as many at that time would have been aware, the whole Celtic concept of sovereignty rested upon. This is really where Arthur comes from ... an ancient *concept* of Celtic sovereignty and national selfhood ratified in the movements of the heavens. This needs to be subject to further examination if we are to realise the real target of Gildas's spleen.

The mythology of Arthur and of the sovereignty of the Celtic lands depended upon the realisation that the stars, seen from Earth, appear to revolve around the Pole Star. They appear to do this of course because the Earth's axis is aligned to the Pole Star. Coupled to this was the realisation that this alignment is not forever fixed, but by virtue of the phenomenon known as the *precession of the equinoxes*, it gradually shifts from one constellation to another. Ancient peoples were well aware of this, even though this movement of axial alignment between constellations could take some five thousand years. As we shall see from the poetry of one of our later Taliesin initiate bards, the Celts had a sound understanding of the phenomenon of precession, and the mythology of Arthur reflects this.

At the time of the first phase of Stonehenge and the construction of the Great Pyramid in Egypt, the Pole Star and Earth's axial alignment were in Draco – the constellation of the Dragon, which Gildas alludes to as *"the bear's stronghold"*. In fact, two thousand years before Gildas, the Egyptians had taken the trouble to align the Great Pyramid to the then Pole Star of Alpha Draconis in Draco. By Gildas's time, the effect of precession had, however, placed the Pole Star (where it still is) in the constellation of the Little Bear, Ursa Minor. The Pole Star was seen as the *peg* (or in currently fashionable 'shamanic' parlance, *tentpole*) around which the heavens in general and the circumpolar stars in particular circled, marking the turning of the year. But this process was more than simply a turning of time and season.

Astrology was, even then, an ancient and naturally accepted part of life to Christian and pagan alike in Wales. This had of course been the case for thousands of years in Egypt, in Greece, in Palestine and indeed in every culture upon the face of the ancient earth. The constellations and planets represented supernatural, or more importantly, archetypal, powers, which came, conjoined and then passed on round in the usual astrological progression. At the centre of all this was that vital axis fixed to the Pole Star (in whatever constellation it happened to be).

As we shall see when we come to examine the role of sacred kings in greater depth, kingship was sacral as well as military and political, and ancient kings ruled very much by "divine right" as priest kings to their people. In this they mediated the powers represented in the heavens, and to do so they were aligned to the axis and the Pole Star. This placed them centre stage in the round of the celestial powers and this was the ratification of their right to rule. A further example of this in Arthur's case is cited later in the Mabinogi in his playing of the magical chess game Gwyddbwyll, which was a talismanic way of establishing his central position to these powers. This central, axial position, of the chess piece representing the king and his right to rule, may further be seen in the sceptre/wand image adopted in the Mabinogi story of *Math*. This axial ratification, shown in Math, is confirmed by the fact that Math gets the star goddess *Arianrhod*, whose name means *"silver wheel"* (implying the circumpolar stars) to 'step over' his wand in an attempt to revalidate his kingship. The image is also taken further in that stepping over Math's 'wand' causes Arianrhod to give birth, so that Math's axial wand /sceptre betrays its phallic significance of a sacred king's ability to mate with the goddess (who was represented in both land and stars) and bring fertility to the tribe and its lands. It goes without saying that this fertility, implicit in the king's phallic axis, was known to be a result of the axial tilt of the Earth, giving rise to the seasonal cycle of nature's fertility.

Celtic mythology readily reflects all this and the later Arthurian romancers understood it. Hence we see the sacred kingship of *Uther Pendraig (Uther pendragon – Uther, chief of the dragon)* whose rule was associated with the old terrestrial axis and the pre-Celtic, Neolithic/early Bronze Age era aligned to the Dragon stars, being succeeded in a new epoch (of precession) by the boy king *Arth*ur ... the son of the great mother bear, when the axis changed alignment to the Pole Star in the constellation of the Little Bear. Thus the *Arth/Bear* alignment was the ratification of the new Celtic epoch of sacred kingship of the land, which Geoffrey of Monmouth and the other romancers later stressed to impel their Celtic revival.

Looking again at the mythology, we can see this confirmed in the person of Bran the Blessed, a carry over into Celtic myth from an earlier era when 'giants' ruled Britain. As far as the Celts were concerned, Britain must have been ruled in the distant past by giants, because only 'giants' could have constructed the megalithic monuments of huge stones which were dotted about the landscape. (One megalithic tomb on Anglesey is in fact called *Barclodiad y Gawres* ... the giantess's apronful.) Bran, as we shall later see, was the fabled giant king of Britain, "the Island of Mighty", who had a great cauldron and whose 'blessed head' continued to advise and entertain his warriors after his death. We shall encounter a number of mythological indications of changeover from the dynasties of the gods and goddesses of the old Bronze Age, especially the giant Bran, to the gods and goddesses of the Celts. But we can for the time being underline the fact that Bran's pre-Celtic cult became, as far as the writers of the later Mabinogi romances were concerned, supplanted by the Celtic cult of Arthur. This is confirmed when we find that Arthur's supposed 'father' Uther also appears as *Uther Ben* ... meaning *Uther of the head* ... and thus Bran – or an ancient king of the Bran type. From this and other evidence which will emerge later in other chapters of this book we can deduce that Bran and Uther are one and the same and that Arthur too knew other mythological lives under other names.

Gildas's Arthur

So now we return to Gildas and his vilification of the Welsh prince Cynglas as a Bear ... an *Arth*. We also note all the accompanying hints about star lore, with which Gildas indicates his understanding of this concept of Celtic sovereignty associated with the constellation of the Bear. In fact he takes all these stellar associations quite cleverly to expand his insults. Following his rebuke about *"rolling in the muck of your past misdemeanours since your adolescence"* he goes on to call Cynglas in Latin *"Sessor"* – which can mean either *ruler* or *rider* – *"of many"*! By using the Latin word *sessor* he can convey the meaning of somebody who sits – or rides – a throne ... or a horse. In that he is aware of the idea of rulership, and the ancient phallic significance of the axis and rulership, in the context of Cynglas's *"misdemeanours since adolescence"* – the double entendre is obvious! More specifically when he calls Cynglas *"the charioteer of the bear's stronghold"* he really starts to show his mettle. He is reminding us that the Little Bear (Ursa Minor) constellation also appears in the sky within the protection of the surrounding Draco/ Dragon constellation, and thus "the stronghold of the bear", and this enables him to take a side swipe not only at Cynglas but another Welsh prince Maelgwyn Gwynedd.

The "stronghold of the bear" is *Din-arth* in Welsh and this just happened to be the name of Maelgwyn Gwynedd's stronghold, above Deganwy. It is here that legend has Taliesin defeating Maelgwyn's bards, chiding them for their lack of mythological understanding, a fault for which (in spite of his other shortcomings) we cannot accuse Gildas! In another round of invective aimed specifically at Maelgwyn, Gildas had brought more of his stellar/animal insults into play describing Maelgwyn as "the dragon of the island" (of Britain). Thus Maelgwyn's fortress *Din Arth,* which Cynglas seems to have occupied at some time, would have been Draco/the dragon's castle, also known in astrological lore as "the stronghold of the bear", because Ursa Minor appears in the night sky, as we have said, to be within the protective embrace of Draco! Gildas is thus belittling Cynglas as being the mere chariot driver, who is playing second fiddle to and under the protection of the much more powerful Maelgwyn. It is also possible that in the chariot imagery of a bygone Celtic age (ancient Celtic chieftains had been buried with their chariots) we see the real slur ... Cynglas and his fellow princes are, as far as Gildas is concerned, living in the fools' paradise of a self indulgent, pagan past, the past symbolised by the mythical, starry Bear King ... Arthur ... or whatever his "bear" name had once been.

If we look, in as far as we can, at what was happening in Wales at the time of Gildas's tirade and his own role in events, we start to see why he was so insulting and why he framed his insults in the way that he did.

The Coming of Arthur

In 540 AD the Romans had long gone and most of what is now England had, through European immigration and/or influence, adopted Saxon culture and language, whilst various opportunist raiders nibbled, as it were, at the edges. The urbanised, Romanised lowlands of central and eastern Britain, in spite of the efforts of Ambrosius and others a generation before, had been easy meat for the Saxons, but eventually the Welsh princes, in spite of their usual bickering, had been able to stem the tide into the West. They had done this on the back of a general dissatisfaction in Britain with all things Roman because Rome had, in spite of appeals for military aid, left the British to the mercy of the heathen invaders. They were therefore Celts again, because the Saxon threat had in effect brought to the surface that ancient *hwyl* (which anyone who attended an international Rugby match at Cardiff Arms Park in the 1970s knows all too well!) In crisis these Celts rediscovered their Brythonic/Welsh identity and this was focused through the princes, of whom Maelgwyn Gwynedd was the chief.

The Dragon's Lair: Maelgwyn's stronghold

The meagre remains of Maelgwyn's court at Deganwy. The most significant traces are of Henry III's castle, wrecked in 1263 by Llewellyn ap Gruffydd. There are also traces of much earlier Roman occupation. Archaeologists were disappointed to find little more than the fragments of a few wine amphorae from Maelgwyn's time.

The irony was that Gildas was castigating Maelgwyn and his fellow princes for exercising the very qualities which were actually holding the enemy back! Such qualities were implicit in the style of the old pre-Roman Celtic chieftains who ruled under the sign of the bear. This was why Maelgwyn's stronghold at Deganwy was called *Din-arth*, "bear's stronghold". It was a place where the spirit of ancient Celticism was rekindled, but it was also a place which reflected the high cultural attainment of Maelgwyn's court, for we should remember that Maelgwyn had been educated by St Illtyd. He could speak Latin and Greek in addition to his own native tongue, and had at one time actually taken holy orders before returning to political life! Din Arth, the stronghold of the bear, was for a short spell – if anywhere could be – Camelot!

But Maelgwyn was not Arthur. Arthur was not a *person* as much as a *people*. It's true that Maelgwyn was the focus and promoter of this revived *Arth* spirit, which is why Gildas had called him *Dragon*, because as we have seen, the mythical Uther Pendragon was the "father" and restimulator of the equally mythologised *Arth/Bear* sovereignty idea. This means that we must find in the further Celtic past a god or demigod who archetypally equates with Arthur … a task which we shall set aside for the moment. In the meantime, we may suppose that Maelgwyn and his fellow princes had spawned a movement whose central motif in modern times might have been *John Bull* or *Tommy Atkins,* or in more elevated terms, *Britannia.* These represent, of course, neither actual historical figures nor deities (although later history, if it had to work with the tools of the Dark Ages, could be excused for assuming them to be so!) They are stereotypes (verging on archetypes) consolidating a patriot battling to defend the sovereignty of Britain. Therefore Gildas did not, could not, insult a *man* called Arthur, or a *god* called Arthur. The name Arthur didn't even exist then. Maelgwyn himself would never in any case have allowed his court to invoke some half heathen *Arthur* "god" … St Illtyd's conditioning would have seen to that … and as we shall later see, it was probably St Illtyd who planted the original seed which Maelgwyn nurtured! In the meantime Gildas was remonstrating not with a man, but with a *movement* and the men who had instigated it.

As to why this should be becomes fairly clear. Gildas was a cleric, and even though he was a cleric in the Celtic church, he was an unashamed Romanophile. He was taken with the romantic image of being an Old Testament Hebrew prophet and therefore in that tradition he had no time for kings or princes, let alone their supposed divine ratification! He saw himself as the Christian conscience of the Brythons and he would have no truck with a return of the old Celtic flamboyance with all the feasting and womanising that seemed to go along with it. Whilst the Celtic church in general went about its business, Gildas was frustrated by its isolation from Rome and by the fact that it could only operate under the patronage of these (in his eyes) jumped up barbarian chieftains. He would be even more irked by the fact that Maelgwyn, the most powerful of these, had been schooled by the great St Illtyd and had at one time, like himself, actually taken holy orders. His insult to Maelgwyn as the "Dragon" would thus, in addition to mythologically/astrologically blaming him as the 'father'/originator of this *Arth* nonsense, equally cite Maelgwyn as "the dragon" mentioned in the Book of Revelations!

Whatever Maelgwyn's shortcomings, the fact remains that Gildas does show us the complexity of esoteric imagery that fifth and sixth century intelligentsia were able to utilise. Whilst in many an instance local Celtic behaviour could be brutish in the extreme, we have to remember that even a regional ruler like Maelgwyn was a cultured and capable man. The very imagery that Gildas uses to infer that we are dealing with a caste of provincial mead swilling nobles with no thoughts in their heads beyond fighting, feasting and womanising is contradicted by the sophistication with which he insults them. Ultimately, the sad fact is that Gildas hated his fellow Celts for being Celts, yet it is only because of this hatred that we have any witness to those supposedly "Arthurian" times.

Nennius, that later monk of Gwynedd, tried to put the ancient slanders of his long dead cleric colleague Gildas to rest, whilst at the same time placating his soul. Gildas is obviously the foremost of the *church fathers* that Nennius cites as a source. To try and set the record straight, as he may have been under some local pressure to do from the descendants of Maelgwyn, he took the name *Arthur*, which by then was in legendary circulation, and applied it to the deeds of Maelgwyn of Din Arth and his fellow princes. For the soul of Gildas and the integrity of monastic history, however, he made his Maelgwyn/Arthur a Roman style *dux bellorum* and assured his readers that along with the church fathers he had also consulted the Roman annals as a source.

The Naming of Arthur

Yet Maelgwyn himself had not long to endure Gildas's hatred. Before a generation had passed, he was struck down by the yellow plague epidemic, dying in a church where it is said he took sanctuary to escape the hallucinations which the fever induced. Gildas lived on for another twenty years or so. If the plague had not taken Maelgwyn, old age would happily have done so to prevent him living to see so much of what he had built around the old Celtic *Arth* impulse shattered. The flower of the next generation of Welsh nobility were slaughtered by the Angles at the battle of Catraeth in 600 AD. As we have seen, the only noble Welsh survivor of that carnage was *Aneirin*, who became the first to take that fateful step of actually writing down the name *Arthur,* some fifty years after Maelgwyn's death.

The name *Arthur* had originally been adopted for popular usage, as we have noted, probably in that stereotypical way that *John Bull* came to be, and this seems to be the sense in which Aneirin uses it. That the children and grandchildren of the Welsh nobility who had fought alongside Maelgwyn should come to adopt it as a Christian name, as they did, is understandable enough ... Geoffrey of Monmouth was baptised *Gruffydd ap Arthur* after all (which may account for a great deal!) That such personalisations should lead later commentators to assume an historical Arthur is also understandable. But if we examine the coining of the name itself we will perhaps find a way into that labyrinth of the Brythonic folksoul where warriors gave way to bards who used names like Taliesin.

Scholars continue to argue about the name *Arthur,* and indeed if there was ever an example of Brythonic bardism playing its phonological games to arrive at the most tangled knotwork of puns and double meanings ... this is it! The very complexity of the possible combinations, and hence implications, in both Old Welsh, Brythonic and late Latin almost certainly tell us that we are dealing with an esoterically designed title embodying the struggle for Welsh sovereignty, rather than the name of some singular mortal ... however glorious. When we considered Gildas's verbal assault on Cynglas we became aware of the way in which so many meanings of cosmological, historical, mythological and even topographical significance could be rolled up in a seemingly straightforward piece of name calling. This displays a bardic technique and wit, of which, in view of his position, Gildas would have been the least likely exponent. What then of others, more practiced in bardic technique and more esoterically inclined? How would they arrive at such a "trick name" to summarise this Welsh spirit of sovereignty? Whatever it was, it would have to work as a spoken rather than a written series of puns ... and it does!

We are already aware of the astronomical connection between *Arth/Bear* and the constellations of both Ursa Major and Ursa Minor, with the latter holding the all important axial Pole Star. These 'bear' constellations have also for many thousands of years been seen as having the same sort of plough shape, and certainly Ursa Major has been known for many ages as "the Plough". The Celtic plough was called an *ard*, a very efficient piece of agricultural machinery that turned the upper soil without drawing up the lower clays and marls. We thus have a Celtic play on words, especially with the later use of the double D: dd and its "th" sound, between the word for a bear – *arth* and the word for a plough – *ard*. In the original Welsh rendering, before Aneirin came to write the name down, Arthur had probably started life as a title for those who fought alongside Maelgwyn, each warrior being a "bear's" man … *Arth-gwr* or *Arth-gur*, which mutated in spoken Welsh to *Arthur*.

All this was, however, a mere starting point for bardic complexity. The next stage brought in the way that the plough was drawn along, by tentatively coupling the Welsh *Arth* with the Latin word for bull … *Taurus*. This would of course produce a nonsensical *Arth-Taurus* (Bear-Bull), but that could easily be overcome by pronouncing the name to sound like *Artorius* … the Latin word for 'ploughman'. Nennius in fact writes down Arthur's name in his bad Latin as *Arturus* This gives room for yet another astronomical pun because *Arthurus* and *Arturis* are both variants of *Arcturus*, the name of the brightest star in the constellation of *Boötes*, which being next to Ursa Major is called *the bear ward*. Thus *Arthurus/Arthur* becomes warden of the sovereignty of the Brythons which the bear symbolised.

Arcturus was also known as the *waggoner* or at least somebody who drives a team of oxen, who pull a plough as much as a wagon, which again brings this round of puns back to *Artorius* … Arthur's Latin/ploughman name. This alternative would be necessary because the word *Arthur* would have been senseless in Latin, but the two versions, Welsh *Arthur* and Latin *Artorius*, would both have carried the appropriate message. The recent Roman military guardians of the sovereignty of Britain were not however forgotten in the bull that drew the plough, because the bull was the totem animal of Mithraism, the religion of the Roman Legions, and the legacy of three hundred years of Roman occupation. Whilst Brythonic pride had to all practical purposes written off Roman help and declared self governance, it would nonetheless still have been remembered how the Emperor Diocletian (at the end of the 3rd century) had hailed Mithras as "the protector of the Empire". Now with the legions gone, the Brythonic Celts needed that Mithraic protection more than ever!

The Bull, the Bear, the Stars and the Land

We have seen that the bull, which could be implicit in Arthur's composite name, was the totem animal central to the Mithraic religion of the Roman armies. Mithras the soldiers' god was a Roman adaptation of the Persian god of light, Mazda, who in his pre-Zoroastrian form was a god of war. Here we must again digress to mention the curious fact remarked upon by Professor Griffen (if not in this exact context) that in one of the biblical visions of Daniel, Persia is also represented as a savage bear! This same biblical passage also seems to have influenced Gildas in his name calling of the Welsh princes. (See Daniel, 7: 4-8)

Be that as it may, the Greeks and Romans, frequently at war with the Persians, admired them as a worthy foe. Mithras was the god who blessed the arms of these all too militarily successful Persians and it would be no wonder that Greeks and Romans would also invoke him for a little of the same help. To the Romans he became *Sol Invictus*, the unconquerable sun. But there was more to it than this. With Mithraism came *dualism* and with dualism's stark divisions between what was right and what was wrong came some very deeply etched moral guidelines. It was this which elevated the cult of the warrior to a new standing, and not surprisingly there was a grade of Mithraic initiation called "soldier".

Mithraism was somewhat wedded to what we would now call "the cult of Hercules", which, as we shall see, was prevalent in the old pre-Celtic Bronze Age mysteries of Britain. Mithras travelled with the legions instilling loyalty and brotherhood, and acting as a bonding force that held soldiers, especially soldiers who were non-Roman native auxiliaries, together. Perhaps this is why it was so popular, or so promoted, in Roman Britain, where there were five major temples to Mithras ... an inordinate number for an occupational force of three legions. Perhaps this is also why in excavations of the Walbrook in London, where it will be remembered the heads of massacred Romans were thrown, a stone head of Mithras was found, indicating, maybe, that Mithras was with them even in defeat and death. This of course bears comparison to Christianity and Renan's famous note about Mithraism that *"If Christianity had been arrested in its growth by some mortal malady, the world would have been Mithraist"*.

We must remember that during the Roman occupation of Britain Christianity was still a fledgling faith, and that much of the tenor and symbolism of Christianity was very similar to that of Mithraism: the birth of the saviour god at the winter solstice, the sacrament of bread and wine, the strong moral teaching, and so on. We have to realise that with the presence of the Legions in Romano Celtic Britain, in addition to the pre-Christian, Druidic worship of the Celts and the Roman pantheistic civil religions, Mithraism would have been a very real alternative to the new Christian faith. In fact Mithraism continued to compete in various Gnostic forms, right through to the thirteenth century, more notably in southern France with such "heresies" as Manicheism and Catharism. In the Templars we have an echo of the Mithraic inspired warrior corps of the Romans and it was at that time that the remnant of Welsh bardism laid down the later romances which brought Arthur into the Mabinogi stories, concocting an association of the Mithraic totem of the bull with some of Arthur's exploits. By this time, the Grail romances were in general circulation and the chroniclers were readily following Nennius to associate Arthur with Roman military practice. At this point we may find that we have closed a circle. At the centre of this circle there seems to stand a cult that has one foot in the legendary military elitism of Rome and another in the old Brythonic validation of sovereignty through stellar, axial sacred symbolism.

The empowerment of the legions had been through the symbol of the sacrificed bull of Mithras, the power that was vested in every *dux bellorum*, every war lord who had been head of the cult holding the initiatory grade of either *Father* or *Heliodormus* to the legions under his command. Such commanders had been in effect local, mortal embodiments of Diocletian's "Mithras, protector of the Empire". The empowerment of the Celts came traditionally through the stars. Notably the stars of the Bear/Plough, and also that "cauldron"/broken wheel of stars called the Corona Borealis or *Caer Arianrhod*.

The symbol of the esoteric Celtic requirement of the name, the impulse for sovereignty, was the bear *arth*. In Latin, *arth* became *ursa* in its role of the feminine/she-bear empowering goddess, and *ursus* in its masculine mode of the one or ones so empowered. The symbol of the mundane military requirement to achieve this sovereignty was the Roman Mithraic bull … *taurus*. Thus we see how the name became the butt of even more bardic word tricks. *Arth-ursa* = *Arth-ur* for example, mating up the little bear, axle holding sacred king with the greater turning around that axle of the great mother bear Ursa Major, which whilst excluding the bull imagery would still have given a power to the turning and retained a Brythonic/Latin combination. But as we know, this would have been unacceptable to a Latin speaker as such, even though it would have doubtless amused the bards. *Arthur*, as we are now aware, needed also to be available and meaningful in some other form for the Latin speaker as

Artorius, or as Nennius has it, *Arturus*, which would give the *Arcturus/ bear ward* combinations which suited his Mithraic role admirably, a role which also has some credence in his appearances in the Mabinogion.

The *Four Branches* which comprise the Mabinogion (tales) proper are above all else *onomastic*; that is they relate mythological events to the landscape as well as the stars to explain such things as place names, because the patterns of the heavens had to be reflected in the patterns of the earth – otherwise sovereignty had no real meaning. We need to find therefore a physical correspondence on the land which may reflect in its history and imagery the symbolism of Arthur/Artorius, "the Ploughman".

God's Little Acre

The earliest Celtic churches were built on circular sites … not least because that had been the style of the old groves and henges, indeed some were actually built within Bronze Age sacred circles. Where a new site was required however, a ploughman was called for and stood at the proposed altar site … the most holy spot. Standing stationery at this point he allowed his oxen to scribe a circle around him to the maximum extent of their traces. This determined the perimeter of sacred soil, of the churchyard … *God's little acre* … and is why so many early Celtic churches are surrounded by a circular wall or embankment. A later superstition said that these churchyards had circular walls so that the Devil had no corners to hide in!

An example of this is the little church at Llanelltyd at the head of the Mawddach estuary, overshadowed by the magnificence of Cadair Idris, the mountain which was the seat of Idris, the legendary star mage and the site of further stages in Taliesin's initiation. Llanelltyd church is one of a number of churches said to have been founded by the great St Illtyd who, before he took holy orders, had, so the Triads tell us, been a knight "of Arthur"! We have already noted that he was the teacher of Maelgwyn Gwynedd. The Triads further cite Illtyd, in the guise of *Elldud,* as the *"holy knight of Theodosius … who improved the mode of ploughing land".* If we need to look to an initiator of the Arthur/ploughman impulse, St Illtyd is probably the culprit!

Whilst the Triads are of themselves notably unreliable, they simply add in this case to a cluster of cross referencing imagery which in its own haphazard way fits remarkably together. We have the curious image of a supposed "knight of Arthur" who was also one of the fathers of the Celtic church and the teacher of Maelgwyn, the powerful prince who was himself a warrior who had been in holy orders. He in turn seems to have been the rallying point of this Arth/bear patriotic impulse, having his court at *Din Arth*, the stronghold of the bear. Moreover Illtyd has a number of circular "God's acre"/plough delineated churches (as of course do many other Celtic saints!) dedicated to him, including this one in the shadow of Cadair Idris, the place where, as we shall see, the 'giant' Idris is said to have mapped the heavens. Then there is the Taliesin connection with Cadair Idris where he was *"in a revolving chair above Caer Sidi"*, which again reiterates this axis/turning motif. As we shall see further on, such a starry initiation stood this particular Taliesin in good stead when he was to further expand upon these matters a few hundred years later, not least in this matter of the Plough, Illtyd and Arthur.

By the time those few hundred years had come round another curious association with this place occurred when a Cistercian abbey, serving this little church of St Illtyd, was built nearby. We shall be examining the Cistercians as one source of the Arthurian/Grail material in their cult of the Blessed Virgin and their associations with that Mithraic reincarnation of mystical soldiery, the Knights Templar, in due course. In the meantime it seems impossible to ignore other later and quite inexplicable 'synchronicities' in the history of this little plough-delineated church of Illtyd and its environs.

With the Reformation, the Cistercian Abbey was of course disbanded and like thousands of others fell into ruin. It was hundreds of years later at the turn of the 20th century that two miners sheltering in a cave in the hills found the chalice and plate from the Abbey, a veritable "Grail" which the monks had obviously hidden. The miners took the sacred vessels, not knowing what they were, to one of the Vaughan family at Nannau, hoping for some reward from these local gentry. The chalice and plate then passed through many hands and were almost lost to Wales, like the elusive Grail itself. But a greater treasure had already passed through the hands of this noble family, its neighbours at nearby Hengwrt and at Peniarth, over the Cadair Idris ridge in the next valley. These were the collated manuscripts which were later to form the *Mabinogi*.

As if this didn't comprise more than a fair share of Arthurian associations with the place, a modern grave in the churchyard of St Illtyd is that of Frederick Bligh Bond, who died here in 1945. Bond is best known for his excavations at Glastonbury and his unearthing of the original Celtic church there beneath the Abbey, a matter of yards from the place where the mediaeval monks claimed to have found Arthur's grave! The church that Bond found is often cited as the first British church founded by Joseph of Arimathea. Bond was however suspended from this project when the Church of England found that he had accurately located this ancient church by mediumistic means.

Whilst this has taken us somewhat beyond our immediate purpose in showing the associations that were implicit in the name of Arthur, it does perhaps serve to indicate how such associations continue to resonate in some curious way down the ages, and like all facets of the Brythonic mystery tradition, indicates an almost alarming immediacy in the power inherent in sacred places upon the Celtic landscape.

The result of all this associated imagery, ebbing out from Gwynedd during and after the Dark Ages, is that in the wake of Maelgwyn's patriotic stance, a lot of bardic effort went into the construction and promotion of the mysteries of Arthur. The objective of this was to instil in the folksoul of a Christian and independent Wales a sense of sovereignty, of a nation which was "God's little acre", whose boundaries were secured by the Ploughman under the auspices of the mighty Bear. In our examination of Arthur's incarnation in the *Mabinogion* we shall see how that construction was achieved and also examine the earlier roots onto which it was grafted.

arthur in the mabinogion

The age of the bardically inspired Arthur is appropriately called the Dark Age, because as will by now be obvious, the distinct lack of contemporary records hopelessly restricts our view of the period. This is a problem with all historical research of the Celtic era, which stems directly from Celtic culture itself and the bardic tradition of transmitting information orally without written sources until the latter days of Celtic decline in the late fifth and sixth centuries. Even then, as we have discovered, the records are scant and fragmentary. What was written down was something of a sporadic record of a few tales which were primarily designed not to be *read* but to be *listened to* in the forms of recitation and song. Welsh, whether in its original Brythonic form or as Old, Middle or Modern Welsh, is primarily about *sounds* rather than *signs*. In itself it has a musical quality and is not for nothing called *iaith y Nefoedd* (the language of heaven)!

After the silence of Gildas, the vagueness of Aneirin, the Welsh Annals and Nennius, Arthur had transformed from a patriotic movement to a personalised legend. As such he then emerges in the *Red Book of Hergest* which became assimilated into the collection of Welsh mythology which Lady Charlotte Guest was to call *The Mabinogion*.

Whilst, as writings, the *Mabinogi* material is mainly thirteenth century and therefore Welsh mediaeval and comparatively late, the myths betray traces of what we can assume to be pre-Christian Celtic tribal lore transmitted verbally by bards, and in some aspects, as in the thirteenth century *Preiddu Annwn* (from the *Hanes Taliesin*), betraying even pre-Druidic (and therefore pre-Celtic) initiatory custom and belief … a point which we shall have cause to return to in following chapters.

We tend to use the term "Mabinogi", but either way the name Mabinogion/Mabinogi (intended to mean "youth tales") as coined by Lady Charlotte Guest is not strictly correct. If any of the collection can be called "Mabinogi" it is only the early material of the *Four Branches*. Lady Guest, the wife of a South Walian, Victorian industrialist, made the initial translations from middle Welsh into modern English with the collaboration of various other current and earlier translators. Scholars now agree, however, that it would be churlish to seek some other title for this collection of mythological tales! Later, arguably better translations, notably that of Gwyn Jones and Thomas Jones, do not incorporate the *Hanes Taliesin*.

The material itself consists of fragments of mythology and folklore, welded together and eventually written down. As ever, the originals from this period no longer exist and what we have are thirteenth century copies. However, we are able to date material fairly accurately by subtle linguistic devices such as *mesotomy* … or lack of, as previously described.

The body of Mabinogi material is drawn from several sources … *Llyfr Gwyn Rhydderch (the White Book of Rhydderch) and Llyfr Coch Hergest (the Red Book of Hergest)* and the *Peniarth* manuscripts. As we have said above, Lady Guest's version also incorporates the *Hanes Taliesin*. By the time the material was originally written down (perhaps from as early as the ninth century) Christianity had been long established even to the extent that its Celtic variant was already largely displaced by Roman Catholicism. Even so, the material encapsulates an oral tradition which seems in some instances to go back way beyond the Druids to its roots in a mystery religion which originated in Bronze Age or even Neolithic times (some three thousand or more years before the documents were written!) It indicates some degree of esoteric tenacity on the part of the bards that they should so faithfully preserve these tales and that they (and indeed their later copyists of the thirteenth century) should feel them worthy of continued preservation. That this preservation was hardly subject to any 'improving' and/or the interpolation of Christian dogma is even more remarkable.

The Mabinogi material itself is collated in three sections:

1) **The Four Branches:** *Pwyll prince of Dyfed, Branwen daughter of Llŷr, Manawydan son of Llŷr, Math son of Mathonwy.*
2) **The Four Independent Native Tales:** *The Dream of Macsen Wledig, Lludd and Llefelys, Culhwch and Olwen, The Dream of Rhonabwy.*
3) **The Three Romances:** *The Lady of the Fountain, Peredur son of Efrawg, Gereint son of Erbin.*

If in any sense we can talk about the Mabinogi 'proper' ... the original and most ancient core of the writing ... it is the Four Branches, summarised by Professor W.J. Gruffydd as:

1) *Pwyll Prince of Dyfed*: Pwyll's descent into Annwn, the meeting of Pryderi's parents, Pryderi's birth. Pryderi's disappearance. His mother's penance, Pryderi's restoration.
2) *Branwen daughter of Llŷr:* Events leading to Branwen's marriage to Matholwch, Branwen's penance, Branwen's vindication, Bran's prowess in Ireland. Death of Bran, Death of Branwen, The Blessed Head ... otherworld theme.
3) *Manawydan son of Llŷr:* Marriage of Manawydan and Rhiannon, the spell under which Pryderi and Rhiannon disappear. Restoration of Pryderi and Rhiannon.
4) *Math son of Mathonwy:* The king and his prophesied death. The unfaithful wife. The stealing of the swine from Dyfed. The death of Pryderi.

Professor Gruffydd's essential thesis however is how the *Mabinogi* turned on the life and death of Pryderi, with characters from other tales being inserted later to nominally replace him in the cycle. Hence the myth of Math son of Mathonwy continues the theme, but taken up in the main with the story of the solar hero/sacred king Lleu Llaw Gyffes ... or Llew as he often appears.

Again however we have the theme, as with Pryderi, of the king and his prophesied death, of the unfaithful wife, and so on. Then we have retribution and restoration.

It is the telling and retelling of an eternal archetypal process ... of the birth, life, betrayal, death and resurrection of the sacred king/hero, the process which Graves says is described by the *"single poetic theme"*. A theme to which Arthur became attached in what is plainly the later material of the collection, The Four Independent Native Tales and the Three Romances.

Culhwch and Olwen, which appears to have been composed of comparatively early (or at least unadulterated) material, and its fantastic tales of raiding and rescuing under Arthur's leadership, parallel Taliesin's *Preiddu Annwn*. In the story, Culhwch addresses Arthur as "Sovereign prince of this Island". The *Dream of Rhonabwy*, which is however the earliest Arthurian story in Welsh, gives us a similar Arthur whom Rhonabwy meets in a dream.

This story has Rhonabwy on campaign, when he and his companions are stationed at a homestead where they are forced to sleep in a cow shed. Rhonabwy settles himself down on an ox hide and thus slips into a dream where Arthur is playing *gwyddbwyll*, a kind of magical chess ... a matter we shall deal with later at some length.

The association of ox hide with a dream of 'the Emperor' seems to bring in the ox/bull/Mithraic association, although the idea of bards sleeping in bull hides to receive *awen* - inspiration - was already well known. The white oxen, reputedly from the Underworld of *Annwn* and known in very old Welsh folklore as *Ychen Bannog*, had existed actually, as well as mythologically, in Wales since before the Roman occupation. Taliesin will be introducing us to them again in a later chapter. The most impressive Celtic representation we have of a recumbent, possibly sacrificed bull, however, is in the inner base plate of the *Gundestrup cauldron* which dates from first century Denmark.

This and other evidence, particularly from Ireland, which never knew the imprint of an Imperial Roman sandal, indicates that the pagan Celts had, like many other cultures, a ready affinity to bull/ox mythology long before Mithraic/Roman occupation and influence. One way of looking at this is to exclude the possibility that Mithraism had any effect upon the symbolism employed in the creation of Arthur. Another view may however be that the very fact that the Celts had an affinity to this symbolism made the adoption of a measure of Mithraism, and its subsequent amalgamation with Arthur, all the more likely.

As we move onto the next Mabinogi tale *The Lady and the Fountain*, which also takes place under the auspices of Arthur, we find that a guardian figure between inner and outer kingdoms, a wild giant of a man, appears. He is a keeper of beasts, and can summon all the wild creatures to him. Charles Williams has bulls fighting around this giant who is himself dressed in bull hide. Why Williams's muse should have directed him to place further emphasis upon bulls in Arthurian material seems uncertain. That this figure should be so like the archetypal stellar figure of Orion or Hercules is probably no coincidence. Mediterranean statues show the lion/solar symbolism shared by Hercules and Mithras, which is also implicit in the Celtic Mabinogi hero Llew (whose name means lion) and as we have noted, what came to be known as a Hercules cult was operative in Bronze Age Britain and subsequently given bardic credence in Celtic times.

This Mithras/Hercules connection to the arth/axis symbolism seems to have been realised in the ancient world. A rock relief in Commagene shows Antiochus I dressed as Hercules, shaking hands with a star spangled Mithras, who holds a staff tilted at an angle to suggest the slant of the earth's axis.

But it is to the older part of the Mabinogion, to that tale of Math and his wand, which we must turn to find the Brythonic roots of this symbolism and with them the roots of Arthur.

Math fab Mathonwy Reborn

The Mabinogi tale of *Math fab Mathonwy* is the fourth of the group of mythological tales known as the *Four Branches*. This section of the writings comprise, as we have pointed out, the more ancient, and in some instances, pre-Celtic mythology of the Mabinogion. *Math fab Mathonwy* may be translated as *"bear son of bear-like"*, which in view of our previous researches will immediately alert us to the possibility that we are dealing with some ancient Arthur prototype.

As we shall see, the parallels between the characters and adventures of *Math fab Mathonwy* (and indeed other myths from the ancient *Four Branches* of the Mabinogi) are deliberately transplanted in the later stories. Incidents and characters in Math, for example, start to show up in the later Mabinogi story of *Peredur Fab Efrawg*, and so on, all of which indicates a deliberate bardic process of reaffirming Brythonic sovereignty in the shape of Arthur in the later tales. Yet in the later tales of the Mabinogion this appearance of Arthur is never as a central character. Arthur, though personalised, is an empowering figure, a source of authority and sovereignty, as Math had been in the earlier Math fab Mathonwy tale. His function is to provide a background which facilitates the deeds of the Welsh heroes. This is of course what we would expect if 'Arthur' was the spirit behind a movement, rather than an historical person at the head of it. Such, as we have realised, was the situation in the time of Maelgwyn Gwynedd and Gildas, which the bards reiterated in their tales. They intended, as we shall see, that the *legendary* Arthur should become a *mythological*, Christianised version of Math. They made him a warrior of the new saviour god Christ and robed him in quasi history, to stand as an enduring *symbol* of sovereignty of the Brythonic Celtic lands into the Christian era. History shows that their work was not in vain.

This then is the whole irony of Arthur. Whereas the majority of heroes pass from history into legend, we have taken Arthur from legend and 'assumed' him into a factual history where he never really existed. That some band of warriors in post-Roman Britain may have nicknamed themselves or their leaders after the mythological hero for a time may have been the case, picked up from the old soldiers' tales which Nennius says that he heard. But we must call as our final witness the bard who composed what have been called the *Graves Poems*, written just after the time of Nennius in the tenth century *Black Book of Carmarthen*. In a roll of the heroic dead from those battles to stem the Saxon advance and preserve British sovereignty, the poet assures us *"Bet y march. Bet y Guythur. Bet y gugaun cletyfrut. Anoeth bid bet y Arthur."* – The grave of March, the grave of Gwythyr. The grave of Gwagan Redsword. Unknown (unwise ... i.e. foolish to seek) the grave of Arthur.

We are deliberately warned that we will never find 'Arthur the man' any more than we will find a physical location for Avalon. Thus perhaps we would do well to take the poet's meaning as: "Though great warriors have fallen, Arthur (the spirit of British sovereignty) will never die." He is *Rex Quondam, Rexque Futurus* ... the once and future king.

CHAPTER FOUR

The Math Heritage

During the latter part of the Bronze Age it appears that the sacred king cultus, which later became featured in the myths of Bran the Blessed, began to be amended by other beliefs. This seems to have been at the time when, as archaeology shows us, there was sudden population expansion and the rise of a specific warrior class. This was the time of the *Urnfield* people, when the first appearances of land demarcation and fortified settlements started to occur. The Urnfield people may be considered to be "proto-Celtic".

It was probably at this time that the cult of Bran became amended by a cult which the later Celtic bards were to identify with Math and Gwydion and which subsequently became written into Arthurian legend.

The Children of Llŷr and Dôn

From what little the Mabinogion and other sources tell us, there had been the first (divine) dynasty of *Llŷr Llediaith*, the father of Bran. Llŷr's name seems to derive from the Irish word for "sea", implying the prehistoric arrival of the early Bronze Age Beaker people. The second part of his name *Llediaith* means "half formed language". In contrast, the dynasty of the goddess *Dôn*, which followed, gave rise to Math and his nephew Gwydion, who was "the best storyteller in the world". The Triads credit Gwydion as the bringer of arts and sciences (graven upon a stone) and he is said to have brought "letters" into Wales. This implies a contrast between two cultures ... that of the allegedly unschooled and unsophisticated Bran culture in contrast to the later accomplished Gwydion culture. The further implications of this are that, at the time that these divine dynasties changed, there was a change of language, affirming the emergence or invasion of another culture. As we shall see the Irish myths indicate, with more precision, the same successions of dynasties and socio-religious shifts in the appropriately named *Book of Invasions*.

When we see the story of Arthur digging up Bran's head in later Arthurian tales, we are seeing the work of the bards milking old myths which featured this cultural and religious change to fit Arthur into the bearskin of *Math fab Mathonwy* – "Bear, Son of bear-like" ... son of the *Mother** bear. This technique of transposing old material to new characters to validate them is universal. St Matthew's gospel uses the technique very effectively by putting the words of the Old Testament prophets into Jesus's mouth. St Paul did the same thing by invoking Melchizadek in his epistle to the Hebrews. To examine this bardic transference from Math to Arthur, we must however give *Math fab Mathonwy* closer scrutiny.

ꝏath faꞽ ꝏathonwy

Math was a sacred king probably reflecting the time when sacred kings were of a new breed, when the self-sacrifice of the cult of Bran began to change to the use of surrogates. He shares a universal peculiarity with many sacred kings however, in that his feet were particularly sacred ... a point which will require later elucidation. His court however, so the Mabinogi tells us, was at *Caer Dathyl*, which has been subsequently identified as the site of an Iron Age fort, *Pen Y Gaer*, in the hills between Conway and Llanrwst. The reason why the later Celtic bards chose to set him in this location may derive from a rare phenomenon in the defensive structure of Pen Y Gaer which archaeologists call *chevaux de frise*. Basically this is the setting of a defensive area of rubble-strewn ground over which potential attackers would break their ankles in the dark! Be that as it may, Math's sacred feet had to be lodged in the lap of a virgin when he was holding court at Caer Dathyl.

---

*   The *mab/fab* in Welsh indicates "son" of "mother", e.g. "Crist mab Mair" – Christ son of Mary, suggesting the ancient Celtic and pre-Celtic practice of matrilinear succession. On the other hand, *ap*, as in "Gruffydd ap Arthur", Geoffrey of Monmouth's original Welsh name, indicates that he is "son of his father" ... in this case a father appropriately named Arthur.

The chosen virgin was a maiden called *Goewin*. Goewin's name, as is usually the case with the queen of a sacred king, contains the adjective "white" ... *wen/wyn/win/Gwyn/gwen* ... and consequently is shown to have come from the Faery realm or Underworld of Annwn. The bards used the same device, as we shall see, for Arthur's queen *Gwynhyfwr* (Guinevere).

Now Math's nephew Gwydion, son of Dôn, had a brother called Gilfaethwy who desired Goewin, and Gwydion undertook to fix things so that Gilfaethwy could have her. He persuaded Math that he could go to Pryderi, the chief of Annwn, the Underworld, and through magic, steal Pryderi's pigs. There is no little significance in this because, as we saw when we met Myrddin's piglet, pigs were sacred to Taliesin's old adversary, the goddess Ceridwen, keeper of the Underworld cauldron. Math agreed, and Gwydion by magical trickery stole the pigs and headed for home. Pryderi came after him however and war ensued, in which Pryderi was subsequently slain by Gwydion in single combat (using a little magic) at Maentwrog. During the campaign however, Gwydion, as he had intended, slipped back to the court with Gilfaethwy whilst Math was still away and incited Gilfaethwy to rape Goewin. (What we may have here is a memory of the rape and shaming of priestesses of an old cult by priests of the new, which may reflect a friction between the two beliefs that we have cited or between later Celtic and Bronze Age beliefs.)

When Math returned from the war, Goewin, not unnaturally, told him what had happened. Math decided to marry Goewin as she could no longer be his foot holder, and in doing so we see the exercise of sovereignty through female empowerment – a point which we shall expand upon elsewhere – when Math says ... *"I will take thee to wife and the authority over my realm I will give into thy hands"*. Then Math punished Gwydion and Gilfaethwy by turning them into animals. However, this didn't solve the problem of having to have his feet resting in the lap of a virgin. Gwydion, having been restored to human form and supposedly wanting to make amends, suggested his own sister *Arianrhod* for the role. Math had to be sure, however, that Arianrhod was a virgin and so he made her step over his wand, for Math and Gwydion were both wizards, but Math the more powerful. As Arianrhod stepped over Math's wand (what turned out to be) twin boys fell from her womb. In fact these were not directly fathered by Math as we shall later see. One of them, later to be named Llew, was however something of a reincarnation of Math himself, but this is something which, again, can await explanation elsewhere.

The revenge of Arianrhod for being, as she saw it, thus shamed and the effects of that revenge upon the destiny of one of her sons, the solar hero Llew, is what the remainder of this Mabinogi tale *Math fab Mathonwy* is taken up with. In fact the story lays out a fairly typical pattern for the process of bardic initiation which developed from the sacred king cult. The original myth undoubtedly explained certain astronomical and astrological lore, but many accompanying tales are long lost (even if they were ever written down) so we have only a partial explanation. What is clear however is that Arianrhod's denial of her son meant that he could not be named, armed or mated; in other words he was denied the sacred king prerequisite of empowerment by the triple goddess. Gwydion, his so-called uncle, yet so obviously the boy's father, uses his magic to trick his mate/sister Arianrhod into providing the three-fold empowerment. Firstly he and Llew go to Arianrhod's court, masquerading as shoemakers. This seems to allude to the fact that Gwydion is determined to have the goddess reveal her feet. At first she sends measurements via her servants and the shoes are two big or too small. This means that our 'shoemakers' have two pairs of shoes into which her feet have been placed, and thus it may be that Llew is on his way to obtaining the right to place his own feet in the lap of a goddess or her representative, as would befit a sacred king like Math, by this act of sympathetic magic which in the third instance is reinforced when Gwydion insists that to make shoes which fit, he (and Llew) will have to see the goddess's feet. This means that Arianrhod is obliged to visit these shoemakers, and to do so she leaves her Caer, comes to the edge of the water (the area of Annwn between the archetypal and natural worlds) and thus makes herself vulnerable. This vulnerability is easily exploited by Gwydion. When she faces Gwydion, not recognising him and assuming him to be the shoemaker he appears to be, rather than the kingmaker he is, she says how she finds it hard to believe that he can't make shoes from the measurements that he's been given. He replies that now she has come to him he definitely can. Of course what he means is that he can now definitely make the shoes' resting place for the feet of Llew! As he says this a wren appears nearby.

In the Brythonic Mysteries, the wren symbolised the sacred, sacrificed king and became his sacrificial animal substitute in ceremonies which later remembered the old and bloody rites of sovereignty in a dwindling pagan folk magic. *The Cutty Wren* folk ballad recalls this, describing the ritual hunting and killing of the wren, including the cooking of the bird *"in a bloody great cauldron"*. The expletive 'bloody' is not included to either describe the gory rites or to give rustic flavour to the song, but originated as *"by our lady"* and so paid cautionary Christian lip service to the Virgin Mary, substituted for Ceridwen, goddess of the cauldron.

Llew aimed at the bird (whether with sling, stone or spear we are not told) and hit it *"between the sinew and the leg bone"*. Again the sacred king theme is brought into play here, in that Llew maims the bird, a feature of many a sacred king, not least *Bran*, who was wounded in the leg with a poisoned spear, and *Bron,* Christianised successor as king of the Holy Grail. In this maiming of the symbol of sacral kingship by the king in waiting, we are probably seeing a memory of the old Bronze Age sacred king rituals where the would-be successor was required to play a prominent part in the mutilation and death of the incumbent king. Seeing this ritual maiming action, Arianrhod is forced to take a step towards recognising Llew as a future sacred king, and (supposedly unwittingly) names him … *Llew Llaw Gyffes … "the lion with the steady hand"*. The *Lion* title again brings the sacred king theme into play, being the totem animal of Heracles/Hercules whose mythology would have typified, as we shall see, the ancient sacrificed king cults. Seemingly angry at being tricked into this affirmation for her son, she lays a *geasa* (prohibition) upon the boy that she shall never arm him. This in effect would deny him any king/warrior status, indeed his very manhood – for only the mother, as representative of the goddess, could arm her son.

What in effect is happening here is that the process of Llew's acknowledgement and empowerment as sacred king at the hands of the goddess, his "mother" Arianrhod, is being ritually thwarted at each stage. Whilst it may be argued that she is in fact saving her son from ritualised slaughter by denying him this sacred king status, her *geasas* are rather like the stages between degrees of magical initiation or intervals in an initiation rite. In reality she is not refusing to acknowledge his sacral kingship as successor to Math, but is making him work for it! There is, after all, in this coming to terms with the empowering goddess, an element of the courtship of some femme fatale by the unhappy candidate.

Gwydion takes Llew away and begins to look for ways around this further prohibition. He eventually decides again to use his magic and present himself and the boy at Arianrhod's court, changed in appearance and dressed as bards. The assumption of this role as roving bards is not difficult because Gwydion is the archetypal bard, being the "best storyteller in the world". He and Llew spend a night as acclaimed bards at Arianrhod's court, then in the morning the court rises to the sound of warning trumpets, for the place seems to be under attack. In the light of this dire emergency, Gwydion urges Arianrhod to arm them to resist the siege. She apparently having done so in all innocence is then told by Gwydion that the arms won't be needed, for the 'siege' was an illusion of his magic. He then reveals to her who he and Llew really are, gleefully reminding her that, in spite of her prohibition, she has nonetheless armed her son.

Again we are told of her rage at being thus deceived, and inevitably this results in a further prohibition to inhibit the boy's validity for kingship. This latest and third prohibition is that the young Llew should never have a wife "*of the race that is now on the earth*". This is an interesting prohibition, confirming the idea that the sacred king should be married not to a mortal but to a Faery Queen, who by definition would be from a race which had passed from the earth, or at least the world! What in fact Arianrhod is doing is, again, not thwarting his destiny to become a sacred king, but defining the terms of his sacral kingship.

The story makes much of Gwydion and Arianrhod's mutual antagonism and appears at face value to place Arianrhod in the role of the wicked witch of the North. Gwydion is said to return with Llew to Math's court and remonstrate with Math, the present sacred king, about Arianrhod's wickedness, but reading between the lines, it becomes clear that in fact Gwydion is constantly presenting Llew to the goddess as a candidate for sacred kingship and Arianrhod is falling all too easily for each of her brother/mate's shape shifting feats, in order to allow the defined steps in her son's initiation.

Math suggests to Gwydion that they overcome this latest prohibition by making a woman by magic, out of flowers, to be a wife (not of the race presently upon the earth) to young Llew. They do so, making her from the flowers of meadowsweet, oak and broom and baptising her with the name Blodeuedd, which literally means "flower face". In fact whilst the Mabinogi romance only mentions these three flowers, the *Hanes Blodeuwedd* says that she was made out of nine trees. A suitable number for a triple (3x3) goddess. Oak would have been sacred to Math, as sacred king, and meadowsweet was sacred to Gwydion (and his Norse counterpart Odin). Broom is mentioned in another poem attributed to Taliesin as the flower of lovers' assignations, but, as Graves points out, its wood was used to make spears. In this we can see a Blodeuedd whose flower construction comprises flowers which are symbolic of characters and events of the story … the two flowers Oak and Meadowsweet indicating her origins in the magic of Math and Gwydion and the broom that was meant to cover the love aspect of things being later changed to become the spear which treacherously dispatches her husband Llew.

Having made the woman-form from flowers she is 'baptised'. This is a Christian gloss upon the magical process of inducing a Faery spirit into the flower form. It is then, having provided this Faery, surrogate goddess to empower Llew's sacred kingship, that Math is able to grant the youth land in what is now Meirionydd. Accordingly Llew becomes a sacred king in waiting.

All goes well, until one day Llew leaves Blodeuedd alone at Mur Castell … the site can be identified as the old Roman camp at Tomen y Mur near Trawsfynydd. In Llew's absence, a certain Gronw Bebyr "Lord of Penllyn" comes by, stag hunting. *Penllyn* means chief of the lake, which identifies him as none other than Ceridwen's husband, Tegid Foel. The appearance of this hunter of royal stags from the deeps of Annwn is the next sequence in Llew's unfortunate adventures as a would-be sacred king.

Blodeuedd, looking out from Mur Castell, sees Gronw slaughter a stag … a symbol of the sacred king Llew, her husband, which is the sign for this sacrificial stage of the rite to be set in motion. The sacred king, having been established, must now be dispatched.

Blodeuedd invites Gronw in and they immediately fall for each other and sleep together; in fact he stays three nights with her. Needless to say, they resolve to kill Llew … but to kill a sacred king is no easy matter. He has been empowered by the Goddess and is thus, except under very special circumstances, invulnerable … and even the gullible Llew has not been stupid enough to broadcast this information. Before he leaves Blodeuedd, Gronw reminds her to extract the secret of Llew's vulnerability and to let him know, and the day before Llew's return he quickly makes himself scarce.

Llew finds Blodeuedd seemingly troubled upon his return, and asking her what the matter is, she eventually says that she is worried for him and wonders what sort of circumstances might put his life at risk. Llew, innocently thinking that she is genuinely concerned for his safety, seeks to reassure her by telling her that he may only be killed under the bizarre circumstance of being stood with one foot on the edge of a bath and the other on a he-goat. As if this in itself isn't a rare enough situation in which to court death, Llew goes on to tell Blodeuedd that even then he may only be dispatched by a specially prepared spear that needs a year to be made. The treacherous Blodeuedd gets this information to Gronw forthwith, who sets to making the spear.

When the year has passed and the spear is ready, Blodeuedd asks Llew to remind her of the circumstances in which he may be at risk. Better still, she insists, he should show her. The bath is prepared at the edge of the river and the goat brought. Llew takes his bath then steps out and stands with one foot on the goat and the other on the bath's edge. Gronw is ready on a nearby hilltop and throws his spear. Llew is impaled, gives out a scream, and then turns into an eagle and soars into the sky and out of sight.

We see from this that the vulnerability of the sacred king involves his feet. One foot has to be in one peculiar place and the other in another, but both off the ground. With his feet thus out of contact with the land, like those of Math, he becomes the true sacred king and so is ready to become the sacrifice. But there is more to it than this. As the one named Llew he has come to the height of his powers and been named at the summer solstice (under the astrological sign of Leo ... the lion). He is killed with his foot placed on the goat, which is the astrological sign of Capricorn at the winter solstice. The lion-maned golden one, the sun hero, has come to his fullness in midsummer and died/disappeared at midwinter. As for the bath, it was probably a cauldron of transformation and rebirth in the original tale, but became a bath to suit the location of the myth at the old Roman camp of Tomen y Mur, where there are the remains of a bath house, fed by the river/stream mentioned in the story.

After Llew's 'death' by impalement ... an aspect of the ritual sacrificial rites of the Bronze Age, later typified as "Hercules" cults ... Gwydion learns what has happened and again seeks Math's aid. The upshot of this is that Gwydion goes looking for Llew, and coming to a farm to spend the night, hears that the farmer's sow exhibits a tendency to wander during the day. Gwydion takes notice of this because (like us) he knows that the sow is the totem beast of the goddess Ceridwen, keeper of the cauldron. After all, the last time Llew was seen was at his death/transformation at the bath/cauldron, at the hands of Gronw, alias Tegid Foel (Ceridwen's husband). The next day he follows the wandering sow and she leads him to a tree. In the tree sits an eagle, alive, yet as rotting as any corpse. Maggots and flesh fall from the bird to the ground which, superficially, is why the sow finds the place so attractive. Gwydion realises that the live but decomposing eagle is Llew and sings an *englyn* to coax the great bird to come down and perch on his knee. When it has done so he transforms it with his wand and the eagle again becomes the emaciated flesh and blood Llew.

The pair return to Math's court from where they gain permission to sally forth to reclaim Llew's kingdom. Llew kills Gronw with a spear and Gwydion goes after Blodeuedd. In her flight to escape Gwydion, her "nine maidens" fall into a lake and are drowned. By now the number nine (3x3) of the goddess and the return of her representatives/servants to the faery lake from where they no doubt originated will be obvious. What may be less obvious however is that in this driving into the lake of the maidens who have aided and abetted their mistress's infidelity, we see a borrowing from the New Testament parable of the Gaderene swine and thus another Christianised reference to the sow totem of the goddess Ceridwen.

Blodeuedd herself is then left to face Gwydion alone, who turns her into an owl. This is a clever piece of imagery in that she now becomes *Blodeuwedd,* which is the word for an owl. Gwydion has thus transformed her from flower spangled Venus to the goddess of wisdom, the Greek Athene, whose totem bird is the owl. The owl is a bird which has a dished "flower face", so that her primal flowery essence is retained, but transformed. She has chosen to mate with the dark god Gronw in the stead of the sun god Llew, so whilst retaining her selfhood, she will forever witness a goddess of the night, rather than of the bright sunshine. Llew is restored to his kingdom and the story, such as we have it, ends.

It has been noted elsewhere that Llew's trials at the hands of the goddess in whatever guise, starry Arianrhod, flower-made Blodeuwedd or the white sow Ceridwen is in fact *five-fold,* with Arianrhod and Blodeuwedd both displaying dual roles and Ceridwen making her single brief, totemic appearance, so that in fact Llew's initiation is at the hands of five aspects of the goddess. As we shall see in chapter six, the rites of sacrifice of a sacred king in the Bronze Age were essentially a five-fold process.

The story of Math fab Mathonwy was written down at a time of early mediaeval Celtic revival, but its origins as oral myth, expounding mystery lore, particularly in relation to sovereignty, are a thousand or more years older. That Young Llew should be destined to become the archetypal sacred king after Math is briefly hinted at, at the end of the story. When Llew was restored, it said that he went on "to rule over all of Gwynedd", the kingdom of the high king Math ... from which we must deduce that "the king is dead, long live the king".

In cosmological terms, Llew is the sun, the axial point of the planets, in apprenticeship to "stepping into Math's shoes" as the son of the Bear axial point, the Pole Star in Ursa Minor. The axial symbolism is indicated in Llew's spear and Math's wand respectively. But as we shall see, the cosmological ideas that these myths propounded were more than just abstractions of the fertile bardic mind. In their obsession with the ancient themes of sovereignty, the bards set these patterns of heavenly destiny upon the landscape and into the folksoul of Wales. Latterly, their most remarkable achievement in this respect was of course the creation of Arthur.

Math and Arthur

In view of our early enquiries, we may now be sure that Math, *the bear who was son of bear-like*, was the ancient proto-Arthur.

His axial wand, which brought to fruition the starry wheel (*Arianrhod*) of the heavens, the empowerment of his sovereignty in his goddess /priestess footholder, Goewin, who was subsequently his queen (later reflected in Arthur's complex relationship with Guinevere) mark him out as the archetypal sacred king.

Math was said to be a guardian of buried treasure, like the great votive hoards at *Llyn Cerrig Bach* on Anglesey for example, and Bronze Age/ Neolithic graves of sacred kings. A horde of artifacts were in fact found at a village named *Mathon* below the *British Camp* on the Malvern Hills. So, as a guardian of treasure, Math – *Bear son of Bear-like* – takes on a role traditionally given to dragons. Was this not the way in which that Little Bear in the heavens, Ursa Minor, held in the embrace of the Dragon, had taken on the role of treasuring the Pole Star from the dragon, and how Arthur, that later bear cub, took on the role of *Uther pen Dragon?*

In the old tales the reincarnation/planned successor of Math as sacred king was, as we have just seen, Llew (or Lleu) whose adventures and imagery are also rejigged to fit Arthur, with the later assistance of another Llew recreation ... *Lancelot.* The child Llew, like the child Arthur ... and indeed the child Christ ... is taken away to be raised in secret to become the archetypal *Mab Darogan ... the prophesied son.*

When both Llew and Arthur come of an age to be named and armed we have further parallels. The naming and arming incidents (albeit through trickery) of Llew by his goddess mother Arianrhod confirm this as Celtic custom, derived from even more archaic practice of the king or tribal chieftain's rank and power being validated by a representative of the mother goddess, often a Faery woman. This serves to provide Arthurian legend with a further, if tangential, connection to the *Math* story, where Arianrhod seems to attempt to thwart this process ... as Morgan le Fey attempts to with Arthur. When Arthur is armed it is, again, by a representative of the goddess, the Lady of the Lake ... a typical *Gwraig Annwn* of Welsh Faery lore. Indeed this imagery of the Lake Faery/ representative of the goddess arming Arthur is also designed to maintain the practice of mother arming son. We can see this when the later writers of Arthurian romance make Arthur's Faery mother Ygraine hail from the flooded Underworld kingdom of Lyonesse. They then have Arthur being armed from the deeps of Llyn Tegid (Bala Lake) which other Welsh legend tells us was a flooded kingdom, whose Underworld associations, as Taliesin has already shown us, are well attested to by the presence there of the goddess Ceridwen. The implication therefore is that the *Gwraig Annwn*/Lady of the Lake who arms Arthur is in fact his mother Ygraine … herself a *Gwraig Annwn* .

Arthur's mating, or hoped for mating, with Guinevere, or *Gwynhyfwr,* and its disruption by the schemes of Morgan, is foreshadowed in the Math tale by Arianrhod's laying a *geasa,* a prohibition, upon Llew that he shall never have a flesh and blood woman/queen. When this prohibition is overcome and Llew does get a queen, Blodeuedd, she proves to be as unfaithful to him as Gwynhyfwr was to be to Arthur. The adultery of queen Gwynhyfwr makes Arthur the same cuckold that Llew becomes through Blodeuedd's adultery with Gronw in the Math story. The romancer's device for Arthur's conception by the connivance of the magician Merlin is also the same as the one used earlier by the bards who wrote Math, using the archetypal bard/magician Gwydion.

In the Mabinogi story, Gwydion gets Math to go off to war so that Gilfaethwy can sleep with Math's queen Goewin. In the Arthurian story, Merlin gets Ygraine's husband, the King of Cornwall, out on campaign so that Uther gets to sleep with Ygraine. Ygraine accepts Uther into her bed thinking (through Merlin's magic) that Uther is her husband, whilst in *Math* the mating is equally illicit, but less subtle. The parallels are exact in detailed events, if somewhat tangled overall in the differing requirements of the old Math and new Arthurian 'versions'.

In *Math,* we start to see that in fact Goewin and Arianrhod are certainly two aspects or items of story about one goddess.

In Arthur then, we have the heritage of Math, an ancient sacred king type, as successor to the even older sacred king cult of Bran. But though Arthur may have been a bardic invention, 'his' effect in galvanising a Welsh, and subsequently British, sense of identity has been very real. He is as real as fifteen hundred years of projection by our national psyche can make him, and that is as real as any national figure can get, flesh and blood or not. The bards did their work well.

Che Bards

It was the job of the bards to make sure that the Celts *knew who they were*. This is why the Romans had been so intent upon suppressing the Druid stronghold on Anglesey all those years before. The Druids, taking over from their Bronze Age predecessors, refined and structured the bardic ideal, and held everything that represented Celtic existence within their lore. It was their job to retain all matters of law, mythology, religious practice, history and genealogy, everything which told the Celts who they were, what their values were and where they came from, and to make sure that none of these markers of Celtic identity were lost from generation to generation. At the decline of the Druids and the rise of the professional and legalistic Christian court bards this task seems to have fallen in some degree to the unorthodox *Cyfarwydd* ... the wandering storytellers who (as Taliesin amply demonstrates in his chiding "englyn" (verses) of the *Preiddu Annwn* ... the spoils of Annwn) were something more than storytellers!

Telling a story was an exercise in ritual sonics to evoke precise magical patterns.

The tradition of telling the tales, of putting across the mythology in such a way that the archetypal gods and goddesses were effectively evoked, demanded a magical technique. Gwydion was the archetypal god of bards and every Taliesin initiate bard saw himself made in Gwydion's mould ... not least in his tribulations with the Goddess! Poetry may, like magic, be described as a technique for making changes in consciousness and in doing so being able to give substance to abstract ideas. Potent key images are fed into consciousness to evoke an inner concept into a tangible thought form. If we couple this idea not only to that of the image being delivered but the technique of delivery itself, we start to get some idea of what the original bards were trained to do.

Sound waves delivered at particular frequencies can do more than make music ... the modern medical use of such techniques as ultrasound to produce pictures and break up kidney stones, indicate that the ability to focus sound waves is a powerful and practical tool. The Celtic languages, as we have observed, were languages which were designed to be spoken and sung rather than written, and this still – even through all the steps from Brythonic to Old Welsh to Middle Welsh to modern Welsh – holds true. Complex sonic exercises in the Welsh choral tradition such as *Penillion* as well the poetic metrical recitation devices such as *mesotomy*, mentioned already, indicate a language which is more interested in *sounds* than *words*.

We have legends that modes of speech could achieve not only the formation of potent thought forms but actual physical effects. It was said that the bards were able to raise boils on a man's face by the use of sarcasm! It may be that it was such questionable and unpredictable abilities which caused the eventual prohibition of certain modes of recitation, the forbidding of cursing and the restriction of certain techniques of composition among the official court bards.

This implies that after the decline of the Druids and the rise of Christianity, official 'tame' court bards were employed who had much political but little magical ability. There were however those of the Taliesin's ilk … the wandering, unofficial *Cyfarwydd,* as we have said, who were under no such prohibition and it is to these that we owe the preservation of the myths and, glimpsed between the lines of verse, a battery of magical technique which we are cajoled into guessing at.

One thing which will by now be clear however is that it is impossible to separate the literary and magical merits of Celtic mythological material. We might even say that it is *deliberately impossible* because the material has been specially crafted so that the efficacy of one aspect depends upon the construction of the other. This ability to use the Brythonic language, or pre-Brythonic language, in a particular way is hinted at, notably in the Irish *Senchas Mór,* where two *fili* (Druids) are upbraided for talking to each other in a *dark tongue,* which the assembled court could not understand. There has been some speculation that this has something to do with "tree alphabets" and Ogham sigils, and also (and more likely) that they were using an archaic form of Irish … *Old Goidelic,* the original Celtic tongue. The use of the adjective which became *Ddu (black or dark)* to describe early Celtic or pre-Celtic (Bronze Age) sites in Wales … *Cae Ddu* and *Ffordd Ddu* are two examples of Bronze Age sites in my own locality … may give the answer. The use of the adjective *black* seems to relate to sites which are old rather than sinister (though a few qualify on both counts!) In that much of the Taliesin material seems to relate to Bronze Age esotericism, one wonders whether the dark speech and the mysteries that it described are part of a complete corpus of mystery teaching which was originally transmitted from the Bronze Age occupants of these islands to the early Celtic settlers who overran and assimilated them. Whether or not this was the case (and Graves hints at the idea of an original Taliesin being of pre-Celtic stock) the fact seems to remain that Brythonic, or a variant of Brythonic, was used in a particular way with sonic effects by the bards. That there were special styles of pronunciation and that, even towards the close of the Celtic era, the use of riddle and mystification in speech was *de rigeur* for anyone (even Christian clerics) who aspired to some form of bardship, has become clear. It is essential that we view Arthur and the "Taliesins" and others who promoted his mythology against this background.

Che Bardic Evolution of Arthur

As we follow the tangled knotwork by which mythologies leapfrog cultural delineations down the ages, we arrive, in the time of the later "Taliesins" (via various strata of British and European mediaeval myth) in twelfth century Provence at the feet of the *Trouvères*. The Trouvères were as much bards, after their own fashion, as were the bards of sixth century Wales, and like the court bards of Wales and Ireland they had powerful patronage. We can immediately think of the legendary *Blondel* who was Richard the Lionheart's Trouvère minstrel. That such a minstrel should be accredited to Richard's rough patronage is not surprising, for the troubadour movement was patronised by the remarkable Eleanor of Aquitaine, Richard's mother. It was Queen Eleanor's patronage of the troubadours which inspired the cult of courtly love and the code of chivalry which developed from it. In this elevation of the feminine we see the old goddess empowerment theme, so implicit in the ancient Math story. Now however, the goddess Arianrhod was replaced by the Christian Blessed Virgin. Pagan shades still however managed to hang to the mythology, with a goddess appearing in some versions as the Shepherdess ... around which many a supposed heresy was built in southern France. But this is where, deriving from troubadour Provençal poetry, influenced by Moorish mystical philosophy, the Trouvères/bards rearranged the ancient Celtic myths of the sacred king's validation by the goddess to subtle interplay between kings and queens, and knights and ladies. At its roots however it was still the Celtic theme of *sovereignty* implicit in the cult of sacral kingship.

The Arthur that the French Trouvères inherited and adapted came from the Normans of northern France. Whilst to some extent the Normans would have touched upon Arthurian tales during their occupation of Wales, the real "French connection" was made not so much through occupation of the dwindling Celtic areas of western Britain but through the Breton minstrels.

Then as now, the Bretons, whilst sharing the Northern French mainland with their Norman neighbours, were literally a race apart. Whereas the Normans were descendents of Norse settlers, the Bretons were descended from a mix of the original indigenous Celts and Celts who had left mainland Britain in the face of Saxon incursion westwards. Tradition places a Welsh prince among the evacuees but the majority would have been Cornish Celts. With their cousins of Welsh and Cornish Britain the Breton Celts therefore shared (and still share) a Brythonic language, culture and mythology. That this, with an Arthurian emphasis, spread to other areas of France seems to be clear, when we note that in the late ninth century Sigisbert VI rises up against Louis II using the title "Prince Ursus" ... or "Prince bear" (the *Arth/bear* of "Arthur" in other words!) Be that as it may, it seems more than likely that the Normans' initial contact with Celtic lore came through minstrel bards from Brittany, but was reinforced some time later in the Normans' occupation of Wales ... later feeding the first of many a 'Celtic Revival' in the twelfth century, when, ironically, much of the Mabinogi material, ancient though it already was, came to be actually written down!

The Arthurian writings of Chrétien de Troyes and Robert de Boron at the end of the eleventh century continued to promote ideals of chivalric knights and their porcelain ladies. Hot on their heels come the British versions ... eventually producing the fifteenth century *Le Morte d'Arthur* of Sir Thomas Malory, one of the first books to be printed. This is the idealised Arthuriad that we tend to know.

Whilst the bards would not have been displeased with the evolution from Math to this idealised Arthur and the continuing theme of sovereignty promoted down the ages, the twelfth century Celtic Revival at the time of the Crusades also seemed to reiterate the Romano Arthur. It may be no coincidence that the rise of the Templars with their peculiar brand of military gnostic spirituality bears close resemblance, and perhaps deliberately imitates, the Mithraic code of the Roman legions. Again, as with the specific Arthur mythos, we seem to be faced with a wholesale (and supremely successful) bardic attempt to put the rich esoteric wine of a very ancient pagan past into new Christian, or at least quasi-Christian, wine skins!

Certainly the Templars in the light of their ready exposure to a good deal of Middle Eastern esotericism can also be held responsible for the introduction of new facets of mystery teaching into that ancient concoction, which attached to and stimulated the Arthurian revival. It is, for example, from such sources that the later material attributed to the Taliesin cultus gets some of its more obvious touches of Judaic esoteric colouring. The late *Hanes Taliesin* is perhaps a case in point, where our initiate undergoes the essential climax of his preliminary initiation … being swallowed as a seed by Ceridwen … upon a threshing floor. The Old Testament tells us that it was upon such a threshing floor that the original Jerusalem temple was founded. It was in these physical foundations of the temple known as the "Stables of Solomon" that the Templars had their Jerusalem headquarters … hence of course they were Templars – "knights of the temple". Given that the European concentration of the Manichean/Cathar heresies and the stronghold of the Templars in southern France was an area of previous Romano Celtic settlement, there may have been pre-existing 'local' sources to further encourage Mithraic/Arthurian ideas as well.

So, while Eleanor of Aquitaine's son Richard Coeur de Lion hacked his crusading way through the Middle East of the twelfth century, the Mabinogi manuscripts were being written in their present form and the bards were keeping the goddess and her latest sacred king, Arthur, alive and well in Christendom. Above all they were Celts, the Church of Rome notwithstanding!

aRthuR and the faeRy Women

Eleanor of Aquitaine's patronage and validation of the cult of *courtly love* elevated the role of women in the pattern of court philosophy and practice, so that knightly endeavour, even the somewhat dubious knightly endeavour of the Crusades, was seen to be initiated and empowered by devotion to the beloved. The lady of Arthurian romance empowers the sacred warrior and does so as an extension of the power of the Queen, who rather like Dante's Beatrice, becomes a quasi-goddess. This courtly love/sovereignty theme is at the heart of Arthurian romance and of the ancient Math tale which spawned it, but before that spawning each porcelain lady of Arthurian romance had originated as a Celtic *Gwraig Annwn*, a "wife of the deep", a mate from Annwn, the world of Faery.

If we de-Anglicise Guinevere's name to its original Welsh spelling, *Gwyn-hwyfyr*, we have a name which indicates an otherworldly being. As we have pointed out earlier, the prefixes and suffixes of *gwyn/gwen/wynn/*

wen and *win* are mutations or versions of the Welsh adjective *gwynn* which means "white". This adjective is employed to describe Underworld beings, because much of what comes from the Underworld of Annwn is white. When Thomas the Rhymer meets the Queen of Fair Elfland, prior to being taken into the Underworld, she is seated upon a *white* horse.

The reason for *white* signification of underworld figures may be because of it being the time-honoured bloodless/death/ghost colour, or it may be for other reasons which we shall set aside for now. This "white" suffixing and prefixing may be further seen in such instances as the Underworld aspect of the goddess … *Cerid-wen,* who, it will be recalled, had a cauldron in which bubbled the stuff which fed the poet bards. *A-wen* inspiration. The Underworld king located beneath Glastonbury Tor was (and for all I know still is!) *Gwyn ap Nudd* (who also becomes one of Arthur's companions/knights in the *Culhwch ac Olwen* romance) and Arthur's ship which travels to the Underworld in the *Preiddu Annwn* is called *Pryd-wen.* Mallory also gives the name of Arthur's shield as *Pridwen.* This may be a confusion of the names in Arthur's martial inventory, but it also gives us the image of a shield used like a coracle. Either way, *Prydwen* literally may be translated as "of white aspect", suggesting a suitably spectral means of transport. In the meantime we should also consider that a shield and a Round Table are not symbolically dissimilar.

The Table Round was Gwynhyfwr's dowry upon her marriage to Arthur, and in spite of such evidence as the mediaeval painted table at Winchester, is a symbol of very ancient provenance. We have seen how "Guinevere" derived from *Gwyn-hyfwr,* which can be taken to mean "white apparition", and like Math's hoped for validation in Arianrhod, whose name as we have seen means "silver round" representing the circle of stars, it validated the axis. Indeed we are told by the romancer bards that this Table Round/Gwynhyfwr's dowry (and Arthur's validation of sovereignty) was brought from the constellation of the Great Bear!

One legend tells of Gwynhyfwr fleeing for refuge to her father's place in the "White Tower" or "White Mound", taken to be an ancient mound, probably a burial mound, on what is now Tower Hill on which the Tower of London's White Tower was subsequently built. Burial mounds may be considered "white" because of the sometime use of large amounts of quartz stones in their construction and/or the Underworld association. The mythology of the Underworld god Bran (who had a magical cauldron like the goddess Ceridwen) says that his severed head was placed in the White Mound to protect Britain. Bran's totem is the raven, and indeed the Welsh word for crow/raven is still *bran*. It is said that when the ravens which occupy the Tower of London leave their habitat, Britain will fall ... all of which substantiates and perpetuates the Bran legend. This is further emphasised by a story that Arthur, seeing himself as the once and future protector of Britain, went to the White Mound and dug up Bran's head on the arrogant assumption that in view of his own powerful protection this Bran-charm had become obsolete. He is said to have quickly replaced the blessed head following a number of setbacks in his struggle to hold back the encroaching Saxon hordes!

If we examine this tangle of myth and legend we realise that beneath the theme of defence of the realm, with the Dark Age Celtic struggles against invaders after the withdrawal of the Roman legions, there is a deeper stratum of meaning. The essential grist of the legends is that the Arthur cult spoiled the ancient burial site associated with the god Bran. This is in fact a memory of the cult of Math/Gwydion overthrowing the cult of Bran, simply being given a Christian update in the person of the New Math ... Arthur. Again, Geoffrey of Monmouth's motif of Arthur pillaging the white mound of Bran is taken up shortly afterwards by the member of the Taliesin cult who wrote the *Preiddu Annwn,* where he has Arthur raiding Annwn, the Underworld, reiterating the incident in *Math* where Gwydion steals the sacred pigs of Annwn from Pryderi. In the *Prieddu,* Taliesin, as we shall see, gave out the names of these *Caers* as puns about burial chambers to shame the metaphysically clueless court bards, so again we can assume that Arthur's 'raid' on the Underworld was via a Bronze Age or Neolithic mortuary complex. There are also tales telling how Arthur attacked various Underworld locations to get back Gwynhyfwr after she had been abducted. The abduction stories include an incident where she is held by Melwas who is at that time the evil resident of Glastonbury Tor, and the episode where Lancelot has to rescue her from Meleagant of Gorre. Both of these locations and their inhabitants are metaphors for Underworld locations and powers, and with these myths Gwynhyfwr begins to take on the mantle of a Celtic Persephone.

We therefore have an association of Gwynhyfwr with the Underworld, and Arthur, or Lancelot in his stead, raiding that Underworld. Again the Mithraic significance of Arthur is hinted at. Firstly the caves/burial mounds may relate to the subterranean chambers of Mithraic ritual, but more convincingly, Lancelot standing in for Arthur is a nudge in the direction of the Celtic sun hero Llew who is the nearest character that Celtic mythology had to Mithras. Sometimes entry is made via the obvious gates of both death and the past, represented by ancient burial mounds, where the sacrificed sacred king Bran the Blessed with his great bronze cauldron is the god of the earlier, Bronze Age, epoch. In seeking out Gwynhyfwr in these, and the association of her name with the Underworld and these sites which are gates to it, we must also assume her to be of an earlier epoch. Nor was Arthur the only raider of Annwn … the god Gwydion and the Christian St Collen also tried their hands, for varying reasons, to get the better of those who lived in the Underworld beneath the sacred Celtic earth.

Why should the long dead, presumably at their rest in the Underworld, be the cause of so much agitation to those in incarnation above ground – and why should Arthur be mated to a queen who hailed from this mortuary kingdom? What did the Underworld beings have which represented such value to the Arthurs and Taliesins of a later epoch? For Gwydion the treasure was pigs! For Arthur it was Gwynhyfwr's dowry which the mythology tells us was the Table Round. Bran had inherited the cauldron which we can assume belonged originally to the Dagda, the chief of the Irish Faery/Underworld race the Tuatha dé Danann … which he later passed back to the king of Ireland with disastrous results. Ireland across the sea, into the sunset of the West, again represented something of an otherworld place to the early inhabitants of mainland Britain. Arthur, in raiding places sacred to Bran, appears to have also been after this wondrous, regenerative cauldron. In the later courtly and Christianised versions of these raids in search of a regenerative cauldron, we have the quest for the redemptive Holy Grail.

These three items of pigs, the table and the cauldron are of much greater import than their intrinsic gastronomic associations, just as the symbols of the Last Supper would seem to somebody coming across them for the first time to be simply those of some sacred feast, yet carry on to have theologically profound implications. Accordingly, these banqueting symbols of roasting pig, a great table that has infinite seating capacity and a cauldron, which, among other miraculous functions, is able to feed anybody and everybody, have much more far reaching consequence. Where the Table Round, the pigs and the cauldron come from in earlier space/time is part and parcel of what they represent. The Celts would have found the cauldrons under the table-like capstones which were revealed when they sacked the extensive ritual and mortuary sites of the Bronze Age. What the treasures of leaf shaped daggers, great cauldrons, boat shaped, crescent lunulas of gold and other relics would have represented to them was a pattern of how things supposedly once were, and if these quests – these Underworld forays – succeeded, may some day be again. Once there had been a golden age … of this they were certain, and they wanted it to return.

CHAPTER FIVE

Cauldron, Grail, Skull and Snake

The Cauldron and the Grail

I F WE ARE to consider what the Arthurian/Taliesin cult was after, we find that our attention is primarily drawn to the mythical cauldron, the source of *Awen*. By the late twelfth century however Chrétien de Troyes and Robert de Boron had transformed this primeval cauldron into the Holy Grail with full biblical provenance as the cup of the Last Supper, yet strangely, Gnostically, associated with the Virgin Mary. She was after all the 'vessel' of Christ's incarnation, and the symbolism of the Eucharist appeared to be all about that. This was emphasised by an apocryphal New Testament gospel known as *The Questions of Bartholomew*, which described how Mary had been visited by an angel who shared the eucharistic meal of bread and wine with her, after which the angel announced that in three years' time she would give birth to the Saviour.

The implication of course was that by taking the divinely materialised body and blood of Christ from an angelic being, Mary, a temple virgin, became impregnated with the material basis for Christ's incarnation. Apocryphal texts with a particularly Gnostic slant, like Bartholomew, were circulated widely in the primitive church of North Africa, and from there made their way to the fledgling Celtic church. The oldest extant version of Bartholomew is in Greek and probably fifth century; the original, again in Greek, was much earlier. Whilst such apocrypha were largely condemned in the fourth century, they continued to encourage a lively body of assorted heresies and found their way into the essentially

British battery of Christian gnosticism which was to provide much of the structure for the Grail legends and the Mary cult which was implicit in them.

The Grail legends as a Christian updating of the old cauldron myths therefore took what had been a pagan goddess/son cult, a very ancient Isis cult around the Mediterranean, added a home grown triple goddess/son cult, as latterly described in Taliesin's encounter (as Gwion) with Ceridwen in Wales, to form a Grail cult of Christ/Mary in the suitably rarified air of courtly love. As this Marian cult began to interweave itself with the Celtic mysteries we have the Welsh bard Dafydd Benfras making poetic declaration to "*Crist mab Mair am pur fonhedd*" ("Christ son of Mary my cauldron of pure origin"). This continues the ancient Celtic matriarchal *son of the mother* (rather than the father) theme but replaces the traditional Underworld Goddess/*Gwraig Annwn*/Faery woman encounter and empowerment with an encounter with the Christian Queen of Heaven. The ancient 'triple goddess' of the Celts was able to fall in with this Christian transference fairly easily, so that the "three Marys" … the *Blessed Virgin Mary*, *Mary Magdalene* and *Mary Cleopas* were able to step into the approximate shoes of the Welsh triad of *Arianrhod, Blodeuwedd* and *Ceridwen*. It is doubtful that any Celtic cleric would actually admit this, even to himself, but certainly this became the way that the symbolism of the Great Goddess neatly rearranged itself without causing any great ripple in the Celtic folksoul. The essential difference was however that the cauldron was no longer warmed and activated by the breath of three times three goddesses but by the breath of the third person of the Trinity, the Holy Spirit, and what issued from the Grail was not the *awen*, the inspiration which had issued from the cauldron, but the power of the Holy Spirit.

At this time it is unlikely that most Celts pondered overmuch on the theology of this; such ponderings were to come later. The transformation from Underworld goddesses, or their Faery representatives, to Mary Queen of Heaven was in any case a sporadic and gradual transference. This is probably why, some two hundred years later, the historical Scottish figure of Thomas of Ercildoune, better known as *Thomas the Rhymer*, assumed that the lady whom he encountered at the start of his Underworld journey was the Queen of Heaven. He was however brought up short by the lady in question who assured him in no uncertain terms that (Holy Grail propaganda notwithstanding) she was *not* the Blessed Virgin Mary, but on the contrary was a real Faery woman, indeed none other than "the Queene of fair Elfland".

The Irish Cycle: Brigid of the Tuatha dé Danann and the cauldron

Perhaps the most outstanding and long lasting example of the absorption of a Celtic cauldron-associated goddess into Christianity was, however, that of *Brigid*, or *Ffraed* as she was known in Welsh (English: Bride). Brigid in fact stole Mary's thunder in Ireland by becoming a Christian saint who was (and is) nicknamed "Mary of the Gael", and whilst this is essentially a study of the Brythonic mysteries, the connections between Ireland and western Britain cannot be ignored.

In the original Irish the name *Brighid* means "high one", for Brigid was originally a 'triple goddess', an exalted triad of three *Brighids* who were sisters. One was patron of the bardic arts of poetry and learning, another was the mistress of smithcraft, the third being the Brighid of healing. These roles became expanded somewhat as Brighid also took on the role of the goddess of Leinster and in time of war became something of a *Morrigan* or war goddess to the Leinstermen. Her patronage of smithcraft would of course have helped in this. She also became a goddess of animal husbandry and was said to have left her cloak to dry upon the sun ... a myth which tends to associate her with the Welsh Ceridwen whose *Caer* or stronghold was the rainbow. Why an Underworld goddess should be associated with the rainbow is a matter to which we will later return. The Brighids were, however, daughters of the *Dagda,* chief of the Irish pantheon known as the *Tuatha dé Danann,* and the essential possession of the Dagda was a magical cauldron.

The Tuatha dé Danann were by no means, however, the original gods and goddesses of Ireland. A compilation of ancient orally transmitted myth and Christian expediency, produced over almost six centuries, eventually resulted in the *Leabhar Gabhála Éireann,* more usually known as *The Book of Invasions.* This work of garbled myth bent by Gaelic monks to biblical compliance does however retain what seems to be the bare bones of Irish mythology. The first occupation of Ireland, according to this, was before the Flood ... by a grand-daughter of Noah! Then after the flood came a battle for Ireland between the demonic *Fomhoire* and the followers of *Partholón.* The followers of Partholón prevailed and

103

started to form the landscape as it is today. They were however destroyed by plague. Then came the invasion of *Nemhedh* but after his death the people found themselves under the evil Fomhoire again. Eventually the people revolted and attacked the island upon which the Fomhoire had their stronghold but only a handful of the partisans survived. Some of these went to Greece and some to the northern part of the world. The descendants of the Greek contingent returned as the *Fir Bholg,* who occupied Ireland again and divided it into five counties. This theme of five-fold division is interesting in that it seems to be imitated, as we shall see, in a number of Welsh Bronze Age sacred sites, and the sovereignty rites which were conducted at them. Associated with this and the cauldron mythology are the references in some Taliesin poetry to "The cauldron of five trees". The arrangement of five counties at points of the compass with one at the centre (*Uisnech*) is also an arrangement that we shall come to when we consider the sacred chess game that was called *Fidchell* in Irish and *Gwyddbwyll* in Welsh. These are games of *sovereignty* which appear to be played between the king and the invisible or Faery powers of the kingdom. The Fir Bholg are also, in respect of this, said to have instituted sacred kingship.

Finally we come to the Tuatha dé Danann, the family of the goddess Danu. These are the descendants of that other remnant of immigrants, the ones who fled to "the north of the world", who in their exile had learned the arts of magic … presumably from the goddesses who elsewhere are the "sisters behind the north wind". Their magical abilities are emphasised by the fact that they bring with them what are considered, even to this day, to be the four traditional magical "weapons" … the stone (of Fal), the spear (of Lugh), the sword (of Nuadha) and the cauldron (of the Dagda). In this instance, however, the chief of these appears to be the cauldron because it is the property of the Dagda who is father of the Tuatha.

The Tuatha dé Danann are pretty much from the same family as the Welsh "children of Dôn" to whom the gods Gwydion and Lleu and the goddess Arianrhod belong, and like the Tuatha are particularly distinguished by their skill in magic. The magical Faery theme is emphasised in the use of the words *tuatha* and *tylwyth* in Irish and Welsh respectively. The Welsh expression *tylwyth teg,* the "fair folk", describes the pre-human Faery races. The Irish mythological story of the Tuatha dé Danann is more specific in placing them chronologically before the "sons of Mil" who are ancestors of the Gaels. Thus the coming of the sons of Mil equates with the Celtic/Gaelic occupation of Ireland, which places the Tuatha dé Danann alongside the Bronze Age folk historically and the pre-human Faery folk mythologically.

Eventually of course the sons of Mil defeated the Tuatha dé Danann and terms were agreed. These terms were that thê Tuatha retained their magic and were to occupy the Underworld of Ireland and the Gaels were to occupy the "upper" material world. At the crossing points of these two kingdoms the Dagda set one of his chiefs to each occupy a *sidhe* ... a Faery mound ... or in mundane terms, a pre-Gaelic burial mound.

The arbiter in this agreement and indeed the pivotal figure in all the dealings between the sons of Mil and the Tuatha dé Danann was the arch Druid of the Sons of Mil ... *Amhairghin*, who is the Irish equivalent of the Welsh *Taliesin* and the later British *Merlin*. It seems something of a coincidence that his name should be very much like the Welsh *Aneirin*, whom we met earlier as an historical poet! Without the magic of Amhairghin, however, the Sons of Mil would of course have been at the mercy of the Tuatha's magic.

Other areas of convergence between the two mythologies may be seen in that the Welsh *Lleu* (or *Llew*) would seem to be the Irish *Lugh,* and the Welsh *Gofannon* would seem to be the Irish *Goibhniu.* There were probably many more such correspondences between these bodies of Irish Gaelic and Welsh Brythonic myth, but as we have mentioned before, the Mabinogi material is fragmentary and we know that there are more mediaeval manuscripts lost than extant. From those which are extant, we get the impression that in the *Children of Dôn/Math fab Mathonwy* fragments, we have but a glimpse of a much more considerable body of (lost) mythology. Be that as it may, it has been suggested that the Children of Dôn and the Tuatha dé Danann were a pantheon common to both Irish and Welsh – Goidelic and Brythonic – Celtic myth originating in *Donu* a mutual mother of the gods. This common mythological base either indicates that a bulk of Welsh myth may have originated from Irish settlement in Wales or, more likely, that the material common to both Brythons and Goidels is very old indeed. That there was even later an encouragement for the two mythologies to be grafted together in Wales would seem to be summed up in the complaint of the 13th century poet Phylip Brydydd. Phylip is outraged that "the speech of strangers" is being encouraged at the court of Gruffydd ap Cynan in Gwynedd, and indeed we know that Gruffydd 'imported' bards from Ireland. We shall see this continuing connection between the Irish and Welsh mythologies as we continue to seek the cauldron – indeed we shall see in our next tale the cauldron itself moving between Wales and Ireland.

In the meantime, the three daughters of the cauldron-owning Dagda ... Brighid who represents its poetic/inspirational/*awen* quality, Brighid who represents its restorative and healing powers (it could bring slain warriors back to life) and Brighid who represents its sustaining (feeding) and making (smelting) qualities, prepared to make the quantum leap into Celtic Christian sainthood.

The triple goddess Brighid became summarised in Irish Christianity as St Brigid, abbess of Kildare. Certainly such a sainted lady did exist in Irish Celtic Christianity, born in about 450 AD. It was said that a hedged enclosure at the Kildare convent contained a perpetual fire fed by nuns for many hundreds of years after the death of St Brigid and that no men were allowed into that enclosure. This fire would seem to represent Brigid's pagan origins, being the fire of inspiration, smithcraft and the sustaining hearth ... which in the Isis mythology had been the fire which made male children immortal (hence the prohibition on letting men near the fire!) St Brigid also became the patron of milkmaids and her feast day came to be celebrated at *Imbolc*, the February festival originally in honour of her pagan sisters.

The myth of her pagan ancestor hanging her cloak to dry upon the sun (probably the vestige of a much more complex cosmology) was brought into service as a swaddling garment for the Christ child, and her milkmaid role was enhanced so that she could be brought into the "Son of the mother" mythological context by being said to have fostered and wet-nursed the divine child from the essence of the Milky Way. It was the use of such powerful imagery overlaid upon her deep-rooted goddess origins which made her all but supplant the Blessed Virgin in Irish Celtic Christianity.

On the British mainland Brigid's impact was less dramatic, though she again became the pagan goddess with a very thin Christian veil as *Bride of Beckary* at Glastonbury in the Arthuriad/Grail legends. Certainly the Brigid cult crossed from Ireland into Wales and the West country. Legend has her landing on Anglesey and setting a turf that she had brought from Ireland at a spot on the edge of Trearddur Bay, where indeed an ancient chapel to Bridget and an extensive cemetery once existed. Whether it was founded by Bridget herself may be open to conjecture, but being so near Holyhead, the closest embarkation for Ireland, would tend to confirm its Irish connection. The remains have since, sadly, been lost to the dunes and the sea, but parts existed and were sketched as late as the eighteenth century. Other legends and place names attest to the Brigid cult in Wales: Llansant*ffraid* in Powys, and St Bride's Bay in Dyfed (another location with Irish proximity) being just two more examples. None of this is surprising because, as has been pointed out, there was sporadic Irish settlement of these areas as well as the importation of Irish bardism. Whether the historical St Brigid herself ever made the journey from across the water is another matter, but her mythological attachment as an ex-pagan cauldron goddess to the 'new' Christian mythology of the Grail is very definite.

Whilst Brigid could not be the mother of the Saviour, the actual vessel of his incarnation with all its Eucharistic attachments, she ran the Blessed Virgin a very close second in what may be described as a 'sub-Marian' cult. Like Mary, who in Christian myth was a temple virgin employed in the weaving of the great Veil which shrouded the entrance to the *Debir*, the Holy of Holies, where the Presence of God was manifest, Brigid became a patron of weavers and spinners. In this spinning/weaving imagery and her Milky Way/stellar associations she also identified herself with that other pagan child of Donu, *Arianrhod*. The hanging of Brigid's cloak on the sun also echoes the rainbow symbolism of *Ceridwen*, Welsh goddess of the cauldron as we have seen. Whilst there is no archaeological evidence of Celtic occupation at the site of Brigid's chapel at Beckary, just below Glastonbury's Wearyall Hill, it is said that Arthur went there and had a vision of the Blessed Virgin. This would seem to confirm Brigid's sub-Marian status and also her cauldron priestess/goddess role as a keeper of the cauldron of inspiration and vision.

A footnote to Brigid's cult presence at Glastonbury may be recorded in that Bligh Bond, the Bristol architect who mediumistically discovered and then excavated the original Glastonbury church, was moved to form an "Order of Brigid" at Glastonbury in the early part of this century. Other members of this order included the Celtic mystic William Sharp, mortal mouthpiece for "Fiona MacLeod". As far as can be ascertained the order worked on Christian Platonic and Celtic themes, though sketches of elemental and goddess themes that I have seen in jottings made by Bond (or perhaps his daughter) tend to indicate that the pagan, magical aspects of Brigid were by no means ignored.

All this would seem to reflect Brigid as the essential bridge between primeval goddess myth and Christian Celtic mysticism, as well as effecting a juncture between the Brythonic and Gaelic Celtic traditions. Another cauldron keeper who also exemplifies this "bridge" is the Celtic god *Bran* whose associations with the Dagda's cauldron were remembered by later Arthurian romance as a Grail/cauldron keeper called *Bron*. Bran (unlike Arthur) also has the distinction of appearing in both the Welsh and Irish mythologies.

Bran mac Febhail

The Bran of Irish myth and the Bran of Welsh myth have their connections, and these are essentially in what the Gaels knew as *echtrai*, tales of Otherworld derring do. The Irish Bran is *Bran mac Febhail*, who whilst out walking one day, hears sweet music which lulls him into sleep. On waking he finds a silver apple branch beside him and taking this to his court, finds himself confronted by a beautiful faery woman, who sings a poem to him outlining the delights of her paradisal inner world. She then disappears taking the branch with her. Bran sets out on a voyage across the western (Atlantic) ocean during the course of which he meets the sea god *Manannán mac Lir*. It is after this sea god that the Isle of Man is named, but of more interest perhaps is the fact that the Welsh Manawydan is also a son of Llŷr. This is the same pantheon to which the Welsh Bran belongs, for the Welsh Bran is also described as a son of Llŷr, so in a roundabout way the connection between the two Brans is made.

As Bran mac Febhail continues on his inner voyage he finds that the sea is like a meadow, the fish are like cattle and the boat seems to be floating through a great apple orchard. This brings to mind the paradisal Avalon that is across an 'inner' body of water. It also makes a further connection with the Welsh Bran in that, as we shall see, our second Bran wades across the Irish sea.

He is able to do this not only because he is of great stature, but also because it is so shallow, and its shallowness depends, we assume, upon another legend which says that Cardigan Bay is the sunken kingdom of *Cantref Gwaelod*, a green plain which once stretched between the Welsh and Irish coasts, but which now lies just beneath the waves. Local legends add that the bells of Cantref Gwaelod may be heard from time to time as they are swung by the waves in their ghostly, submarine towers. Both of these points establish a Bran making a journey west over the sea and the connection with the dynasty of Llŷr.

Bran mac Febhail eventually reaches the paradisal *Island of Women*, where it is hoped that he will mate with a faery woman ... the empowerment process of sacral kingship. However, one of his companions becomes homesick so Bran and his party return to Ireland, only to find that they have been standing outside of time and that their paradisal wanderings have been going on for what turns out to be hundreds of years in the time of the real world. Thus he and his companions are just a legend when they get back, indeed the first of them to step ashore – back into real time – is dissolved into the dust that he would have become had he stayed in the real world! This theme of timelessness, broken by one member of Bran's company who breaks the spell, also occurs in the Welsh Bran story, as we shall see.

Bendigeidfran

Bran's major appearance is in the Welsh Mabinogi as *Bendigeidfran* ("Bran the Blessed" – *Bran*, coming after the adjective in Welsh, mutates to *Fran*). Bran is the giant who appears in the Mabinogi story *Branwen daughter of Llŷr* ... although Branwen herself has more distinction in the tale as a device of the plot rather than a central character. Bran, however, means "raven" in Welsh, and Branwen therefore means white raven. As ever, we should take the "wen" suffix as signifying her Underworld status and thus, as Bran's reason to make his journey, she somehow parallels the faery woman who appears in the Irish Bran mac Febhail story.

The Welsh Bran, however, was the king of Britain and Branwen was his sister. When Bran and his brothers were at Harlech one day, some thirteen ships came across from Southern Ireland bringing the Irish king Matholwch and his retinue, and it transpired that Matholwch wanted to marry the beautiful Branwen and set up an alliance with Bran. This was agreed, and they set out for Aberffraw on Anglesey where Branwen was living and concluded the pact with a banquet, and that night Matholwch slept with Branwen. During the night, however, one of Bran's brothers, Efnisien, a disagreeable man, found out that his sister was sleeping with the Irish king, and as he had not consented to this he maimed Matholwch's horses. When Matholwch heard about this he proposed to leave for Ireland, but Bran, sending messengers and finding what had happened, brought him back and replaced the maimed horses. Even so, Matholwch seemed in low spirits so to make further reparation for the insult, Bran gave him a cauldron. When Matholwch asked where this magical cauldron (which could restore slain warriors to life) had come from, Bran told him that it had been brought from Ireland by a Llasar Llaes who, with his wife, had escaped to Wales from the "Iron House", a kind of oven in which they were incarcerated. Bran added that he was surprised that Matholwch seemed to know nothing of this, to which Matholwch replied: "I was hunting in Ireland one day on top of a mound overlooking a lake and it was called the lake of the cauldron. And I beheld a big man with yellow coloured hair coming from the lake with a cauldron on his back. Moreover he was a monstrous man, and had the evil look of a brigand about him, and a woman following after him. And if he was big, twice as big as he was the woman, and they came towards me and greeted me". He went on to tell how he took the couple in, not least because the woman was pregnant, but they became so disagreeable and caused so much trouble that his people insisted that something be done. His ministers decided that an iron chamber should be built, and the couple and their offspring placed in it and roasted alive whilst drunk. However, when the couple and their son had been placed in the chamber, and the chamber became white hot, the great man charged the heat-softened iron wall and he and his wife escaped – with the cauldron – and thence to Wales.

Bran having received them, and the gift of the cauldron, explained that they had since multiplied and settled the Island of Britain and they had built fortifications everywhere.

The origin of Bran's cauldron therefore becomes clear. The lake which Matholwch came across is Llyn Tegid, or its Irish equivalent, and the couple are Ceridwen and her husband Tegid Foel. The fact that Matholwch was "standing on a mound" overlooking the lake suggests a burial mound to emphasise the Underworld theme, in that, as we shall see, Ceridwen's Underworld kingdom is reached via burial chambers … the *sidhe-mounds* occupied by the chiefs of the Tuatha dé Danann, who by then were assumed to be living in the Underworld. Ireland … the island across the western ocean, also suggests an Otherworldly or magical place. The west was, after all, the place where the sun went down at the end of the day to hide in the Underworld. As we have said before, parts of Wales, particularly south west Wales, were often thought of as "Ireland" because they had been settled by Irish tribes. The ordeal of Ceridwen by an iron furnace suggests the conflict between those who had the old Bronze cauldron technology and those who had the new Celtic iron smelting technology, but the admission is that the older race represented by Ceridwen also had the power of magic at their disposal, with an ability to transform matter and even bring the dead to life. The fact that Ceridwen and her husband bred so profusely and occupied areas of Wales seems to echo tribal encroachment from Ireland by a more primitive culture.

With Branwen and the gift of the cauldron, Matholwch seems happy and goes back to Ireland. All goes well initially and Branwen is treated with great honour. At about the time that she becomes pregnant, however, the rumour starts to get around of how Matholwch was disgraced by Branwen's kin in the episode of the horse maiming, and resentment builds up. Eventually bowing to public pressure, Matholwch makes Branwen a kitchen wench, who has her ears boxed daily by a butcher, so that he can be seen by his people to be humiliating her for the humiliation her brother Efnisien inflicted. Matholwch is also urged by his advisors to ban all sailing between Ireland and mainland Britain, and to imprison anyone who comes from Wales, so that Branwen's plight may not come to the ears of Bran. So things continued for the next three years until, having reared a starling, taught it to speak and how to find her brother Bran, Branwen set the bird free and Bran learned of her predicament.

Bran then took a force to Ireland, and being of giant stature, he waded the Irish Sea towing his ships. As we have said, this echoes the shallowness of the sea in Cardigan Bay and the legend of the flooded expanse of Cantref Gwaelod. At the news of Bran's invasion, Matholwch withdrew to the West side of the river Liffey and destroyed the bridges, because it was thought that the Liffey could not be swum or waded. But Bran made a bridge of himself and his army went over him and gained the other side. Matholwch then sent messengers to say that he would resign the kingship of Ireland to his son, Bran's nephew *Gwern*. This, however, was not enough, so Matholwch additionally proposed that a vast house be built for Bran and that he would meet him in it and come to some agreement. Bran went along with this and the vast house was hastily built. Before Bran got there however, his brother Efnisien went ahead to check the place.

Efnisien saw some two hundred bags hanging from pegs in the house, and coming to the first of these he suspiciously enquired what was in it. "Flour" came the reply. However in surreptitiously feeling the bag, Efnisien realised that there was a warrior inside it (as he had suspected), and he squeezed the life out of the man silently. He then asked what was in another bag, got the same reply and again squeezed the bag, killing the warrior inside … and so on for all the bags until he had killed the last man. He then sang an *englyn* making it clear that he had rumbled the Irish ruse. After that everyone sat down and terms were discussed and it was agreed that Branwen's son Gwern should take over the kingship of Ireland.

Efnisien's reaction to this was drastic. He took the boy, who was after all his nephew, and hurled him into the fire – after which, understandably, fighting broke out. As men fell, the Irish kindled the cauldron of rebirth to resuscitate their dead warriors. Seeing this and the ever mounting stack of British dead, Efnisien, overcome by remorse, hurled himself into the cauldron, stretched himself out and in one supreme effort, burst the cauldron, and in doing so died.

This shattering of the cauldron also occurs in one version of the Taliesin myth, where after Gwion has supped from the cauldron of Ceridwen, the vessel issues a great cry and self destructs.

This is similar to the later Arthuriad idea of the purpose of the Grail being misunderstood – and the Grail, rather than being a Christianised version of the earth-based communal and sustaining cauldron, becomes withdrawn to levels of spiritual abstraction. As such it becomes a dangerous vessel, in that potentially it becomes a vessel of death rather than life. The lesson in either instance is all too plain … that when something which is given to provide for and sustain the many is misused selectively or divisively by the few, it gets taken out of circulation. At the risk of writing Gildas's sermons for him – this bitter lesson was one which Gildas would have gleefully drawn attention to – that the ungodly behaviour and squabbling of the British leaders of his epoch had lead to the withdrawal of the sustenance and protection of the Pax Romana and consequent Saxon oppression. An earlier commentator may also have pointed out to the original Celts that their abuse of the resident British Bronze Age folk, the "cauldron people" who knew the pulse of the land,

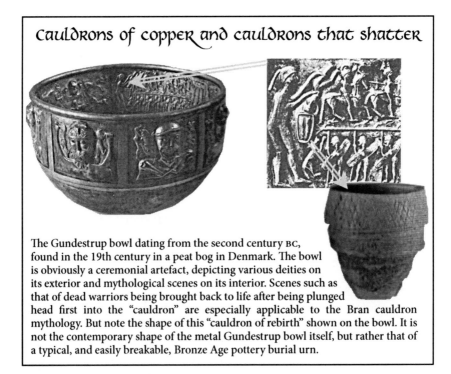

cauldrons of copper and cauldrons that shatter

The Gundestrup bowl dating from the second century BC, found in the 19th century in a peat bog in Denmark. The bowl is obviously a ceremonial artefact, depicting various deities on its exterior and mythological scenes on its interior. Scenes such as that of dead warriors being brought back to life after being plunged head first into the "cauldron" are especially applicable to the Bran cauldron mythology. But note the shape of this "cauldron of rebirth" shown on the bowl. It is not the contemporary shape of the metal Gundestrup bowl itself, but rather that of a typical, and easily breakable, Bronze Age pottery burial urn.

may have caused the land to become blighted and the tribes divided ... as it became in the Arthuriad. This is also a lesson for today of course, in that our abuse of the sustaining mother earth for selfish ends is leading to the withdrawal of natural resources and benefits. Morality tales may be found lurking in every nook and cranny of our mythology, and were certainly there before the Christian scribes made their own theologically prompted amendments!

Because of Efnisien's action, the Welsh or Brythons, "the men of the Island of the mighty", won the day, but at great cost. Of the original force only seven men survived unscathed. Bran, however, was mortally wounded by a poisoned spear in his foot. There is great significance in this. Of the seven who survive, Taliesin is mentioned, who later in the *Preiddu Annwn* describes another campaign in the Underworld to win a cauldron, from which only seven again survive, but this time the leader is not Bran but "*Arthur of mournful memory*".

Bran then tells his seven companions that they must cut off his head and take it back to Britain. In Celtic terms this idea of the head as the microcosmic seat of the soul allows the natural assumption that the spiritual vessel of his head should be returned to his sacred land. In terms of the Bronze Age rites of sacrificed kings, the epoch which this tale remembered, the inference is somewhat more specific as we shall see. We have a further cauldron image, of the skull as the cauldron which contains not only the soul but also inspiration. It was said that the Celts, in addition to taking the heads of enemies, also used their skulls as drinking vessels, which gives the connections between chalice/Grail, skull and cauldron. A further connection may be added in the imagery of the wounding of Bran's heel by a poisoned spear ... a typical sacred warrior king taboo which we seem to have come across in *Math* and which we shall examine in some detail later.

Che Blessed head

When Bran tells his seven companions that they are to take his head to Harlech in Gwynedd, he implies that his spirit shall remain with them. They are then to take the head, after a period, to "Gwales in Penfro"

The passing of Branwen

The scant remains of the Bedd Branwen near Llanddeusant on the 'sacred island' of Anglesey where Branwen was said to have been buried after her rescue from Ireland and subsequent "death from grief". In actuality the now unimpressive mound and the few stones which remain above ground give lie to what was once an impressive Bronze Age tomb, allegedly the largest on Anglesey. Now indistinct, the circular mound was originally some 18 meters in diameter.

In 1813 an urn was excavated from the mound which contained the burned bones of a young woman, appearing to lend a measure of historical credence to the myth. Further excavation in 1966 revealed that this had in fact been accompanied by seven other urn burials. Whilst this might seem to confirm that Branwen returned, as the myth states, with seven companions, along with the severed but still animated head of her brother Bran, both the archaeology and the mythology go on to refute this.

The archaeology shows the site to have been a henge with a standing stone, long before it became a burial place. Some centuries later, three urn burials were placed on the site and a ring of stones set over them. Slabs were then placed between the circle of stones and the original central standing stone, and the whole covered over with the mound. Four more urn burials were added shortly afterwards.

The mythology does not, in any case, say that the seven companions laid themselves down to die with Branwen. They took the still animated head of Bran to an Otherworld island where it entertained them until its eventual demise and subsequent burial in the White Mount, the present site of the Tower of London. The mythological ideas of the companions being able to hear the song of wisdom of the postmortem head of Bran in their Otherworld island (that such sites represented) may account for the macabre supplementary burial of infant earbones found at this site, or, more likely, they relate to the court butcher striking Branwen about the ears each day during her incarceration in Ireland. Either way, these archaeological correspondences to the mediaeval Mabinogi story are remarkable, and suggest that Bronze Age traditions of the hidden features of the site were preserved in oral tradition for maybe three thousand years before the myths were written down!

(Pembrokeshire). There, he tells them, his head will remain uncorrupted until a door is opened which faces towards Cornwall. The mention of Cornwall may well be an addition in the light of Geoffrey of Monmouth placing Arthur's birth at Tintagel, thus the incoming Arthur cult (or its Math precursor, coming into these islands via the Bristol Channel) is prophesied to bring about the decay and decline of the Bran cult ... not least as those who are its supposed guardians lose faith and transfer allegiance – "opening the door" to the religion of the new incoming tribes.

So, with these caveats and instructions, the seven with the head returned to Britain, the "Island of the Mighty", accompanied by Branwen, landing at the mouth of the river Alaw on Anglesey. On their arrival Branwen looked between Britain and Ireland, grief stricken at the slaughter done because of her, and died. Aneirin, whom we have already met, laments:

"Softened were the voices in the brakes
Of the wondering birds
On seeing the beautiful body ... "

They buried her on the banks of the Alaw in a "four sided grave". In fact a burial mound on the banks of the Alaw near Llanddeusant, variously called *Bedd Branwen* and *Carn Branwen,* was excavated in 1813. It was found to be a cist burial with its typical "stone box" (our four sided grave) with an urn containing human ashes, a burial of the late Bronze Age. Other urn burials were found in a 1966 excavation.

On their way to Harlech the seven companions of the Blessed Head got news that Caradawg, whom Bran left in charge of Britain, had been slain and that Caswallen had usurped the throne ... a brief admix of pseudo history! In spite of this they took the head to Harlech as Bran had instructed them, presumably to the castle rock, the actual *Twr Branwen* where Edward I later built one of a network of castles to suppress the Welsh. Here the seven sat with the head of Bran, feasting and drinking and hearing and telling tales ... obviously reminiscent of a sacred funeral feast, some rite of sacral kingship in days gone by. As they feasted they heard the sweetest songs from the birds of Rhiannon, but these were nowhere to be seen. This ritual went on for seven years ... another reference which may allude to the internment of a sacred king's head ... a matter that we shall deal with shortly.

At the end of the seventh year they set out for "Gwales in Penfro", modern Pembrokeshire, and arrived at "a great royal palace overlooking the sea and a great hall it was". Recent tradition gives this as the island of Grassholm, but I am more inclined to believe that the island was in fact

Lundy in the Bristol Channel. My reason for believing this is the weight of older tradition which cites Lundy as *Ynys Gweir,* the island sacred to the Welsh god Gwydion. According to Peter Beresford Ellis, this island fulfilled the same function for the Welsh that *Tech Duinn* did for the Irish. Tech Duinn means "the house of Danu", which gives us another association with the Underworld of the Tuatha dé Danann and/or the Welsh divine dynasty of Dôn (which Gwydion belonged to). It would certainly therefore be more appropriate for the blessed head, having spent the ritual seven years at Harlech, the stronghold of Bran in life, to be transported to an island which represented Annwn or Avalon. We note that when the head is moved there it becomes re animated ... "*nor was it more irksome having the head with them then when Bendigeidfran had been with them alive*". The copyist is perhaps a bit vague here but the implication is that the head is taken to Harlech for seven years ... or maybe seven lunar months (a seven-fold unit of time in any case to allow the head/spirit to assimilate the seven stage Underworld transformation). After this first part of the ritual it was taken to perhaps Lundy. On Lundy they had arrived at the paradisal heart of the Underworld, where they abide with the head for "fourscore years", during which time none of them get any older ... a usual state of affairs on an Underworld sojourn as we have seen. But then, after this time, disaster strikes. If the bard says "after fourscore years" meaning that something happened during the fifth year of this sacred king rite, then this follows an appropriate pattern of Bronze Age ritual practice. The disaster which strikes in the story is that one of the seven, like Pandora, wonders what *would* happen if the door that faces Cornwall is opened!

What happens, as prophesied, is that the head dies and decays. We have noted that the head was said to have been buried subsequently in London, but again this may originally have been Lundy – with a gloss on London to onomastically explain the mound and Roman fortification which became the Norman fortress of the Tower of London, with its ravens (*bran* is, even today, the Welsh word for raven).

So ends the tale of Branwen daughter of Llŷr.

The Bite of the Serpent

The fact that Bran is wounded in the foot draws attention to another sacred king in the Mabinogi: Math fab Mathonwy, who as we saw in our last chapter, had to have his feet resting in the lap of a virgin, unless he was away at war. Graves quotes other instances of such sacred kings in *The White Goddess*, starting with the idea of the "Achilles heel" being a universal feature of all sacred kings.

Many mythological themes have a universality, cropping up across wide chronological and cultural boundaries, and the myth of the Achilles Heel, named after the Greek hero, is one of them.

Achilles the son of the goddess Thetis and the mortal Peleus was said to be the only one of Thetis's seven children to survive. Versions of the myth vary; some say that Thetis held her child Achilles in the flames of a fire, others that she plunged him into the river Styx ... both acts intended to coat the child with immortality and thus invulnerability. As we have seen, the Bran story shows a deviation of this practice when Branwen's son Gwern is thrown into the fire. In Egypt, however, a story similar to the Achilles one was told of the goddess Isis. To hold the child during immersion in either fire or water, the goddess grasped him by the heel (an image perhaps preserved in the old Tarot card of the Hanged Man) and due to this part of his anatomy being covered by her thumb and finger it remained the only part of him to remain vulnerable. Achilles was killed by an arrow to his heel in the battle for Troy. The Celtic mythographers would have been aware of this story and also of the biblical Edenic myth in which, as a sign of banishment to mortality, God tells the serpent that "They shall strike at your head *and you shall strike at their heel*". The image of the serpent and the poisoned spear are of course synonymous. Sacred kings were usually considered to be partly of immortal, divine stock, as was Achilles, the son of a goddess. As such they were deemed to be invulnerable except in being susceptible to death from a wound in the heel, as we saw with Math, or in some other bizarre circumstance, as we saw with his nephew Llew.

Graves discusses at great length the whole idea of the vulnerable heel and the sacred king, whereby certain kings developed a kind of hip swinging gait so that the vulnerable heel never touched the ground, and how this became associated with the foot of a bull and hence sexual potency and fertility; an idea with which serpent and spear imagery can be readily associated. Such a "bull foot" may well result from a serpent bite making the foot become swollen and inflamed so that the victim would not be able to place his foot upon the ground. The "bite of the serpent" appears to have been literally, as well as metaphorically, the lot of many a sacrificed sacred king.

We can see how this could have linked the imagery of sacred king cults with the sacrificed bull of Mithraism. Some Roman images of Mithras show him as lion-headed (an association with Hercules which we shall discuss later) and entwined with serpents. The Underworld sacred king cult therefore made Mithraic associations with Arthur. That no Arthurian mythos filtered to Ireland, despite ready interaction between Wales and Ireland at the time that the Arthurian Mabinogi myths were being composed, tends to underline the fact that there was a Roman/Mithraic content to the mythology, which would have been spurious in an Ireland which had never known the impress of the Imperial sandal.

Mithras was in effect the priest who slaughtered the bull associated with the sacred king, that the land may be fruitful. In many respects the cult of Arthur killed off the cult of Bran and attempted to capture Bran's "cauldron" from the Underworld with the same intention.

Graves further cites the imagery of the bull foot with the apparent foot fetishism indicated in (the sacred king archetype of) Lleu making buskins (shoes) for his mother Arianrhod … and retaining two pairs. As pointed out in our last chapter, this seems to be something more than a foot fetish, in that these shoes/buskins are a goddess symbol into which the foot of the sacred king fits. In fact the symbol may indicate a sacred king new born of a virgin goddess, literally in the process of emerging from her womb with his feet being the final part of him to emerge in this birth/rebirth process from her "lap". The symbolism of the snake, both as an adjunct in dispatching a sacrificial sacred king and in its sexual "mating with the Goddess" symbolic context, is obvious.

The use of snakes to guard sacred places was universal. Native Americans say that sacred places are so guarded, and our own experience in New Mexico bears this out! The Egyptian cobra hieroglyph, *ara*, meant both "serpent" and "goddess", and the Hindu goddess *Kundalini* is associated with the "raising of the serpent fire" and the opening of centres of higher consciousness. Certain classical and other temples and sacred places were associated with oracular serpents, links with the Underworld and divination. The priestesses who used to make prophetic utterances at Delphi were called "Pythonesses".

Snakes, whilst having an inclination to sun themselves, are generally active in caves and the dark, the quiet places that sacred sites so often are! The image of a snake going through changes, shedding its skin, and being so intimately associated with death, phallicism and poison or hallucination make it an ideal creature to be associated with altered states of consciousness and initiation. Hallucinogens, like sexual arousal (not to mention the adrenalin surges caused by abject terror!) have always been a time honoured universal (if precarious) aid to inner experience.

Graves goes on to talk of a certain synchronicity in his own experience of getting bitten by a snake, having his foot swell and going into an hallucinatory state. During his hallucinations he says he saw what appeared to be an island, which could be compared with Avalon-type islands of the Otherworld, and how the image began to revolve, as it does in the Celtic myths.

It seems likely that a number of sacred kings would, prior to their ritual slaughter, have met their deaths – or at least their anaesthetisation – through intentional snake bite. The image of inner transformation preserved in early seventeenth century Rosicrucian lore of a snake within a skull, is not, I think, entirely metaphorical in its much earlier origins. Both of these symbols of snake/spear-bite and skull are central, as we have seen, in the Bran myth, to sacred kings and head cults.

The cult of the head and the Grail

The cult of the head is one which became especially associated with the Grail. The story of Bran associates head cultism with the cauldron, and subsequent stories of Celtic saints who lose their heads (and have them restored) as well as beheading themes in the Arthuriad, notably that of *Gawain and the Green Knight,* indicate an enduring cultism based on the image of the severed head. As we have said, the Celts considered the head to be the microcosmic seat of the soul, which gives some credence to the Celtic practice of taking heads as battle trophies in the light of the Bran story. Presumably by taking the head of an enemy, and thus the dwelling place of his soul, he could not be resuscitated in the cauldron of rebirth. The Celtic *torc* worn about the throat was a spiritual and (to a lesser extent) practical device to inhibit such decapitation. The skulls of heads taken in battle were used by some Celts as cups … probably a degradation of a Bronze Age rite which emphasises the Grail/cauldron connection. Bran doubtless instructed his own head to be taken by his companions so that it would not fall into enemy hands. Nobody would be drinking to victory out *his* skull. Over and above this, as we have mentioned, he would have wanted his head to be returned to his sacred land so that the proper rites to ease his passage through the Underworld could be undertaken.

Bran became the archetypal Celtic god of the dead in relation to this head cultism, but such cults were by no means exclusively Celtic. The Underworld cult (of the singing head) of the Greek Orpheus and the subsequent Orphic mysteries are an obvious example. Be that as it may, we have seen how the identification of the head "as seat of the soul" and receptacle of inspiration (*awen*) could be identified with both the cauldron and the Grail and how this could be carried across from the pre-Christian myth of *Bran* and his cauldron to the Arthurian myth of *Bron* as a Grail keeper. This becomes even more interesting in the light of Robert Graves's discussion of the ancient Hebrew shrine of Hebron in *The White Goddess* and Taliesin's mention of Hebron in the *Hanes*.

paradise in palestine

In the *Hanes Taliesin*, Taliesin, or at least a bard of that cult, makes the poetic boast *"I have conveyed Awen to the deeps of Hebron"*. We have seen how in the Christianised Arthuriad it became convenient to change Bran's name to Bron, but why should a Celtic seer be particularly interested in Hebron, an ancient Hebrew cult centre of South Judea in ancient Palestine?

The answer seems to figure around an early Christian legend. The legend ran that the head of Adam was taken aboard Noah's ark, and after the flood, was buried "at the centre of the world". This has shades of the legend of Bran's head being buried at the White Mound upon which the Tower of London now stands ... unless we believe that it was on Lundy. The legend goes on to say, however, that the personage who was responsible for this action was none other than *Melchizadek*, whom we have mentioned before.

Robert Graves in effect takes up the story from here, without mentioning the legend, but says that a group of Hebrew heretics who were called the *Melchizadekians* had a shrine at Hebron where the head of Adam was said to be buried in a cave. He adds that Hebron had been considered by the ancient, pre-exilic Hebrews to be the sacred centre of the earth, but that David later changed this to be Jerusalem, where his son Solomon subsequently built the first temple. Whilst Graves implies that David in a sense "sold out", we have to realise that David was, like so many kings, swayed by expediency. He was on home ground at Hebron and had been proclaimed king and anointed there, but he knew that politically it would be impossible for him to have his capital there. For a start, had he been based there the northern tribes would never have gone along with him. Even so, Graves notes that Hebron is where these early Hebrews reckoned that the Garden of Eden had been … hence the Adamic association and hence the place where the temple needed to be.

The Temple of Paradise

To gauge the full significance of this we need for a moment to look a little more closely at the symbolism of the first Jerusalem temple before the Babylonian exile and the demythologising of Judaism by the Deuteronomists … and (contrary to fundamentalist wishful thinking) Israel *did* have a mythology! The first temple was synonymous with the Garden of Eden, where the un-fallen Adam had walked with God, until he and Eve were expelled and the way to the garden guarded by the Cherubim with the flaming sword. The innermost part of the Jerusalem temple, the *Debir* or Holy of Holies, was intended to be the place where the presence of God, the *Shekinah*, continued to be represented in Earth. The Debir was entered by the High Priest, who laid aside his ornate robes to don a simple white robe, thus representing an angel and also identifying with the Cherubim, who barred the Edenic gate. He and only he could enter, and then only once a year. He entered through the veil, that great triple curtain, one version of which was said to have been woven by the virgin Mary*, which as we have seen was embroidered with exotic vegetation to give the impression that the High Priest was entering the garden, as Adam had in the beginning, to talk with God. The symbolism of Mary assisting in the weaving of such a curtain behind which the Presence

---

*   This inevitably evokes the obvious heresy that perhaps Mary was impregnated not as a result of archangelic visitation but by the 'visitation' of the High Priest! Such a straightforward conclusion obviously has horrendous theological implications! See *Polarity Magic. The Secret History of Western Religion*. Berg and Harris. Llewellyn 2002.

AWEN

of God would manifest in earth, in the great high priesthood of Christ, becomes obvious, as does the rending of that curtain at the crucifixion.

The *Shekinah*, the Presence of God in Earth, was said to manifest upon the *Kapporeth*, the Mercy seat, the chariot throne of God formed by the outstretched wings of two great guarding Cherubim carved in wood, overshadowing the Ark of the Covenant. The Ark of course held the tablets of the Torah ... the result of such Edenic conversations with God, experienced by Moses, who lead the children of Israel to a second promised land/paradisal garden, after Adam's original failure!

The Debir was Judaism's holiest place in the world, the absolute spiritual centre of God's good earth. Beyond this absolute centre, this paradisal room, the spiritual intensity of the Shekinah radiated out, like the ripples from a pebble dropped into a pool ... in ever widening circles yet of decreasing intensity, encompassing the holy land of Israel, and ultimately the world.

The ideals of ancient pre-Deuteronomist Judaism were that Israel's king should be a priest king, a sacred king, and like the Patriarchs should be the one who essentially acted as the mediator between his people and the presence of God in Earth. He should be the successor of Adam and of Moses, who entered the paradisal state to talk with God in the garden. This was not, as we shall see, dissimilar from the ancient Brythonic ideas of sacred kings in ancient pre-Celtic Britain who entered Annwn to mediate with the great mother on behalf of the tribe.

In some senses, and without any exercises in theological hair splitting, what the Ark of the Covenant was to the Jews, the Grail was to Christians, the cauldron of Annwn and the sacred skull was to the pagan Celts and the blessed head of Adam was to those heretical Melchizadekians! All these things represented an absolute paradisal focus where the soul looked upon its own origins and knew the pattern for its evolution.

This paradisal focus where the door of Heaven stood ajar was guarded, in the Hebrew context, by the Cherubim. In fact Cherubim in Hebrew means "the strong", obviating any ideas of the chubby cherubs who grace stereotypical painted ceilings! As well as guarding the Edenic realm they drew the chariot throne of God and their action may be equated with wind or breath and fire. As the writer of the eighteenth Psalm says (verses 9-11, NEB):

"He swept the skies aside as he descended,
thick darkness lay under his feet.
He rode on a cherub, he flew through the air;
He swooped on the wings of the wind

He made the darkness around him his hiding place
and dense vapour his canopy"

The Cherubim are storm angels. They equate with the strength of the storm. The Hebrew word for wind, *ruah,* also means "spirit" ... as in the "spirit which moved over the face of the waters" in the origination of creation.

Here we may notice some Celtic echoes in the Cauldron/Annwn mythology. The cauldron is warmed "by the breath of nine maidens" ... and the Kaballistic number of Yesod, the sephirah to which the Cherubim are assigned, is nine! By the same token, not only does Taliesin say that *"my original country is the land of the cherubim"* but adds that he has been *"three times in the Caer of Arianrhod."* Now the Celts equated (as the Welsh still do) the *Caer Arianrhod* with the stellar constellation of the Corona Borealis which literally means "the crown behind the north wind". Our Taliesin initiate is trying to make sure that we make the link with esoteric Judaism and the Hebron legends.

It will be remembered from the story of Gwion/Taliesin that the Cauldron of Ceridwen was originally made for the goddess's own son Afagddu. Squire associates this name with "storm cloud", and though this would not be the literal translation in modern Welsh, the "ddu" does appropriately mean "dark" or "black." When we associate this, however, with the mythology of Afagddu's mother Ceridwen, whose *caer* was the rainbow, we begin to see an interesting run of symbolism.

Llyn Tegid at Bala, the site of Taliesin's initiation at the hands of Ceridwen, has its own flood myth. In the biblical account of the Flood, Noah released the raven, the totem bird of Bran, after the storm. Then when the dove (perhaps the white raven signified in the name *Branwen*) had been sent and the ark came to rest on dry ground, he gave the sign of the rainbow:

"This is the sign of the Covenant between myself and you and every
living creature with you to endless generations:
My bow I set in the cloud
sign of the covenant
between myself and the earth.
When I cloud the sky over the earth,
the bow shall be seen in the cloud."

To compact the two myths together, Ceridwen's rainbow is the sign of the covenant, and the sustenance and inspiration of the cauldron enables God's side of the covenant, of bountiful nature, to be kept. Afagddu was

Adam, the original child of nature, of the goddess, to whom the Edenic provision was first made. After the flood, when the rainbow had appeared, Melchizadek is said to have left the Ark and buried the head of Adam at Hebron.

Meanwhile we may also reflect upon the role of the Cherubim as conveyers of divine breath, even as Taliesin boasts of having *"conveyed awen to the deeps of Hebron."* Graves also cites another Taliesin poem, *Y Awdil Fraith*, which again sets an emphasis on the original paradisal creation being set at Hebron.

"The All being made
Down the Hebron Vale,
With his plastic hands
Adam's fair form"

That *Awen* is the inspiration of the cauldron that could place the initiate poet in touch with the paradisal, and that such a theme should be linked to the focus of Judaism at a time when Christianity was established, is understandable enough. Early Christianity took a great deal more of its symbolism from archaic Judaism than we realise. Even so, what is not understandable is why "Taliesin" should have chosen a place that had ceased to be considered of optimum spiritual significance long before the existence of a Celtic Britain, let alone over a thousand years later ... by which time even the third Jerusalem temple had long ceased to exist.

Graves suggests that some archaic and heretical beliefs of Judaism might have reached the Christian world via the *Essenes* ... and certainly they had reason enough to believe in the old pre-exilic temple traditions.

What we have here is a head cult operating in Wales, originating in the Bronze Age. The mythological location of Branwen's tomb was, after all, found to be where the myth described it, and to be of Bronze Age origin! Then perhaps more than a thousand years later this cult was able to find other strands of its mythological roots in archaic and suppressed legends from halfway around the world in Palestine! Graves manages to show in his ingenious and convoluted way how this could be accounted for in the movements of early sea peoples as well as the Essene connection, but our own view would lay the blame somewhat later, with material imported through the Celtic church's connection with the (so called) primitive church of Ethiopia and Egypt. This, the first of the Christian churches, was heir to a great deal of Gnostic, Essene and pre-Christian apocryphal material. It is also said with some justification that the Ark of the Covenant, along with the lost tribe of Israel, made its way to Ethiopia. Certainly, during the crusades, the Templars sent emissaries to Ethiopia to try and get hold of the Ark, and certainly one of our later Taliesins would have known of this.

The figure of Melchizadek features in a lot of Essene writings and the legends of Hebron were absolutely suitable to our sacred head/Grail/cauldron mythology. As we have discussed, the cauldron cult became a Christian Marian/Grail cult. The associations with the temple and the paradisal symbolism would have settled well with that apocryphal gospel *The Questions of Bartholomew*, relating the tale of Mary as a temple weaver of the veil, taking the bread and wine to invoke the incarnated presence of God in Earth. These are the symbols of God's archetypal high priest Melchizadek, and "the Great High Priest of the Order of Melchizadek" Jesus Christ in fulfilment of the ancient sacrificial blood rites.

The original inhabitants of Hebron were Edomites. *Edom* is in fact the word from which *Adam* derives. As such they would have been aware of the challenge of Abraham having to overthrow the "four kings of Edom whose kingdoms are unbalanced force", after which he met Melchizadek who gave him bread and wine. Melchizadek, who is synonymous with the wanderings of the tribes under Abraham in about 2000 BC, is described as being "king of Salem which is peace". Obviously this Salem, this paradisal peace, had not always been synonymous with Jeru-Salem, at least not before David made his political decision to relocate the Edenic centre of the world! Graves has shown through his tree alphabet endeavours that the titles SAL, SALM and so on, embody this idea of a lamed, sacred king. Melchizadek in the biblical account seems in no way to be lame but he is certainly a sacred king, and like the lamed Fisher King of Arthurian myth called *Bron,* he has profound associations with the Grail. On the one hand, like Merlin, he is "without father, without mother, having neither beginning of days nor end of life." On the other hand he is the archetypal priest king invoked by St Paul to explain the role of Christ, whom he likens to "a great high priest of the order of Melchizadek".

What we seem to have here is a whole body of loosely associated mythology which the bards of a Celtic "Taliesin" tradition, with all its Underworld lore of cauldrons, severed heads, serpents, sacred kings and sovereignty, found they could use to enhance their lore and, as and when the need arose, give it biblical provenance. This was important for the bards who were for the most part Christian priests. Celtic neo-paganism still finds it difficult to come to terms with this historical fact, remaining somewhat in denial that were it not for the erudition (and elaboration) of these cunning and heretical early clerics they would have no Ceridwen, Arianrhod, Branwen or Rhiannon. That provenance however came not with the Christianity of Peter and Paul but of John, which is essentially why a Johannine Celtic church found itself at odds with the Church of St Peter in Rome.

In the light of the foregoing it will be obvious why John the Baptist, whose hermit-like existence reflected that of itinerant Druid and early Celtic saint alike, should appeal to the Celtic mind. But there were perhaps other connections. Whilst there has been quite an amount of esoteric speculation that Jesus Christ may have been an Essene, a convincing case has yet to be made. Certainly there are Essene hints in many of the sayings of Jesus, but these may stem from an intermediary source. That source may well have been his cousin John the Baptist, for whilst the case for Jesus being an Essene is flimsy, the case for John is a good deal stronger! There were other Johns of course. Taliesin says so: *"Johannes the diviner I have been called by Merlin"*. He means St John the divine, writer of the fascinating book of Revelations. There was yet another John, the beloved disciple.

How natural for a fledgling Christian church being presented with the biblical writings to identify itself with "the disciple that Jesus loved" rather than St Peter. That made three Johns ... another triad of semi-divine beings that could sit to the mythology.

The Knights of the Temple

It is sometimes difficult to see the cult of Taliesin in its later days in mediaeval Wales in this context of a wider world. The fabulous, fairytale claims that we have quoted from the *Hanes Taliesin* are still associated in the mind's eye with Celtic knotwork, Druids and all the stereotypical paraphernalia that the word "Celtic" induces. The fact is, however, that when the *Hanes* was written, as one of the later declarations of the Taliesin cult, Wales was part of a larger world and a larger philosophy. As we have seen, this embraced not only the myths of the Celts and their Bronze Age predecessors, but the myths and esoteric philosophies of the Middle East too. The Taliesin cult certainly believed in the "native tradition" and fought to preserve it, but as a mystery cult its stance was essentially *evolutionary*.

This meant that it voraciously acquired knowledge that could enhance its traditional philosophy and understanding. A parallel can be drawn with modern mystery schools whose initiates may study traditional teachings such as *Qabalah* on the one hand yet find useful extensions of their knowledge in such fields as quantum mechanics. It cannot be over emphasised that the Taliesin cult and indeed other traditional mystery schools of the time were only too willing to import Middle Eastern ideas. By the time that the *Hanes* was written in the thirteenth century, the earlier Middle Eastern sources provided by the churches of North Africa became supplanted by a much more viable source. That source came from the Crusaders in general and those esoteric Crusaders, the *Knights Templar*, in particular! This is probably how and why our latter day thirteenth century Taliesin became so interested in Hebron!

The Knights Templar were formed in Jerusalem 1118, as the *Order of the Poor Knights of Christ and the Temple of Solomon.* Their stated purpose was to defend the pilgrim routes to Jerusalem (which had been captured by the Christians nineteen years earlier) but there is no record of their doing this, and with their initial membership restricted to nine members for nine years they certainly didn't have the capacity to do so! Neither were they "poor"; by the time their power was culled and the order disbanded some two hundred years later, their wealth had become (and still remains) legendary. In the "nine times nine" allusions to membership we know that we are dealing with a mystery cult, and when we recall that the Celtic cauldron was "warmed by the breath of nine maidens" we have a good idea of the cult's leanings.

After this very restricted beginning the Templars were officially recognised at the Council of Troyes in 1128 after which they suddenly expanded. The younger sons of the noble families of Europe in general but France in particular, flocked to join their ranks, signing over their possessions, including all land and property, as they did so. Much of the propaganda which attended the order's expansion may be laid at the door of St Bernard of Clairvaux, who praised them as *"the militia of Christ"* and gave them the organisational parameters they needed, including the drafting of their essentially monastic rule. This was hardly surprising, as André de Montbard, one of the founding knights of the order, was St Bernard's uncle. The tract of rolling countryside at Clairvaux where St Bernard was to build his monastery and headquarters, from where he re-organised and radically expanded the Cistercian monastic order, was given to the him by the Count of Champagne, another Templar lord.

Initially the expansion of the Templars and the Cistercians went, not surprisingly, hand in hand. In 1139 a Papal edict from a Pope who had been a protégé of Bernard placed the Templars solely under Papal allegiance, rather than to the monarchies of the countries in which they were variously established. Their name became synonymous with high level diplomacy and political intrigue. It was the Master of the Temple of the Knights Templar of England who stood beside King John and watched him sign Magna Carta. Astonishingly the order generally maintained diplomatic connections to the Saracen enemy and even it is said to their own Saracen counterparts, the much feared and fanatical *Hashishim*. The Templar headquarters at Acre were something of an open house to all ideologies of the Middle East. This included Judaism, with which the order had ready contact both in the Holy Land and through its considerable presence in Southern France and Spain. Templar preceptories were to be found throughout Europe, not least in England ... and Wales!

The connection with the Jews in general and the Essenes in particular is an interesting one. The Templars took their name from the Temple of Solomon, where they were quartered in Jerusalem. Of course the third temple had been destroyed almost a thousand years earlier so that only the foundations, the temple cellars known as "the stables of Solomon" remained. Rumours abounded (then as now) of the great treasures both mystical and pecuniary which had been taken from the temple and their possible whereabouts. One of the many Judaic sects who seemed to have been privy to these secrets were the Essenes, although they had absented themselves from the third temple and its customs, seeing it as corrupt. They did however keep scrolls, some of which were subsequently discovered as the Dead Sea Scrolls which held inventories of temple treasures. The Essenes also called themselves *"the Keepers of the Covenant"* a term which could easily have been misconstrued as being the "possessors of something", not least the Ark of the Covenant, rather than simply a sect remaining *true to* the Covenant.

All this, plus the prominence given to the Essenes by classical writers, would have made their traditions of interest to anyone looking for the contents of the obliterated third temple! Much of Essene tradition featured Melchizadek and it was probably Essene tradition which prompted the early Christian myth of the head of Adam being buried by Melchizadek at Hebron. We have also cited John the Baptist as being an Essene ... as well as a ready candidate for the perpetuation of severed head myth ... and the Templars were considered to embrace among their heresies the Johannite heresy ... as indeed, at some junctures, were the Celtic church! The Mandaen (Gnostic) heresy, of which they were further charged, held to an emphasis on baptismal rites, on the soul's journey after death through a seven stage journey (not unlike the initiatory journey in Taliesin's *Preiddu Annwn*) and held Adam as a key figure. It seems likely that the Templars were exposed to quite a lot of Essene and other Jewish esotericism and tradition such as this ... which they adopted and adapted!

The Templars' wealth (whether they found the Temple treasures or not!) success and influence inevitably attracted powerful enemies, but whilst they controlled the situation in the Holy Land with Papal backing they were untouchable. Their fighting ability, however, was as legendary as their arrogance, a fatal combination which caused them to make a series of strategic, if heroic, blunders in the Holy Land, notably the battle of Hattin in 1187, shortly after which Jerusalem was lost to the Saracens. Their last stronghold in Palestine, the coastal fort of Acre (where the garrison predictably fought to the death) was not, however, lost until 1291. After this, however, with the Holy Land finally lost, their enemies had an opportunity to sow the seeds of their downfall.

Phillipe IV of France, who had been humiliated by their refusal to allow him to join their order and by their setting up something of "a state within a state" in his kingdom, was their principal enemy. By intrigues of his own he managed to install his tame Pope, Clement V, and simultaneously question the useful continuance of the Templars now that the Holy Land was lost. In 1307 Pope Clement ordered the Templar suppression on grounds which included heresy and sodomy. In Phillipe's France the suppression was carried out with relish, and a number of Templars were tortured and put to death. In England and elsewhere the suppression was rather lukewarm. Their sister orders of the *Knights Hospitaller* and the German *Teutonic Knights* continued to exist, but the Grand Master of the Templars, Jacques de Molay, was burnt at the stake in France in 1314.

The charges of heresy arose from confessions under torture in France, where the Roman church had always been uneasy about the sympathetic links between Cathars and Templars in the southern province of the Languedoc. The heretical Cathars (who even now enthusiastically refer to themselves as "Celts"), had previously been persecuted for their Gnostic beliefs in the Albigensian Crusade. Now charges of even worse heresies were levelled against the Templars. Among these were charges arising from a number of confessions that admitted that they worshipped a bearded head called *Baphomet.*

Given their connections with the Middle East, this would seem to be the Arabic word (many Templars spoke Arabic) *Abuihamet* which means "Father of wisdom". Such a 'father figure' accords with the appellation of *Father* ... variously of wisdom, truth, etc ... as the supreme deity of Gnosticism. The title was also one used for the Magi of the senior grades of Mithraism, which had sprung up in another military elite centuries before and sprung moreover from the same Gnostic dualist heresy! They were also said to have worshipped a goat-footed figure. The lame/cattle-footed sacred kings of Celtic myth, and the head of Bran, do not seem too far away from these. Nor does the head of Adam. It is known that the Templars had connections with the Essenes which gives a further connection to John the Baptist, who, as we have pointed out, probably was an Essene.

Whilst a good deal of the charges may have been without foundation, it does seem clear that the Templars were by no means conventional Christians. The 'head' worship seems well attested to and even in more sympathetic times, some hundred years before, Pope Innocent seems to have had to admonish them for "necromancy" … which would square with the practice of rituals focused on a severed head! Their Grail interests (another grey, if not black, doctrinal area for the Church of Rome) coupled to a Marian cult cannot be doubted either. The Marian cultism came through the Cistercian order and St Bernard of Clairvaux, who had so enthusiastically aided and promoted them in their early years. Indeed their white surcoats were probably modelled on the white habits of the Cistercian monks. All Cistercian abbeys were dedicated to the Blessed Virgin Mary and we are again reminded of that telling phrase of the Welsh poet Dafydd Benfras, linking Grail origins to Marianism: *"Christ, son of Mary, my cauldron of pure origin"*. We also know that certain Grail mythographers had very definite connections with the Templars. Wolfram von Eschenbach visited the Templars in the Holy Land in the late twelfth century and subsequently presented an idealised picture of them in his *Parzifal* as the *Templesin,* knights who guard the Grail sanctuary. *Le Grand San Graal* by contrast, the romance which served as a later model for Malory *(Le Morte d'Arthur),* emulates the Cistercian rather than the Templar position. This is the influence which gave that originally Brythonic hero *Gwalchmai* the name of *Gawain* and set the image of the Blessed Virgin upon his shield.

It is beyond our brief to take this into greater detail and discuss the many flowerings of Grail Romance which attended the Crusades. This is a task which has in any case been done ample justice by others. Our purpose is simply to indicate the origins and evolution of Brythonic myth and draw attention to its continuance against the background of wider history into which the Welsh bards, who were still calling themselves *Taliesin,* and the tradition they represented, merged with ease.

Let us again examine that merging, as a Taliesin of the thirteenth century tells us in the *Hanes* about some of the places he has visited. Here's a selection:

1) *"I was in Canaan when Absalom was slain"*
2) *"I conveyed Awen to the deeps of Hebron"*
3) *"I was at the place of the crucifixion of the merciful Son of God"*
4) *"I have been with Noah in the ark"*
5) *"I have witnessed the destruction of Sodom and Gomorrah"*
6) *"I am now come here to the remnant of Troia"*
7) *"I have been with my Lord in the manger of the ass"*
8) *"I have been fostered in the land of the Deity"*

Graves meticulously dissects this poem in terms of furthering his tree alphabet/calendar thesis. His reconstruction is ingenious, but unlikely, in terms of the evidence available. We shall take a less convoluted approach, and have taken a selection of the predominantly 'biblical' lines, using Lady Guest's translation of the Mabinogi version.

"I have been in Canaan when Absalom was slain"
When the Israelites overran Canaan, Hebron was given to the priestly caste of the sons of Aaron. (Joshua 21 v.13). Absalom was a son of David who rebelled against his father and died as a result. Had Absalom succeeded, however, the temple would have been located at Hebron. Absalom had himself anointed as king there, as his father David had been, prior to going to Jerusalem. David had been told by God to go to Hebron and had only defected to Jerusalem after going there to defeat the Jebusites. (2 Samuel 5 v.6). Similarly, Absalom says *"If the Lord brings me back to Jerusalem, I will become a worshipper of the Lord at Hebron"* (2 Samuel 15 v.7-8). Indeed when David had gone to Jerusalem and Absalom was at Hebron, the people flocked to Absalom. This was because Hebron, not Jerusalem, was considered to be the original holy place of the Israelites (hence it had been allotted to the priestly caste of Aaron, who were of the tradition of Melchizadek) .

What Taliesin is emphasising here is the place of the *true* temple ... an important thing for men who called themselves "Templars"! It was after all considered to be the site of the garden of Eden (the *raison d'etre* of the temple as we have discussed) and the place where Melchizadek had placed Adam's head.

"I conveyed Awen to the deeps of Hebron"
Hebron again! The one who did "convey Awen to Hebron" was presumably Melchizadek. The head of Adam being the cauldron in which the *awen* was conveyed. Again the point is made!

---

* See *Merlin's Chess*. Published by Ritemagic 2006 (www.ritemagic.co.uk)

"I was at the place of the crucifixion of the merciful son of God"
This at face value means that he has visited the site of Golgotha, but Golgotha is translated as "the place of the skull" ... and Jesus was the second Adam. The point is yet again made.

"I have been with Noah in the ark"
The head of Adam was with Noah in the ark according to the legend... so was Melchizadek, who was responsible for later placing the head at Hebron.

"I have witnessed the destruction of Sodom and Gomorrah"
The sins of Sodom and Gomorrah were supposedly the sins of the Knights Templar. Sodomy – the sin which caused the destruction of Sodom – was particularly cited. So to witness the destruction of Sodom in this instance might mean to witness the dissolution of the Templars.

"I am now come here to a remnant of Troia"
This is addressing the original Brythons ... all true Brythons! If we remember Geoffrey of Monmouth's "history" we will recall that Britain was supposedly founded by a handful of men who came with "Brutus" from Troy. Britain was the second Troy, or *Troia Nova* ... the new Troy. Brutus and his remnant of companions were expelled from Troy by the son of Achilles ... whom we have discussed earlier in relation to the vulnerable heel. It may be, however, that our Taliesin (and Geoffrey of Monmouth before him) are playing with one of those puns so beloved of Welsh bards. *Troy* may in such a case be a play upon the Welsh word *troi,* which means turning or revolving. Those who knew the place which was *troi*/turning, were those who had come from *Caer Droi* ... the turning castle (the *troi* has mutated to *droi,* coming as it does after the noun!) In other words they are gods or heroes or bards who have gone through the initiation of the spinning castle. Taliesin says elsewhere in this poem "*I have been in an uneasy chair above Caer Sidi (the turning castle). Whirling around without motion between three elements*"

"I have been with my Lord in the manger of the ass"
Under the clever veneer of the standard nativity setting, Taliesin is waving his Gnostic credentials. "*On the third day, Mary went out of the cave, she went into the stable and placed the child in a manger and an ox and a donkey worshipped Him*" says the apocryphal gospel of pseudo-Matthew, continuing "*Then that which was spoken through the prophet Isiah was fulfilled. The ox knows his owner and the donkey his Lord's manger*". After this the infant Jesus requests that he be known not as a child but a perfect man. The "perfect man" title parallels the Cathar title "Parfait", but more

than this reflects Taliesin's own story ... that when Elphin finds Taliesin, the 'child' speaks up and tells Elphin that he is a bard and he is forty years old! The references to the cave and the ox also have Gnostic/Mithraic overtones.

"I have been fostered in the land of the Deity"

This simply means perhaps that he spent time in the Holy Land, although the word 'fostered' is worth some consideration in the light of the Brigid mythos. As we saw, Brigid 'fostered' the Christ child. Brigid in her more pagan origins was however a cauldron keeper ... so again perhaps Taliesin, the cauldron-born bard, is playing his riddle games!

This sampling from the poem appears therefore to give us some fairly sledgehammer hints. What we have here are not mere boasts drawn from a random selection of scripture. What we have is perhaps a bard of the period at the end of the Crusades whose allusions show a tremendous grasp of Templar/Gnostic lore, as a latter day development of the old Celtic head/cauldron cults. Whilst one flinches at laying anything else at the door of the poor old Templars, who have been the butt of so much supposedly arcane speculation in recent years, it does look as though this particular Taliesin was a Templar, or at least one privy to their secrets as a bard turned troubadour. That he visited the Holy Land, as did a number of the Grail romancers, also seems likely!

In our next chapter however we must consider why he would have explored ancient sacred sites that were somewhat closer to home.

CHAPTER SIX

The King Under the Mountain

BEFORE WE ENTER that insubstantial inner world of death and rebirth in the poetic company of Taliesin, it may be as well to understand in some measure the mortuary customs of our far ancestors so that we can more easily unravel the imagery that the poet uses.

The Gates of Death

The practice of selective burial of the dead in specially constructed subterranean chambers took place in various forms in these islands from about five thousand years ago until, with later infrequency, approximately 700 AD. There are some forty thousand round barrows in England alone and more than a thousand stone circles. Once there were many more, the outlines of which can sometimes still be detected in crop marks and aerial photography, the ground level signs of these having been obliterated by agriculture or dispersion of their materials for other purposes. Place names, especially Welsh place names incorporating the words *Bryn* and *Carn/Garn* sometimes, however, serve to indicate locations of tombs even if the tombs themselves have long since disappeared. A few sites do remain which are not known to "official archaeology" or to the general public. Inevitably many more probably remain and will remain undetected by anyone at all!

The first constructions in the Neolithic period were simply long mounds with no internal chambering. Then in the late Neolithic period the purposeful construction of chambered tombs, often known as *long cairns* or *long barrows* began to appear. These later incorporated passages (thus 'passage graves') leading generally to one or more chambers at the broad end of the barrow with the whole arrangement seeming to depict a journey into the womb. That these were something more than places to dispose of corpses may be seen in the care with which the tombs were sited and constructed.

Frequently we find that care has been taken in choosing elevated sites, often with spectacular views, but many sites have been additionally proved to have been set in locations which are geophysically significant and along particular astronomical alignments. In the care taken in construction, the labour of placing huge capstones over chambers and the intricate drystone walling and corbelling of passage and chamber, as well as in some later instances the intricate carving of stonework (*Barclodiad Y Gawres* on Anglesey is an outstanding example) we can see that our ancestors went to a lot of trouble. Moreover the tombs were often constructed with false entrances, and care was taken to seal and guard them. *Belas Knap* in Gloucestershire is a good example of such a tomb, where the remains of some thirty individuals were found in the chambers with the isolated skull of a man found placed behind the false entrance.

It is discoveries such as this which indicate the juncture of myth and actual religious practice. We are reminded, by this solitary skull, of the head of Bran set in the White Mound to guard the Isles of Britain. Doubtless the priests who attended the burials at Belas Knap were especially intent upon the tomb not being interfered with. Thus they arranged not only for a false entrance but for some individual's head (the receptacle of his soul) to act as a further (psychic) line of defence, just as the head of Bran, as the myth of *Branwen daughter of Llŷr* tells us, had been set at the supposed site of the Tower of London to guard Britain. This would indicate that 'head cults' long predated the coming of the Celts to Britain and further suggest that much of our apparently "Celtic" mythology had its basis in much older spiritual customs. The Neolithic *Capel Garmon* tomb also has a false entrance, and white quartz pebbles were found in a ritual vestibule area. The preponderance of quartz at prehistoric sites, especially in Wales, seems to be related to some understanding of geophysics by its builders, a matter which we shall return to in due course. The fact that Neolithic burials were well sealed with large stones during their sporadic use is understandable. What is less understandable is that when tombs like *West Kennet Barrow* in Wiltshire ceased to be used, the passages were filled with rubble before finally closing the entrance. This would seem to indicate an obsession with security more usually associated with the burials of Pharaohs in ancient Egypt. In the latter case such security would be understandable in view of the rich grave goods interred with the royal dead, but the grave goods of our Neolithic ancestors were meagre and mundane, so we must assume that such security was for religious reasons.

The passage inside Bryn Celli Ddu, Anglesey

As to the burials themselves, these seem to have been essentially of disarticulated bones, and very recent theories suggest that some time during the Neolithic period in Britain "sky burials" were practiced: leaving the corpses open to the elements for a time, with the bones, usually without the skulls, being placed in the barrow later. In the late Neolithic period, remains seem to have been cremated before being placed in the barrow.

Whilst the Neolithic burials were multiple and perhaps dynastic, the Bronze Age immigrants tended towards individual burial. Their tombs are characterised by being set beneath circular rather than oblong mounds, of varying styles … bell barrows being bell shaped, disc barrows and so on. Some elongated barrows and passage graves were also constructed however, and some Neolithic tombs were reopened and used by the Bronze Age culture. The religious overlap between the two cultures is especially apparent in the construction of Stonehenge, which whilst not being primarily a necropolis, was a Neolithic site extensively elaborated by the Bronze Age Wessex culture. As the wealth of metalworking and trading evolved, bodies began to be interred with more elaborate grave goods, the gold grave goods found in the Bronze Age barrow near Stonehenge being an outstanding example.

The internal construction of Bronze Age barrows generally employed a stone box called a *cist* covered by a capstone, and whilst there may be several of these within a mound, they were completely separate. The body of the dead nobleman or king was laid within the cist in the foetal position … again suggesting a return to the womb that the Neolithic tombs had symbolised. Later burials were of cremated remains in a burial urn placed in the cist. In some instances cists were set within stone circles rather than mounds, as at *Moel Ty Uchaf* in Gwynedd and *Temple wood* at Kilmartin in Scotland. Some mortuary circles, especially of late Neolithic origin continuing into early Bronze Age use, were later covered with barrows, as at *Bryn Celli Ddu* on Anglesey.

By the time the Celts arrived in Britain the Neolithic burial sanctuaries were already as distant in time from them as those early Celts are from us. Celtic burials within mounds are comparatively rare finds in Britain, the most outstanding being the *Arras* burials in Yorkshire. The most spectacular Celtic tomb to be found in Northern Europe, however, dates from about the time when the first Celtic influence began to find its way to the British Isles, and this is the *Hochdorf* burial near Stuttgart in Germany. This particular burial, excavated in the late 20th century, seems to have been a one-off affair with the body having been preserved in salt whilst the substantial burial chamber and grave goods were assembled.

The dead man was of middle age and there is no indication of how or why he died. Among the great variety of grave goods were, significantly, a cauldron and a hat of birch bark. We have already seen the mythological importance of the cauldron in the mystery literature of our Taliesin cult. Soon we shall see how a simple hat of birch bark laid at the head of a dead Celtic chieftain from central Europe again confirms that the riddles we are examining are not mere poetic embellishments but guarded description of actual mystery practice, and what is more, mystery practice which was preserved in Britain well over a thousand years after the Hochdorf chieftain drew his final breath.

The death of a King

We have briefly noted already how what has come to be called *the cult of the sacred king* operated in general terms, in that the chief/sacred king as father of his tribe was required to consummate his relationship with the land, the sustaining 'mother' of the tribe. If the chieftain could successfully be seen to mate with and fertilise the mother goddess, the land, then the tribe would know a fertile mother nature, and be nourished and prosper. This is the origin of the concept of *sovereignty*, summed up in the oft quoted phrase *"The king and the land are one"*. We have seen the survival of this concept in later Arthurian myth when Arthur fails to consummate his relationship with *Gwynhyfwr*, his Faery Queen surrogate of the goddess. The cauldron Grail of plenty (the symbol of the fertile womb of the goddess) is lost, the land becomes waste and the people suffer.

The consummation between the chief and the mother goddess of the land, and the fertilisation of her cauldron womb of life and plenty, depended in Neolithic times upon the chieftain's voluntary sacrificial death. In death the king/chief's essence, his blood and generative organs, would be scattered upon the land, his disjointed body would be allowed to decompose with due ritual in the forecourt of the tomb or in a pit adjacent to the tomb, like the ones at *Tinkinswood Cairn* in South Glamorgan and *Bryn Celli Ddu*. After a suitable time his bones would be entombed in the cauldron/womb-like burial chamber (with the bones of earlier ancestral chiefs) to place final emphasis upon the consummation and assure the king of rebirth in the deep dark where the stars shone. The final emphasis of that consummation may account for the phallic standing stone to be found within the womb-like chamber of such burials as *Bryn Celli Ddu* (below), signifying his desire for the starry goddess as the axis upon which the Earth turned. All the stages of the sacrificial death seem to have been aligned to a particular time scale, including the time that the king's

bones were sealed, guarded and undisturbed in the tomb to allow his being to meld with the Mother goddess/land and subsequently find its place among the "stars within the land". The time scale for all this was governed by the movement of the heavens, seasons, solar and lunar phases and the rising and setting of stars. This is one reason why particular tombs and ceremonial circles/henges may be found to align to particular constellations.

As time went on the sacrifice of the king would be taken on by a surrogate who would be treated with all honour and given the best in food drink that the tribe had to offer ...

treated in other words like a king for the traditional "year and a day" and then sacrificed. As we shall see, the supposed "year and a day" was probably, originally, five years. This treatment of a surrogate as king seems for a time to have included access to the queen's bed, which was hardly surprising as the queen was herself a surrogate for the goddess.

The importance of the queen as surrogate for the goddess seems to date from the Bronze Age when tribes appear to have enjoyed a matriarchal society, or at least to have had matrilinear succession, a practice which endured into the Celtic era. The Brythonic Celtic *Boudicca* is an obvious example of the powerful queen/priestess, as is the legendary Irish *Queen Maeve of Connaught*. There were certainly, as classical commentators attest, female Druids, and the prestige of female saints within the early Celtic church seems to point to this being a carry over of the prestige of Druidic priestesses. Even Brigid the saintly nun of Kildare is said to have been the daughter of a Druid and a Druidess herself (presumably in the *goddess* Brigid's name) before she embraced Christianity. This seems to be confirmed in the placing of her abbey at Kildare, an Irish combination of words which translates as *"church of the oak,"* the oak being sacred to Druidism (*Druid* derives from the Welsh *Derwydd* – oak seer) and to the pre-Druidic Hercules cult/sacred king practices in Britain. As the myths show us (not least that of Arianrhod being tricked into arming her son Llew, in *Math fab Mathonwy*) it was the tribal queen as representative of the Faery woman, and ultimately the goddess, who empowered the warrior/ruler caste. This practice reappears, as we have seen, in the guise of *courtly love* expressed in the later Arthuriad.

As representative of the goddess who thus confirmed the king's standing, early queen/priestesses in the Bronze Age and perhaps into the early Celtic era appear to have thus taken surrogate sacred kings as their consorts, prior to the surrogate's ritual death as Hercules at Midsummer. Archaeological and other evidence also indicates that at certain times certain tribes also found it appropriate to sacrifice children. Again mythical confirmation of this occurs in the Bran legend, when *Gwern*, Branwen's son, is thrown into the fire. In terms of the Hercules cults which we shall discuss in a moment, the mythical accounts of the *rages of Hercules*, which were attended by an inclination to kill children, seems to back this up. There are indications of a Brythonic cult which sacrificed children to a bear goddess, which also seems to be confirmed by the known practices of parallel cults around the Mediterranean.

The hercules cult

Graves identifies the practice of the sacrifice of surrogate sacred kings with the widespread classical cult of the sacrificed Hercules, and indeed Hercules does appear as *Ercwlf* in a Taliesin poem *Marwnad Ercwlf* which Graves cites to indicate that (the) Taliesin (cult) was familiar with the Hercules mythology. It appears however that the myth of Hercules (originally the Greek *Heracles*) grew from, rather than originated, Bronze Age cult practice which extended from the Mediterranean and through Northern Europe and Britain. The chalk figure of the sexually potent *Cerne Abbas* giant in Dorset appears to be an obvious example of a later British devotion to Hercules, and his ability to initiate fertility. Recent research points however to the probability that the figure did not exist before the seventeenth century.

The Hercules cults, it is said, made their victims drunk (or, I suspect, administered adder venom to them or had them bitten by adders), then tied them to an oak tree at the centre of a ceremonial circle. The victim, Graves claims, was fastened in the *five-fold bond* inverted on a lightning blasted oak tree with the five extremities of neck, arms and legs secured in an inverted pentagram/star posture. He was then put through the five-fold death of scourging, blinding, castration, impalement and, finally, dismemberment with his successor in sacred kingship cutting off his head as an act to symbolic continuity. This ceremony would take place at the time of the Summer Solstice, when the sun is at its zenith, because as a representative of the sun god the victim would be assumed to be at the height of his Herculean powers and therefore able to fertilise the land most potently. His vital blood would be caught in an urn to be sprinkled on the tribe and, after disjointing, parts of his flesh may have been roasted and eaten by a selected group of warriors who would thus share in his strength. This leads us to wonder at the occurrence of Bronze Age trough hearths which were supposedly for "cooking game"! The finding of assorted jumbles of charred bones in tombs also seems, in some cases at least, to point to the remnants of such feasts. The inversion of funerary urns in tombs containing cremated remains would also seem to have been intended to represent the skull of the sacrificed victim, which in later Druidic philosophy came to represent the seat of the soul within the human body.

Much of this would seem to be conjectural, even given Graves's convincing arguments such as the "Tal" of the name Taliesin being related to Talus-Hercules, and the ingenious unravelling of poetic clues by the Ogham/Tree alphabet. Archaeological evidence does however seem to bear much of this out. Upon considering two late Neolithic/early Bronze Age sites which are particularly well known to me, I was surprised to find that in each instance the sacrificed victim would have been put to death within a five-fold settting ... the five-fold death in the five-fold bond of Hercules. The stone circle at *Moel Ty Uchaf* in Gwynedd was shown by Professor Thom to be laid out in perfect pentagrammatical geometry, with its open burial cist at the centre of the pentagram. The burial chamber in *Bryn Celli Ddu* is five sided and has five small stones at its entrance, and the two chambers of *Dyffryn Ardudwy chambered cairn* are each of five sided construction. Additionally, there are five carved stones set purposefully in the chamber at *Barclodiad y Gawres*. Further research shows that this five-fold symbolism crops up in other Bronze Age and Neolithic sites where we might expect the five-fold sacrificial death of a sacred king to have been enacted ... *Cashtal yn Ard* on the Isle of Man is a five chamber tomb, as are *Hetty Pegler's Tump* and *West Kennet Barrow*. Five-fold cairn groups occur at *Kilmartin Linear Cemetery* in Scotland and *Porth Hellick Down* in the Scilly Isles, as well as countless other places, and even a Bronze Age ritual site *Waun Oer* on the hillside below *Cadair Idris*, which is very well known to me, consists of an alignment of five stones. I am also grateful to Margrit Hugle who on one such site visit drew my attention to the fact that the majority of standing stones used in such sites are themselves five sided. The most obvious example of this use of five-fold symbolism in the setting of Bronze Age sites may however be found in the impressive horseshoe of Sarsen Trilithons at *Stonehenge*.

The habitual use of pentagram symbolism in modern and mediaeval magic is of course well known, as is the pentagonal construction of Egyptian pyramids (four base points and an apex), obelisks, and so on. There is, however, implicit in all five-fold symbolism the idea of *empowerment,* not least the empowerment of language in the use of five vowel sounds. What is difficult for our modern minds to encompass is the idea that such a barbaric death could have anything to do with 'empowerment', but everything to do with de-humanisation and degradation, even though in the Christian theology that most of us grew up with, the degradation and barbarism is translated into salvation!

The idea of the Herculean sacrifice being set to an oak which is blasted by lightning is also worth some consideration. To (so called) primitive man, lightning was something more than the flash from the sky when the gods were angry. Lightning could be a symbol of fertility, in that it announced a storm and rain after which the rainbow, known to the Celts as the *Caer Ceridwen,* appeared as a promise of fertility in the sky. Lightning also appears in the myths (like the Mabinogi story of the *Lady of the Fountain*) as an announcement of a door opening between this world and the Otherworld. The motif is however universal … from the lightning impaled mystical tree of the *Qabalah*, to the burning bush, to the lightning bolts of an angry Zeus. If however, as some deduce, the ancients had a grasp of and/or were able to sense, as animals can, the changes in geo-electrical magnetic fields, then lightning would have carried a much more subtle message to them of the implications of their Hercules sacrifices. The burning bush of biblical record is paralleled in the *tree aflame* of Celtic folklore. The silver birch/silver branch that we have already discussed was also a symbol of lightning and the chevron/zigzag-like markings on stones at *Barclodiad y Gawres, Bryn Celli Ddu* and other tombs were probably also intended to depict lightning. The preference for elevated and exposed ceremonial sacrificial sites may well have, all things considered, been not so much to secure an impressive view but to actually attract lightning.

a hercules of many names

Another memory of the Hercules cult in Britain associated with sacred kings may be seen in the Arthurian myth of *Gawain and the Green Knight*. Gawain was originally the Welsh hero *Gwalchmai ("the hawk of May")*. The story begins as 'a Christmas game', with the giant 'green knight' having a club made from holly wood, then runs into a seasonal and onomastic cycle (the town of Holyhead on Anglesey … holy head … figures in scenes set in North Wales and the Wirral). The usual tests of arms and moral nerve complete the tale's initiatory theme. The Green Knight, like Bran, becomes anything but 'dead' when decapitated, and in fact replaces his severed head. The Bran myth is also to some extent located at Holyhead/Anglesey as a embarkation point for Ireland … which at times of confrontation across the Celtic Sea may have brought in the "guarding head" theme. The 'Chapel in the Green', where Gawain goes to undergo his own three-fold beheading test, turns out to be a "green mound" … a burial mound in other words. And again, as well as the more obvious comparison with the Bran myth, we may have in this Green Chapel an onomastic association with the *Bedd Branwen,* the grave of Branwen on the banks of the Alaw on Anglesey. It should also be mentioned that in this area of North Wales/Wirral where the Mersey estuary runs into the Celtic Sea, we also have the town of Holywell (Holy well) where the Celtic *Saint Winifred* performed the same Green Giant feat of replacing her own decapitated head!

The lion/tree symbolism of Hercules in the death of a sacred/solar king again crops up in the *Math fab Mathonwy* myth, where the resurrected *Llew* (or Lleu) who has been impaled by a spear and whose soul has flown away like an eagle, is found roosting in a oak tree. Beneath the tree a sow (sacred to Ceridwen) is rooting after the rotting flesh which drops from the bird. By now the oak tree and sow symbolism will be obvious; the impalement by spear and perhaps the idea of a death ritual with an allotted time for decomposition/"sky burial" which is also implicit in the imagery. Llew's name, originally *Lleu (light)* seems to have purposely been spelt *Llew* at times because this means *"lion"*, a sure reference to the totem of Hercules.

Hercules attained this lion totem after tearing a lion apart with his bare hands and thereafter wore its pelt. As De Santillana and von Dechend note in *Hamlet's Mill,* the attributes and adventures, including betrayal by women, of Llew, Hercules and the biblical Samson (in the book of Judges) are pretty much identical. The "betrayal by woman" which this composite Hercules suffers may well reflect the temporary affection given to the sacrificial victim prior to his death.

The evidence therefore seems to indicate that late Neolithic and Bronze Age sacrificial practices were remembered and/or adopted and perpetuated in Celtic mystery practice, but came to describe the mythical death and rebirth of the initiate bard, the Taliesin, rather than the actual slaughter of a priest king. That these practices had originally been preserved in Greek, and later Roman, mythology, affirmed them as the practices of an *Ercwlf*/Hercules cult to the Celts, who later came under Roman occupation and influence. It was probably at this time that the sacrificed hero of the Mabinogi *Math fab Mathonwy* tale, Llew/Lleu, took on his lion name to line him up with the Hercules hero, which also fitted nicely with some of the symbolism of the Mithras cults which were prevalent among the occupying Roman forces. Interestingly, the site which the Mabinogi offers as the Caer of Llew, *Tomen y Mur* near Trawsfynydd, was a Roman military camp whose occupants would have been adherents of the Mithras cult.

This reinforcing effect of the new imported Hercules myths upon the ancient British mystery practices which it had come to describe, may also be seen in such things as the Greek myth of *Jason and the Argonauts*. It is said that the Greeks admitted to various classical commentators that Heracles/Hercules was an Egyptian deity that they had imported. This gives us a more powerful cross reference to a culture who were very much preoccupied with the death rites of priest/kings, and (tenuously!) draws in the speculation of mythological exchanges through the links between the early Celtic church and the primitive Christian church of Ethiopia and

Egypt ... links which were being forged during the Roman occupation of both Egypt and Britain. Both had in their own ways a mutual heritage of their ancestors building their mortuary and/or initiatory structures in five-fold symbolism ... the pyramids with their five angles, for example. More important than such speculative connections, it was this Egyptian Hercules who had been the original Jason of the *Jason and the Argonauts* myth. Here we have a *Hercules/Jason/Gilgamesh* who was said to have slept with fifty women in one night as Bran had done in Celtic myth. Whilst the *fifty* again introduces the five-fold symbolism, this may also reflect the pleasures awarded to a Hercules victim prior to his death. Hercules was also *Briareus*, who in Greek myth had fifty heads ... the crew compliment of Argonauts, whose Argo/Ark was built of oak, the Druidic tree of Hercules. The oars of the Sumerian equivalent, Gilgamesh's *Magan* ship, which also had fifty sailors, was cut from five particular trees. Taliesin mentions "five chief trees", a point taken up by Graves in his linguistic/calendrical thesis. Perhaps here, in these voyages of Hercules/Jason/Gilgamesh and their companions, we have the Arthur of the *Preiddu Annwn* and his ship *Prydwen* voyaging, as we shall see shortly, into the Underworld realm of Bran, the British proto-Hercules, and the other sacrificed and beheaded ancient kings of Bronze Age times.

It is fascinating to read Graves's account of how he came to write *The White Goddess,* and of the synchronicities which attended this. The most fascinating synchronicity of all, which Graves seems to miss, is however the fact that he was suddenly moved to write such a study of the ancient Hercules cult in Britain and its poetic Celtic renaissance whilst also writing an historical novel based upon *Jason and the Argonauts!*

hercules in the heavens

The sacrificed hero/king cults in Bronze Age Britain appear on the archaeological and mythical evidence therefore to have been introduced by Neolithic or early Bronze Age visitors to these islands, and subsequently to become a central feature of early rites of sovereignty. There seems little doubt that this was the basis of continental and later (500 BC on) British Druidic practice, although in Celtic times it appears to have continued in an initiatory, if not actually sacrificial, context in the practices of the Taliesin cult.

All this would seem to be beyond doubt, until explorations are made into the stellar symbolism of Celtic mythology. Despite sporadic mentions of *Ercwlf* (Hercules) in the bardic literature, the Celts plainly were not overtly concerned with the constellation of Hercules. The Celtic references and/or allusions to star groups are much more concerned with the *Corona Borealis, Ursa Major, Ursa Minor* the *Pleiades* and the *Milky Way*. These were after all the ancient stellar patterns upon which the magico-religious practices of their British predecessors were based. The Ursa Major and Ursa Minor stars were, as we have seen, relevant to the Bear/Arth mythology and also to the Plough aspect of Ursa Major and the opening up and fertilisation of the mother Earth through the principles of sovereignty. The rising of the Pleiades on the shoulder of Taurus were related to this symbolism. The stars of the Corona Borealis, the *Caer Arianrhod,* as it is called in Welsh, whose shape is remembered in certain Bronze Age circles and later Celtic *torcs,* was the constellation of particular interest to the Taliesin initiate bards – not the constellation of Hercules where Greek mythology had placed this hero.

Yet in the night sky it is Hercules who stands at the open circlet of the Caer Arianrhod, just as the sacrificial victim would have stood at the entrance to the enclosure of the five-fold *Moel Ty Uchaf* circle in Bronze Age times, even as the Greek Heracles had stood at the Underworld cave of the Delphi oracle.

The Caer Arianrhod/Corona Borealis was to the Celts and many ancient peoples "the bear cave in the sky". It was the cave-like entrance to the burial mound and thus to Annwn, and it was the entrance to the Avalon of the Hesperides at which Hercules stood holding the axis of the Earth for Atlas. Whilst the original sacrificial practices of Neolithic and Bronze Age settlers in Britain may have been shared by their Mediterranean and even Middle Eastern contemporaries, the later importation of the classical Hercules, with his special constellation in the sky, to Celtic Britain, never changed anything for the initiate bards … it just confirmed things!

The five and the seven

A problem may still seem to remain, however, in assuming this carry over from Bronze Age sacred king practices into a Celtic mystery system which was still being poetically promoted by the Taliesin bards well into the Christian era. Whilst we have been indicating the numerical stress on *five-fold* symbolism in a magical Bronze Age tradition, the majority of Taliesin poetry and Mabinogi material lays stress on the number *seven*. All the constellations cited as being of significance to the Celts are constellations which consist, at least to cursory naked eye observation, of seven stars. The Taliesin bards were particularly interested in the Caer Arianrhod/Corona Borealis, for this is where one Taliesin initiate bard says that he has been *"in the prison of Arianrhod"* and thus cites it as the symbolic and gruelling 'place' of his initiation. By taking such astronomical assertions of the Taliesin poems on the one hand and seeing how they translate in a sacred site of Bronze Age origin on the other, we are able to draw Celtic mythology into its context of Bronze Age mystery practice and see the seven-fold symbolism of the former and the five-fold symbolism of the latter fit together.

Moel Ty Uchaf stone circle is a Bronze Age site of particular significance, in that whilst being comparatively small, it is probably one of the best preserved and least tampered with prehistoric sites in Britain.

As we have already said, Professor Alexander Thom found that this circle was constructed on exact pentagonal geometry, a task undertaken some thousand years before the Greeks were credited with devising the geometry of dividing a circle into five. It consists, as our illustration shows, of a horseshoe or corona of stones in a *torc* shape imitating the shape of the Corona Borealis, Taliesin's 'prison of Arianrhod' in the stars and his place of stellar initiation. A further seven stones are set apart in the 'mouth' of this corona which ancient people of a number of cultures knew as a "bear's cave" in the stars. The main circle/corona area consists of a further thirty-five (i.e. 5 x 7) stones, with the burial cist at the centre. There are subsidiary cist burials below and around the circle, partly covered with white quartz and some evocative earthworks.

What we have therefore is an elevated ceremonial burial site, purposefully constructed on pentagonal/five-fold geometry, with five times seven (thirty-five) stones set out in the shape of a constellation to which sacrificed kings and latterly initiates were bound to go. We may suppose from this that the Hercules rites of sacrificial and sacral kingship, "the five-fold death", were performed every seven years, and for this site we may tentatively reconstruct this sacrificial rite as follows:

1. The voluntary victim would first be drugged, possibly by snake bite or the administering of venom in some other way. The Gundestrup cauldron image of the sacred king (often erroneously called a "shaman") holding a serpent and a corona shaped torc may be an illustration of this. His eyes

The apple and Annwn

Moel Ty Uchaf in the Berwyn Mountains, North Wales

A well preserved Bronze Age site surveyed by Professor Alexander Thom, who found that the circle was constructed on an exact basis of pentagonal geometry. This would seem to accord with the expression of the number five which appears to be inherent in so many late Neolithic and Bronze Age sites. Indeed five burial cists lie immediately below this circle to the south west.

The natural pentagram at the heart of an apple; the star at the centre of the circle, making the cut apple the perfect metaphor to explain the five-fold geometry of these ancient sites as gates to the Under-world of Annwn.

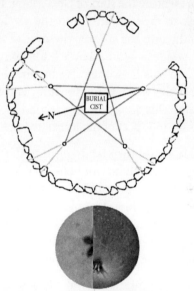

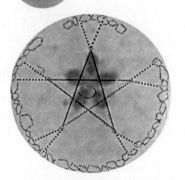

The Red and the White

The cut apple, red on the outside and white on the inside, with its integral pentagram core. White was an adjective (gwyn, wyn, wen) embodied in Welsh names to signify beings and facets of Annwn. The red "outside" of the apple would contrast as the "blood red" mortality of the outer world.

The red and the white is a frequent esoteric motif, especially in regard to Glastonbury, whose Tor has provided a time-honoured gate to Annwn.

are closed which seems to indicate a semi-conscious state which snake bite would, mercifully, induce. In this hallucinatory state, he would be presented at the inner stone at East of North which would align to the Midsummer sunrise. Here at sunrise the first bloodletting would occur with what Graves describes as scourging. This being the case, the victim would undergo the first stage of shedding his mortality in the symbolism of shedding his flesh. This shedding of skin/changing would also align to the symbolism of his being drugged with venom and "having the vision of the snake". This first blood on the ground would also give the goddess the first of five "fertilisations" aligning to the five years of the victim's kingship as her consort.

2. Moving sunwise, he would then be taken to the next point of the five-fold circle facing the ever rising sun and the central of the seven stones representing the stars of Ursa Major. Here he would be blinded and turned back to face inwards into the circle/corona. Thus he would be facing blindly into the corona, the cave of the bear and the secret dark place of the goddess – in darkness – for no man may look upon her directly and live. In this he would also be directly facing his own tomb … where in effect she was waiting for him, and no man may (normally) foresee his death. This would be the second blood letting which would rob him of the second facet of his mortality, the ability to see.

3. He would then be dragged to the third point of the summer sun at its zenith, though he would be unable to see it. At this point of the sun at its most potent he would be castrated, his genitals and blood fertilising the earth. Some blood would possibly be preserved at this stage to sprinkle on the tribe to make them fruitful. This castration, the taking away of the human ability to enjoy the pleasures of the flesh and procreate, would discontinue yet another facet of his mortality.

4. At the point almost at the west of the circle, the place where the sun sets in winter, he would be killed by impalement on an oak spear and thus cease, at the position of the going down of the sun, to be mortal any longer.

5. His limbs would be separated from his torso at the point west of north.

6. Finally, back at the point of origination in the circle, where the rite began, the victim's successor, the "new" king, standing at the start of the cycle, would cut the victim's head from the torso, thus taking on the "soul" of the kingship. He would keep the head elsewhere enshrined for oracular or guardianship purposes, possibly burying it beneath a standing stone.

7. Warriors of the tribe would roast and eat particularly significant parts of the corpse to share in the strength of the ex-"king". The remains of the corpse might be placed on a flat stone nearby or within the central burial cist, left open to the elements to allow decomposition. This would be for a specified time, probably until the Corona Borealis showed her "eighth star" to signify that the dead man had joined the stars and was secure in the heavenly cave of the goddess, and had achieved "the crown behind the north wind". In token of him then being secure within the goddess's starry cave the remains, including charred bones from the roasting, but except of course the skull, would be finally buried in a chamber or cist.

After burial, the stars would turn to align the deceased ancestor/king to reform his relationship with the tribe. His remains would lie in the deep dark awaiting the alignment of the "stars within the earth" with the tribal stellar patterns to which the tribal lands were seen to conform. It

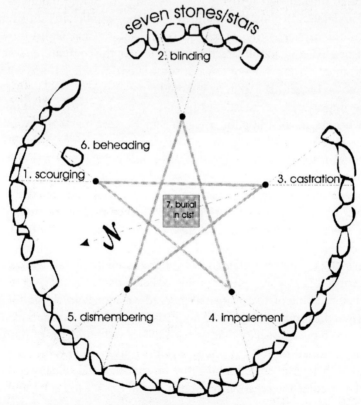

Moel Ty Uchaf showing the ritual stations and the pentagonal geometry indicated in Professor Thom's survey. The pentagram points indicate the centres of longer and shorter arcs from the numerically plotted outer circumference.

would be during this interval that the companions (perhaps as many as the seven companions of the Bran myth, signifying the seven-fold stellar constellations) would be required as 'ghostly guardians' of their king. Although such practices seem to have ceased by Iron Age/Celtic times, the Hochdorf burial indicates that the trappings of this 'tradition' remained. The Hochdorf chieftain was buried alone, yet seven 'drinking horns' were displayed in his burial chamber, presumably for his companions. The horn, again bringing to mind Mithraic and Taurean stellar symbolism, was a potent symbol of the forces of polarity and of regeneration and rebirth. In the Taliesin poem *Preiddu Annwn*, mention is made of "the horns of light".

Any companions of the 'king under the mountain', or at least his bones, would be chosen with little notice, and death would be sudden. But to be thus chosen, to be the king's discarnate bodyguard, was perhaps at one time a great honour. We do however have reason to believe that some later 'companions' preferred dishonour to death. Either way, such companions did not go into the 'great turning', as the king did, but remained, as we would understand a ghost to remain, to guard the chamber. In the technical terms of the mysteries they would be 'bound souls'. Thus, whilst the king established his 'root' in the sacred land, the soul of the companion/s would be 'restrained', to be given quittance at some later time when it was felt that the tomb no longer needed to be guarded.

The importance of guardianship and of 'door keepers' is a concept which occurs in all initiation rites. It can be seen particularly in the Mabinogi romance of *Culhwch ac Olwen*. It also existed in the sacred king rites, in the sense that any disruption may not only be a premature interruption of the sacred king's assimilation of earth/star patterns, but may latterly 'profane the pattern'. There seems to be archaeological evidence of such 'guardianship' practices in the finding of individual, whole skeletons adjacent to the disarticulated bones laid out in the chamber itself. At *Camster Round Tomb* in the Scottish Highlands, for example, the chamber contained burnt bones whilst the passageway to it was "guarded" by two unburnt complete skeletons.

When the king or surrogate had merged with the land/the goddess, it seems that the tomb could be used for initiatory and/or oracular purposes. We can perhaps appreciate that, as with the sacred buildings of our own era, they fulfilled more than one role. Westminster Abbey, for example, is used both for the coronation/initiation of kings and queens and as a place for regular intercession on behalf of the British folksoul, and as a necropolis of the great. On the other hand not all religious structures contain burials and it may be that some prehistoric chamber structures which contained no sign of burial, or of normal domestic activity, were of this type. The Scottish *souterrains* and "empty tombs" like *Carn Gluze* barrow in Cornwall seem, rather like the pyramids, to suggest this. But not all empty tombs are of course "empty" for this reason. The spoiling and robbing of burials by amateur archaeologists in recent times or hostile tribes in ancient times are more often, if not invariably, the reason.

The king and the land are one

As we have seen and shall see, the secrets of ancient burials as routes to the Underworld and folksoul of the race/tribe were assiduously defended, latterly by the bards, because to know and overthrow the gods of a folksoul/culture was considered, in ancient times, a prerequisite to the physical conquest of territory. This is universally apparent, particularly in the history of the Jerusalem temple which was despoiled and razed to the ground by invaders on three occasions. Since the third desecration and destruction in 70 AD with Titus tearing down the veil which concealed the Holy of Holies, carrying off the sacred vessels and destroying the building, it has never been restored. The Romans took the same trouble with the Druidic heart of Celtic religion that they had done with Judaism, by invading the Druid stronghold of Anglesey and burning down the sacred groves. They knew that such sacred sites were where a race had its roots in the land, and that in such cases kingship was implicit in the symbol of a sacred king being wedded to the land as the embodiment of his people. The Celts and their predecessors considered that the land and the goddess, whose splendid body it was, owned them – rather than vice versa. The king and the land were one so the people and the land were one. The king and the goddess were one so the people's relationship to the goddess was ratified by the land that they occupied. To undo the sacred places where this ancestral bond was seen to be forged was to cut the heart out of a people so that they may be easily suppressed. This necessity to defend the linkages of the folksoul to the land was of no less relevance at the time Taliesin was writing the *Preiddu Annwn* in the twelfth century than they had been in Bronze Age or tribal Celtic times. To cut this umbilical cord between a people and their land was to sever their potential for bringing to birth the paradisal aspirations of the national folksoul.

CHAPTER SEVEN

The Defence of Annwn

THE GATES OF the Brythonic mysteries are the gates of Annwn, and they were well guarded. The exchanges of question and answer and "riddle me a riddle" between "porters" at the gate and would-be entrants, shown in some Mabinogi stories, particularly *Culhwch ac Olwen*, betray a bardic obsession with Annwn's security. There was good reason for this.

To the Celts, Annwn was that substructure lying between, and overlapped with, both the natural and archetypal worlds. As we have seen it was entered through burial mounds as well as mountains, lakes, and other natural features. The ancestral king or hero therefore passed into the landscape and into Annwn, then through Annwn to the starry paradisal worlds where the true pattern appropriate to his tribe could be grasped. King Arthur, as we shall see, is one who made that journey, though the Arthur of folklore appears to be ready to return, waiting – with or without his knights – under at least six mountains in Wales! Looking at the literature and films which deal with his exploits, one might say that to all intents he has returned, which paradoxically makes the point of the purpose and power of myth.

The mythical (and even the historical) king venturing or sleeping under his mountain, earth mound or *Caer* is, however, a universal theme. In voluntary death he enters Annwn to seek, secure and mediate the true pattern of being, of sovereignty, exemplified in the goddess, to his people. In psychological terms he is seeking the *Gestalten,* the patterns, appropriate to the well-being of the collective national psyche. The secret of the Taliesin initiate bards, and indeed other initiates in all mystery systems and all cultures, has been that they have been able to make the journey into these inner realms … and return. They have entered the gates of death in the surrogate death of initiation, and indeed the Celtic initiate bard was (and is) a surrogate for the ancient sacred kings, and the later surrogate kings, who were put to ritual death in the Bronze Age. The Celtic initiate's surrogacy was both in the fact that he stood in the place of a priest king of his people and that his 'death' was a surrogate 'living death' of initiation at the hands of the goddess. He romanced the goddess and thus tapped the seven-fold experience of Annwn, returning to implement what he had learned for the benefit of his people. Hence as we shall see "only seven returned from Caer Sidi". The bardic throne that he attained, what Taliesin called the "uneasy chair", is in effect his attainment of the status of a priest king. His trials to attain that throne are at the hands of the triple goddess who holds the keys of those qualities presumed in a true king ... wisdom, knowledge and understanding.

The idea of inner creation and indeed the inner constitution of humanity being seven-fold is also met with in a number of mythologies and philosophies throughout the world. Our latter day Taliesin initiate who wrote the *Spoils* may even have been familiar (especially if he was a Templar and/or Gnostic as we might suppose) with *the Book of Enoch* and the seven 'mountains' of Enoch's inner landscape.

"I went beyond it and saw seven magnificent mountains, each different, whose stones were magnificent and beautiful ... the seventh mountain was in the midst of them and it excelled in height, resembling the seat of a throne. Fragrant trees encircled the throne."

If we wanted to overlay one mythology on another, we would find the Celtic mythological images falling into place. Here we have the sacred trees, the seven mountains/*Caers* and the chair/throne of bardic knowledge. In the meantime we must look at *Caer Sidi* as an overall complex which consists of seven Caers in total, and may be, as Graves notes, the word which derives from the Irish *Sidhe*. As we described elsewhere, the *Sidhes* were gates to the Underworld (Annwn) where the Tuatha dé Danann held sway. Each Sidhe was a stronghold of a chieftain of the Tuatha and these were generally held to be located at ancient burial sites. The Sidhe of the Dagda himself was said to be at the impressive Newgrange tomb.

The Welsh *Sidi* was generally taken to mean "revolving", a point which we will expand upon later. What is clear however is that a definitive and universal cosmology is being expressed here and that Caer Sidi and its sub-Caers are not so much inner places as inner *experiences* ... they are experience of the goddess of all nature, terrestrial and cosmological, mundane and spiritual, confronting human nature in the most profound and intimate way. Caer Sidi is the overall seven-fold inner experience of *Awen,* and *Awen* is the stuff of Annwn.

To understand Annwn, we can say that in broad terms it is that matrix of inner consciousness which Jung called the *collective unconscious* and which has variously been described as the *Underworld, Inner Planes, Folksoul* and so on (the terminology has become hopelessly confused in the last forty years or so!) What is clear however is that whilst it is very definitely an Underworld, it is not one of the classical Hades type. It is not some static, ghoulish realm of sad or particularly evil souls. It is a dynamic place which, whilst having its beauties and dangers, just like the material world, comprises the dynamics behind the life of the physical world. That mythology should choose to personalise these dynamics (because they embody modes of consciousness) is no less valid than seeing them in the scientific terms of quantum mechanics or the wavelengths of the electromagnetic spectrum or even in the (typically Celtic) spiral of DNA. Annwn is an area of dynamic catalytic action utilising the substructures of both consciousness and matter to enable the *becoming* (or in psychological terms, the *integration* of the collective psyche) of a people and their environment. It is over this *becoming* that the goddess rules as mistress of Annwn.

The Mistress of Annwn

The Goddess rules primarily because of her femininity, her ability to foster what is in the process of *becoming,* the embryonic future, within her being. This embryonic future is however a transformation of the past, hence she *breaks to make,* and is the repository of spent life and spent events as well as new life and new opportunities. Her aspects are, as we have seen, not only those of an archetypal earth mother. As she brings all things to birth ... and death and rebirth, she is an *empowerer.* In the aspect of **Arianrhod,** for example, she is an initiatrix, initiating and arming her 'son' Llew. Initiation is of course of itself a new beginning, a birth, or at least rebirth following a psychological and spiritual 'death'. Arianrhod's cauldron/cave/womb is in the stars, because as the initiatrix of cosmological events she holds those patterns which the stars were seen to embody.

Arianrhod is however every bit a 'mother' in this broader sense, as is **Ceridwen,** who more literally gave rebirth to Gwion as Taliesin. This more homely image is shown both in her bubbling cauldron and her totem animal of the white sow, a creature of startling fecundity, which in no way subordinates her to Arianrhod. Arianrhod's wisdom provides its insights into human destiny. Ceridwen's understanding provides for the stuff of creation by which that destiny may be implemented.

Blodeuwedd, on the other hand, represents that impulse of vibrant life which can be both attractive and deadly. She is not a goddess of love in the classical sense, but she endows the initiate with a knowledge of that raw and reckless power in nature and human nature, called *hwyl* in Welsh, which impels events. In psychological terms she may be thought of as *libido*. In some ways she is the irresistible apple on the tree of Eden, the knowledge that is implicit in the bitter sweet lessons of life. It is only, however, through the arousal of human endeavour that knowledge of life, and the wisdom (the owl into which she is ultimately transformed) which stems from that knowledge, may be attained.

It will be clear from our preliminary perusals of the Welsh mythologies that these functions and titles of the triple goddess tend to overlap and combine. She is after all *one* goddess, one power, albeit of myriad aspects, encapsulating that area which enables *becoming*. She is, in all her aspects, the muse of poets, the initiatrix of bards and the Beatrice of mystics. Her subsidiary titles, not least of spinner and weaver, are of course implicit in her activities, as is her patronage of smithcraft, cauldron keepers and milkmaids. She is associated with all the breaking down, creating and sustaining roles embodied in human activity, facilitating these functions between the natural and archetypal/paradisal worlds. She embodies in fact the cauldron/catalyst in which pre-material forces and the consciousness of human, once human and other non-human modes of being participate and interact. She is therefore the "space" of Annwn itself.

The seven Caers of Caer Sidi

Whilst the various "Caers" tend to give an idea of seven defined inner regions of Annwn, almost as a sop to the definitive tendencies of human intellect, this was probably a late Celtic interpolation. Caer Sidi implies one total experience in Annwn. What is however fragmented into seven 'separate' Caers or stages is human perception … hence from this experience "only seven return" … it is a seven-fold *perception* of ONE reality. It is therefore the journey of human consciousness which is seven-fold, not Annwn itself. As our illustration shows, the seven supposed milestones upon this journey are in fact the seven junctions or gates between archetypal, paradisal aspirations and the physical, natural world in which they are intended to be expressed.

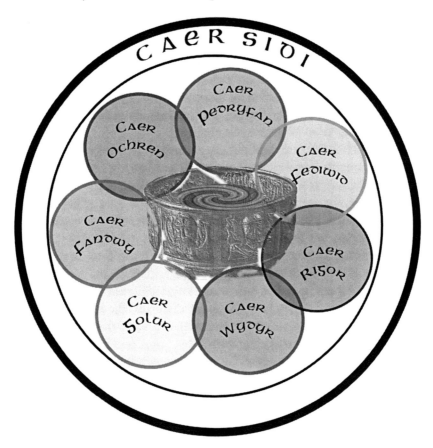

The seven-fold symbolism, which, as we have indicated, is a pretty much universal way of categorizing human inner experience, must be realised as an anthropomorphism which feels comfortable to human perception. Again (if one wishes to use the rather limiting terminology and philosophy of psychology) this is the *Gestalten,* the configurations, or patterns, through which the human psyche deals with its aspirations and needs. The natural world shows us seven directions (above, below, forward, backward, one side another side and a centre). It also shows us seven days to a week, seven notes on a musical scale, seven rainbow colours, seven continents and so on, and many of the major stellar constellations appear as seven-fold to the naked eye. In the philosophy of magic, Celtic and otherwise, the seven planets were also seen as the intermediaries between mundane creation and the archetypal patterns of the constellations. The fact that the cauldron of this catalytic process occurs in the Taliesin material as being "warmed by the breath of *nine* maidens" can be accounted for by the fact that the two lunar nodes were often taken by the ancients as an additional two 'planets' to the traditional seven. Be that as it may, we have seen it was important to the Celts, as it was to other cultures, to have their inner and outer worlds seeming to reflect each other. Intangible inner territory therefore generally became seven-fold to match up to the tangible territory of the natural world. In creating such a reflection, a potent and supremely successful conduit was set between the archetypal, aspirational worlds and outer life.

The tools and techniques used to enable such a conduit were those of consciousness, and essentially the practice of magic, the art of making changes in consciousness in both oneself and in others. Magic's *prima materia* is the human imagination, a material which is equally vital to the world of the poet and storyteller. This imaginative material was what the Celts called *Awen* ... yet Awen once primed, once invoked, seems to have an ability of independent action. The reason for this is plain. The conduit formed between Annwn and the outer world enabled a flow in both directions. The results of this two-way flow, especially in terms of consciousness, may be respectably described in Jung's theories of *synchronicity* and the content of particular dreams, but the ability of such prophetic bards as the *Awenyddion* are a more spectacular example, as are Graves's descriptions of the action of the poetic muse.

True poetry and true magic are one and the same thing. Both seek, by causing changes in consciousness, to reveal facets of an inner reality. In this inner reality intellect can find few footholds, for the poetic myths from which magic is made and the magic by which poetic myth is forged both speak to the soul. Intellect can pick at the structure of myth just as it can pick at the structure of music, but cannot grasp its essential quality. As we have seen, however, the application of bardic technique in its setting of both traps and clues for intellect, of itself demanded considerable intellectual skill, but this was simply the packaging of the mystery. Intellect was, in a sense, encouraged to such contortions, at least in a trainee initiate, in trying to unwrap the mystery that it would soon fall aside and allow intuition to take over. It was a kind of Celtic Zen.

The defence of sovereignty

The practical implications of this are obvious however. In the strategies of sovereignty, the ability to tap the archetypal and paradisal blueprint of a folksoul enabled those who made it their business to do so, to set long term racial aspirations. In more immediate, tactical, terms, it gave access to pre-matter and pre-events, and thus enabled precognition (usually, but inaccurately, called prophecy) and the means to 'adjust' the embryonic future in the light of what was foreseen. This is the province of practical magic, though modern psychotherapeutic techniques such as *Neuro Linguistic Programming* claim to be able to do the same … at least on an individual basis.

As far as the bards were concerned, therefore, anyone who could activate Awen and thus find their way into the racial substructure of Annwn, was either friend or foe. This was sensitive territory, as secret and sensitive as any military installation might be in a modern state. In the ancient world the ability to know the names of the gods and goddesses of an enemy was a prerequisite to conquest. To be able to penetrate the enemy's inner reality, to capture what made him 'tick', his reason for being, his folksoul, and to be able to anticipate and tamper with his future was, as we have seen, to be able to strike at his sovereignty, his roots in the land.

Whilst all this may sound fanciful to our logic-chopping contemporary consciousness, we should remember that we have modern examples of the power which may be exercised by penetrating these archetypal, mythical levels of the psyche of a race. We might for example reflect upon how Adolf Hitler managed to penetrate and wilfully manipulate the underlying archetypes of the German folksoul by playing upon the potent keys of Germanic myth. That the Nazi hierarchy was mythologically and esoterically driven is well documented, and evidenced in their obsession with Grail mythology, with Catharism, and with Himmler's formation of an occult order – the *Knights of the Holy Lance* at Wewelsburg, attended regularly by such high ranking SS marshals as Himmler himself, Heydrich, Bormann and Peiper.

The bards, mindful of such abuses in their own times, therefore set a series of defences at the gates to Annwn and seeded them with riddles, as readily as any modern garrison commander might seed the approaches to his stronghold with landmines!

In many of the poems of the Taliesin cult and the myths upon which they are structured we are presented with both the minefield and a route through it. We are shown the seemingly barred gates of Annwn but also tiny gaps, usually signified by puns and double meanings, by which we might safely squeeze through. The ability to penetrate to such levels, of what we are variously calling the folksoul and racial psyche, and what Jungian psychology would call the collective unconscious, and what initiates of Bronze Age times may have known as "land star patterns", is after all something of a double edged sword. As we have shown it may be used to undermine a race but it can also be used to heal and inspire. The true bards had an image, a paradisal ideal to which the Celts should aspire and which they needed, they thought, to stimulate. They sought 'treasures', archetypal images from the Underworld and the past, but especially the cauldron of transformation, of plenty, and of rebirth. This was the key, for it was from the cauldron that true Awen arose. This is why the mythologies place so much value upon this vessel which was later to be embodied in Christian ideal ... perhaps the too idealised Christian ideal ... of the Holy Grail.

The Celts would also have been aware of the sanctity of severed heads and skulls of the ancient Bronze Age Hercules cults and latterly, by the Templar epoch, would have been able to align this to the legend of the head of Adam as a paradisal marker, being the supposed seat of the original soul of mankind that had known paradise. Again the practical applications of this will be apparent. Indeed, as we have seen from the Bran mythology and the practices of the Bronze age 'Hercules' cults, the severed head was the forerunner of the cauldron. Indeed the Bran story shows the transitional stages between two cultures and these two 'sources' of Awen .

We have seen that in the pre- and post Romano Celtic era there was certainly tribal feuding. Whilst much of this would be about things like cattle and status, the more fundamental invasions which involved desecration of sacred sites, even though there were myriad tribal and local deities, albeit with the same archetypal functions, seems to have been avoided. The credit for much of this may be placed at the door of the Druids, who holding a common philosophy among them, were able to meet as ambassadors from their various tribes and unravel and settle the more fundamental conflicts that went beyond stolen cattle and hurt pride. It does however seem likely that the stories of Arthur invading ancient tombs, as in the *Preiddu Annwn* poem which we are soon to consider, hark back to earlier invasions of Bronze Age Britain, and the suppression of the Bran cult by the Math cult, when sacred sites *were* deliberately interfered with.

We have told how "Arthur" took a wife from the ancient Faery race, *Gwynhyfwr,* to ratify and empower his sovereignty. When she was in

danger of abduction, however, she sought refuge in her father's Caer …
the "Tower of London" (the myth was eventually written down, as most
were, during or after the Norman occupation!) As we have seen, the
Tower of London was on the White Mound and was sacred to Bran. It
is where (my speculations about Lundy being suspended!) his head was
buried, the head which Arthur insisted on digging up. From this we see
that the cult of Math, later resurrected as Arthur, was spoiling the sacred
places of the Bronze Age cult of Bran, whose "white" underworld Caers
housed the cauldron/skull of *awen*, and thus of inspiration and validation
… the paradisal pattern by which the king and the land were believed to
have been harmonised in the distant time of an earlier, golden age.

patterns of Sovereignty

That they were believed to be so harmonised is taken up in an
extraordinary piece of material from the gifted scholar and seer of the
Brythonic Mysteries R.J. Stewart. Stewart believes that earlier prehistoric
races living in what were much later to become the 'Celtic' kingdoms,
expressed the concept of sovereignty and the ownership of land in a
rather different way. His assertion, which our own researches confirm,
is that whilst local tribes were comparatively small, perhaps numbering
only fifty or sixty people in one locality, clan cohesion and influence
extended to other groups of people scattered over many hundreds of
miles. Originally this appears to have been achieved without a plethora
of local chieftains treading on each other's toes, and a strict protocol on
these matters was maintained. To break the protocol was unthinkable, for
reasons which will soon become clear.

Obviously these patterns of scattered clans were not originally based
on outer territorial 'frontiers' which could be extended or retained by
force of arms, or peacefully delineated by topographical boundaries
such as rivers and highlands. Tribes were not even 'related' by blood
kinship (except no doubt locally). What seems to have qualified
membership of such an 'extended' tribe, however, was identification
through a particular inner pattern or *harmonic* of the land on which
they happened to live. Strange though this seems to our modern
minds, such a way of being attuned to particular areas of land may still
be understood from aboriginal tribal elders who are still, thankfully,
prepared to promulgate the indigenous beliefs of their cultures in
various parts of the world.

THE DEFENCE OF ANNWN

Expressed in terms of the landscape of Britain, this would mean that a tribe centred on what we now call Cornwall may well have had 'tribal members' in a small part of north west Wales, whilst most of north west Wales may have been the centre for yet another tribe which had scattered members in, say, Cumbria … and so on. In other words, the tribal harmonic was literally 'geo-logical', rather than 'socio-logical' … or topographical. If a precise inner pattern in the land existed essentially in one place, but sporadically in others, then, as I understand it, those of the one place became the kernel of the tribe and the others became parts of its extended membership.

Whilst this seems odd to us today, we can see such scattered allegiances through unseen characteristics in the distribution of particular animal and bird species. We can also see the inner links between such places, delineated by the routes of animal and bird migration. Nomadic peoples still, to some degree, show the same characteristics, but the obvious example of an 'extended tribe' tied to a particular sacred land is still of course, the Jews. If Graves's speculations about Hebron being an 'oracular centre', in other words the place where the head of a sacred king (Adam) was buried, and thus the place of the essential inner earth 'harmonic' of the children of Abraham, then this example becomes particularly clear in the light of what follows.

Such harmonic patterns through the land are dimly realised in our recent acceptance of *ley lines*, some of which appear to individually extend over many hundreds of miles. The convergence of a number of ley lines onto a particular Neolithic or Bronze Age site, does in some instances seem to indicate the inner drawing together of harmonious strands in the body of the land – forming in their convergence, at the site of a sacred king's burial mound, the completion of a pattern. If we think of this in musical terms, with each far flung part of the tribe sounding its particular 'earth note', then we can see how all these notes vibrating on the 'strings' of the ley lines could be imagined to come together as the tribal 'chord' at the burial place of the sacred king, where the tribe made its own particular accommodation with the goddess.

If such beliefs had been exercised with practical effect for most of the Bronze Age, this would account for the ease with which certain undertakings were managed, such as the bringing of the Stonehenge *bluestones* from South Wales to Wiltshire, with the vital inter-tribal cooperation necessary to such an undertaking, rather than conflict. It would also account for the stones themselves, which presumably sounded the right geological "earth note" required by the tribe, or extended tribe, at Stonehenge.

161

What in fact we can see built progressively at Stonehenge through Bronze Age times is a representation of the same five-fold Corona Borealis horseshoe/corona symbolism, set at the heart of that great enclosure. This is of course the same symbolism in stone which occurs at Moel Ty Uchaf. At Stonehenge the "horseshoe" of Sarsen Trilithons also forms an open skull or cauldron, and the bluestones brought from the mythical western shores of Wales to be set within it would seem to represent the Awen which rises from that cauldron. This is why Excalibur, or more correctly *Caledfwlch*, the sword of Arthur's destiny, may with equal validity be drawn from a "cauldron"/lake or from a "skull"/stone … a matter that we shall address in detail later.

It is, meanwhile, interesting that Stewart's inner informant in his book *The Underworld Initiation*, a long dead sacred king, claimed to have attained the title "Stone king". Not only had the sacrificed king made the 'round' of the stones at his death, as described in our previous chapter, and also become an integral part of the living earth, as the rocks were, but he had become a king in the stars which the settings of stones represented. When the tribe looked to the stars, there he was turning with them. When they looked to the polygonal hewn stones of circle or chamber, there he was too. Stone king and Star king.

Under the ancient 'sacred king' procedures the extended clan system was able to preserve its delineations and protocol. R.J. Stewart mentions that any breaking with this protocol would have resulted in an almost unbearable 'loss of face'. In fact Stewart's contact/sacred king described such a situation as 'loss of root in the family ground'. We can see how, with his remains in the earth and his representation in a standing stone being embedded in the earth, this phrase of being *rooted* in the family/tribal ground would be so apt. Under the taboo of the possible loss of such a *root*, we can also see why 'guardians' were necessary to deter any violation which would disrupt the intricate tracery of the earth patterns to star patterns, kings to tribes and the tribe to the *family ground*. Any disruption of the pattern could sever this vital umbilical cord between the tribe and its mother, the goddess who was the land. The effect of such a catastrophe would be that the tribe would to all intents lose its very '*being*'.

Obviously a time did eventually come when these ancient protocols began to break down, particularly when peoples of other beliefs began to infiltrate the old tribal lands. This seems to have started to happen, as we have shown, towards the end of the Bronze Age, when a time of unrest and upheaval seems to have followed hard on the heels of a population explosion. When this started to happen, it follows that some raiding and despoilment of sacred places did occur. This, as we have seen, seems to be recalled in the myths as a conflict between the beliefs of what appears to be the old Bronze Age cult of *Bran* and the "new" cult of Math, which was later summed up in *Arthur.*

The myths and the poetry tell their own tale. Arthur fails to mate with his Faery spouse Gwynhyfwr, who significantly appears in one romance as the 'Daughter' of Leodegrance. In the name *Leodegrance* "the great lion" we have both the Hercules/Llew symbolism which connects her to 'the old way', and another bardic trick! Gwynhyfwr is a composite of Olwen, whose father was also a 'giant', and Branwen and Blodeuwedd and all the other "white" ladies who hail from Annwn. Her father being called Leodegrance is also a corruption of *Ogyr Fran* – Bran, but not the blessed hero so much as Bran in the guise of the malign raven of death, picking at the exposed remains of the recently sacrificed sacred kings.

This failure to acknowledge Gwynhyfwr (and the tradition that she represented) as the surrogate of the goddess (like Matholwch's failure to acknowledge Branwen) causes a disruption in the pattern, and that vital umbilical cord between the people and the land is broken. What the later romances called the Quest for the Holy Grail was a belated realisation of this, and an attempt to recover the cauldron of Awen and restore the severed link between the Brythons and their goddess.

Recovering the cauldron ... the single poetic theme

The gates of true poetry are, as we have seen, the gates of death. Alun Lewis, whom my father knew slightly before the poet's death in Burma in March 1944, talked about the *single poetic theme* in terms of life and death and what survives, beyond death, of 'the beloved'. This, according to both Graves and Lewis, was what true poetry was all about. Graves discusses the theme in terms of the poet's love affair, virtual death and resurrection at the hands of the power that he calls the *White Goddess.* All sovereignty, the right of the tribe, indeed the right of the whole tribe of mortal humanity to *be,* is vested in her. Her role is mediated and exemplified in poetic terms by the Muse, whilst in terms of the initiate of the Brythonic Celtic mysteries her mediatrix is the Faery Queen, or Thomas the Rhymer's *Queen of Fair Elfland*. It is the destiny of human beings to know her through such mediation in a very intimate way, for only by doing so can the great fear of death and the anxiety of *unbeing* be conquered. Her cauldron, as we have seen, could restore the dead to life and, more than this, resurrect them to realise the paradisal pattern of what *being* should be. Until this is realised, and such a realisation is in itself a kind of death, this primeval anxiety will continue to produce all the aberrations that human nature is heir to.

The failure of patriarchal, theistic religion to accommodate this into a practical theology is lamentable ... and in many instances downright demonic – in that 'the demonic' seeks to exist in and promote *unbeing*. Original, paradisal innocence became forgotten in Augustinian theological (even pathological) obsession with *the woman* Eve as the source of original sin. The result of this was that, in the more extreme instances, an insidious form of spiritual fascism was allowed to masquerade as love. To know and be confident in *being* and realise the place of one's own human nature in *all* nature, is to be touched by what the bards called *awen* ... the poetic inspiration of love and wisdom which the archetypal bard Taliesin supped from the goddess's cauldron. In the original myth the goddess Ceridwen had, after all, made the cauldron for her own son, the ugly Afagddu, to convince and console him in his own misshapen destiny. We should never forget this, for whatever the frightful rites and rigours of the cauldron may entail, it was originally constructed in the unselfish love of a mother for her child.

In the bard's love affair with the goddess, the cauldron symbolism is earthy and obvious, but nonetheless 'true' for all that. Elizabethan metaphysical poets also sought to expire in the laps of some idealised beloved creature, and the sacred kings of Neolithic and Bronze Age times went through death either to enter the vaginal like openings in burial mounds, where passage graves opened out into womb-like subterranean chambers, or to be laid in the foetal position in their cists, or to be poured out upon her, to seep into her splendid body in that final, gruesome orgasm of death. But there is more behind the graphic symbolism of this unconsummated love affair with some divine femme fatale than even Sigmund Freud would have dreamed of, and the objective of the single poetic theme is something more than a religious projection of male Oedipal longing.

The goddess is realised by men and women alike but in differing ways. The woman must *become* the goddess and her man must be her priest,

THE DEFENCE OF ANNWN

champion, lover and friend. Just as she must become and forever remain the muse, the mate … and the mystery.

This fulfilment of these archetypal roles in the mundane modern world is, of course, easier said than done. The mythological trials of the would-be illuminated bards can seem as nothing to the agonies of trying to make such a vision work, to express the *single poetic theme* in everyday life. The problem for both men and women is that the beginnings of empowerment come in the first instance through what amounts to an unconsummated inner love affair. In this, desire becomes a power with which to make transformations in consciousness. Unless the nature of such an inner relationship and the handling of the powerful desires it arouses are properly understood, however, its recipient will attempt to deflect the power by projection … the *contra sexual images* of Jungian psychology … upon the first member of the opposite sex who comes along. As the inner endeavours and/or upheavals which activate such empowerment are not usually undertaken or experienced before one gets into one's thirties or forties, the mundane results can be quite disruptive. The practical reasons for this are all too clear in that with approaching middle age, one's circumstances have usually become so concrete that there is little room for painless manoeuvre.

The tangled emotional lives of male poets like Robert Graves and female initiates like Dion Fortune tend to bear this out! Like the sacrificed sacred king, the would-be initiate poet is frequently hung emotionally between two states of being in a kind of death. Such a 'death' is, more often than not, the psychological catharsis, the hard way by which the lessons of the single poetic theme of initiation are realised. But what may be the rewards, the Spoils of such an adventure?

CHAPTER EIGHT

The Spoils of Annwn

THE BRYTHONIC CELTIC dream that had been embodied in Arthur faded finally with the death of the second Llewellyn at Cilmeri in 1283. Welsh aspirations to Brythonic sovereignty had, at least in any political sense, passed from the hands of the Celtic kings and princes into other, stronger, hands. The dream had foundered as surely as Arthur's quest for the Grail had foundered in the plethora of new Arthurian romance, in which Guinevere, like the goddess that she had represented, was consigned to the precincts of a Roman Catholic convent. To the Welsh, that umbilical cord of sovereignty attaching people to landscape had been replaced by a string of English fortresses stretching from Rhuddlan to Builth. The English king had seen to that, by having the Glastonbury monks discover "Arthur's grave", so that Arthur was not the living spirit of Celtic sovereignty but just a very dead hero. Ironically the king had done what Arthur himself was reputed to have done. Arthur had dug up the remains of Bran – and now King Henry was, in his turn, digging up the remains of Arthur in a further symbolic transfer of sovereignty … assuming of course it was Arthur! The bards knew that it wasn't, but this was nonetheless the very breaching of Annwn, the disruption of the Brythonic Celtic folksoul that they had feared.

The Taliesin cult were however still active, and still expounding principles of sovereignty and destiny which their forefathers had learned from the Bronze Age initiates of some eighteen hundred years before. Against this background we must make our way into Annwn in the company of one of the last of the Taliesin bards, with his "Arthur of mournful memory". Yet whilst all appears to be lost politically, the poem scorns any invasion of the Welsh folk-soul itself, scorns the men of "trailing shields" and "drooping courage" and castigates the fat court bards who should have done more to understand and cherish what had been placed in their charge.

It was inevitable that in doing this, our Taliesin bard should still present himself as a soldier poet, defending this sacred territory by laying down the poetic riddles, clues and challenges in the time-honoured manner. Here is his poem. For easy reference the names of the Caers are in (my) italics.

The Spoils of Annwn

Praise the Lord, supreme ruler of the heavens,
Who has extended his kingdom to the shores of this world
Absolute was the imprisonment of Gweir in *Caer Sidi*,
Because of the spite of Pwyll and Pryderi.
He was the first to go there
Then a heavy blue chain held that youth.
And for the Spoils of Annwn, gloomily he cries.
And till doomsday he shall go on crying.

We were three times the capacity of Prydwen going there
But only seven escaped from *Caer Sidi*.

Am I not a candidate for fame, one for bards to sing of?
In *Caer Pedryfan*, four times revolving.
And when was the first word spoken from the cauldron
That is gently warmed by the breath of nine maidens?
The cauldron of the chief of Annwn
That has pearls about its rim.
It will not boil the food of a coward.
No, he will see the flashing sword.
The sword entrusted to Bedwyr
That now guards the portals of the cold place
Where the horns of light are ablaze.
And when we went to this place, to *Caer Fediwid*,
With Arthur (in his splendid labours)
Only seven returned.

Oh yes, I am a candidate for fame.
To be remembered in song,
In the four cornered enclosure,
In this Island of the Strong door
Where twilight and the black night touch
Where blood red wine was the drink of our host

For though we went to *Caer Rigor*
With three times as many as Prydwen may carry
Only seven returned.

I will not praise the lords of literature.
Further than *Caer Wydr* they can never see Arthur.
Thrice twenty hundred men stood on the wall.
It was difficult to speak with their sentinel.
Oh yes, three times the capacity of Prydwen, we went with Arthur
But only seven came back from *Caer Golur.*

I won't praise men with trailing shields.
They don't know the day or the cause,
Or the hour of that splendid day of Cwy's birth.
Or what stopped him from going down the dales of Devwy.
They don't know the brindled ox with the thick headband,
And seven jewels on his collar.
But when we went with Arthur, of mournful memory,
Only seven returned from *Caer Fandwy*

I won't praise men of drooping courage
They don't know the day that the chief arose.
They don't know the hour of that splendid day, that the owner was born
Or what silver headed animal they keep,
When we went with Arthur of mournful memory.
Only seven returned from *Caer Ochren.*

The structure of the caers

The narrative of the 'Spoils', as its title implies, centres on a supposed 'raid' on the *Caers* (collectively *Caer Sidi* or *Sidin*) in Annwn, by none other than King Arthur, in whose company the poet as one of the surviving "seven" returns from the seven-fold Underworld journey. This brings to mind, as it was no doubt intended to, the Bran myth in which Taliesin was said to be one of only seven to return from Bran's fateful invasion of

Ireland. So the poem is presented in terms of the all too common Celtic experience of men (and women) going to war in great hopeful bands of which only a few ever come home again.

The 'Spoils' that 'Arthur' and his men were after were, superficially, grave goods, but the essential trophy was of course the cauldron of *Awen* (inspiration), which after the high middle ages and an audience beyond Wales had taken Arthur to its chivalric heart, became the Holy Grail. By the same token, what the high middle ages called the 'Quest' (the initiatory journey) is described in the *Spoils* largely in the spirit of the traditional Celtic pastime of cattle rustling. Gwydion had made a similar expedition to Annwn to 'steal pigs', but the pig, being the totem beast of Ceridwen, the goddess of the cauldron, made Gwydion's raid as much an esoteric 'Quest' as this foray of Arthur, Taliesin and their companions.

That these forays into Annwn were in general terms considered to be successful may be judged from Taliesin's statement in another poem, where he appears to have found within Annwn something of a paradisal state: *"Perfect is my chair in Caer Sidi, plague and age cannot hurt he who is in it."* This is reminiscent of the paradisal island of Avalon. Physical locations for Caer Sidi have been cited as Puffin Island off Penmon Point on Anglesey and Lundy Island in the Bristol Channel, to which we have said Bran's head may well have been taken, and which was known as *Ynys Y Gweir*, "Gwydion's island." In that Gwydion was the brother/lover of Arianrhod and the revolving *Caer Arianrhod* has been so closely connected with Caer Sidi, this latter location seems to be reasonable.

In 1995 a *bluestone* standing stone of the type taken from Pembrokeshire to make part of Stonehenge was found on Lundy. Whether this was purposefully taken to be placed there or became stranded on its way from Pembrokeshire to Stonehenge, and subsequently set up there, is not of course known. If the latter, this would make Lundy an important cult centre/sacred island in Bronze Age times. Be that as it may, Caer Sidi then gives us the general experiential Underworld setting within which the other seven Caers are grouped.

The immediate images of Taliesin's poetic riddles are Celtic. His Caers present the picture of high fortified places like Iron Age hillforts or simple defensive enclosures built upon a rounded mound of earth, as had been Celtic, Roman and Norman practice in Wales. Yet the fundamental pun of *The Spoils* is that these supposed Caers were not *upon* mounds but *beneath* them, and in this we are back to the Bronze Age. Taliesin's Caers are burial mounds, or at least they are experiences of the Underworld, Annwn, encountered via burial mounds. When we come to translate the names of the Caers this will become self explanatory.

These are:

1. *Caer Pedryfan* ... which means what it says. It is the four square castle, the four sided place in which Branwen was reputedly buried. As we have noted, this burial would have been a square stone *cist* within a mound, at least in Bronze Age burial terms. We can be fairly sure that it is a Bronze Age burial mound that is being referred to because it is "four times revolving". Of the few later Celtic burial mounds found, a handful are square mounds but unlike the Bronze Age mounds, they are not built on a 'revolving' plan. That is to say they are not square cists set within circular mounds or stone circles. Bronze Age cist burials were generally placed within a stone circle which was sometimes, but not inevitably, later covered over with a mound. The *four times* revolving of such a circle would seem to refer to the seasonal orientation of such circles, either to the quarters of the Vernal and Autumn equinoxes and winter and summer solstices or to the Celtic seasons of the "cross quarters" now commonly called Samhain (Nov 1st), Imbolc (Feb 1st), Beltane (May 1st) and Lammas (August 1st).

Another way of describing such a four fold enclosure is, according to Charles Squire in *Celtic Myth and Legend*, to use the title *Caer Bannawg*. In Malory's Arthurian romance this then becomes anglicised as *Carbonek* the Grail castle. It is, however, just possible that the copyist has intentionally or otherwise mislead us in this. If he had written *Caer Bannog* the meaning would have been changed and we would be considering a Caer which is "elevated" or even "horned". The former may more readily describe the spiritually "elevated" Grail castle but the latter reminds us of the eleventh line of the second stanza of the poem *"where the horns of light are ablaze"* which we shall consider next in *Caer Fediwid*.

2. Caer Fediwid translates as the "castle of the perfected ones", which again brings to mind Taliesin's assertion *"perfect is my chair in Caer Sidi..."* etc. This contrasts with the *"uneasy chair above Caer Sidi, revolving around between three elements"*, which we have cited earlier. The use of "perfect" again makes us wonder on this particular Taliesin's Gnostic/Templar leanings, but such a chance use of a word, even in the case of a Celtic bard, would make pursuit of the point trivial. The reference to *horns of light* mentioned in the previous paragraph is however interesting. Perhaps this is the horned god *Baphomet* whom the Templars were said to have worshipped ... the bull footed sacred king ... whose name as we have already observed appears to come from the Arabic *Abuihamet* ... Father of wisdom, *Father* being a grade in Mithraism which again throws us back to the possible Mithraic aspirations of an earlier Arthur cult. Indeed, as we shall see, the poem has further allusions to the sacred bull … the Celtic *Ychen Bannog*.

Squire and others translate *Fediwid* as "Revelry" and cite the feasting and storytelling which the seven companions of Bran's head experienced in that place beyond time. Curiously the same image may be applied to this Caer whatever the literal translation of its name, for the seven who attend the head are the prototypes of Grail achievers, they are seven who are able to make the inner journey successfully and return as "perfected ones". They become perfected because they attend the king on his journey and by virtue of fulfilling such sacred duty are given quittance to join him in his paradisal state. It will be remembered that one of the companions of the head was Taliesin himself; that is to say one of the Taliesin tradition, or indeed the archetypal Taliesin.

3. *Caer Rigor* – this is the Royal Caer. In this we are in the imagery of burial chambers, because burial in the great mounds of Bronze Age and latterly Celtic times was only accorded to nobility, as may be seen from the grave goods found in Bronze Age tombs in the Stonehenge area. Traditionally the one who went to meet the goddess on behalf of his tribe was a sacred king, so in this sense too the tombs were "royal". As we have seen, however, Taliesin's poetic asides are littered with star lore and in this instance the pun may be that *Rigor* refers to the star of *Rigel* in the constellation of Orion. A number of star myths throughout the world in fact saw Rigel as the star of death and/or as an entrance to the Underworld.

4. *Caer Wydyr* is the glass Caer and "the castle of glass" is something of a universal Otherworld theme. There may however be a more exact reference implied here, especially with the onomastic and physically specific tendency of Celtic mythology, and the role of Arthur in this poem. Before the poem was written, it was claimed, as we have noted, that the graves of Arthur and Guinevere had been found by the monks at Glastonbury, the 'holiest earthe in England'. The choice of Glastonbury as a glass castle would also have provided our Taliesin not only with an Arthur connection but with an irresistible pun, especially if, as seems likely, he was able to speak Welsh, Anglo Saxon and Latin.

The Welsh word for 'glass' is *(g)wydr*, whereas the Welsh word 'glas' means 'blue'. Some say this refers to the "blue" water which once surrounded the Tor and its environs when Glastonbury was an island. But here we must digress to consider the otherworld island theme as a whole.

There is, for example, the distinct possibility that Bardsey Island, off the North West Wales coast, is being indicated here.

Bardsey is what romantics would still like Glastonbury to be, a restricted Avalon, close enough to the workaday world of the Welsh mainland to almost touch, yet separated by treacherous waters and a place only visited by prior appointment and then only if sailing conditions permit.

It was once a place of pilgrimage and there is a tower there, the thirteenth century ruined tower of St Mary's Abbey. There are no striking prehistoric remains, although Bronze Age graves and a Neolithic flint arrowhead "factory" have recently come to light. Some years ago a bird watcher there was seen using apples as a lure, which he had casually picked on the island. These lemon scented apples were found to be a unique variety which had been cultivated perhaps some thousand or more years previously. This makes Bardsey an "Avalon" – an "apple island" – with its own unique variety of *afal* cultivated through the years during which the Avalon and Merlin mythologies were formulated and perpetuated. Bardsey's isolation and quietude, laid like a memorial slab over those turbulent inner churnings of the awen, certainly suits it to be the alleged resting place of Merlin himself, where he is reputedly buried alongside some twenty thousand Celtic saints. This, then, introduces another "Avalon" – indeed another "Glass Island" – where, floating between two worlds, with only the saintly dead for company, Merlin called, as he had in Celyddon, to his otherworldly partner in magic, Gwendydd. For only Gwendydd could build for him the Ty Gwydyr, the house of glass between the worlds. This house of glass, like Taliesin's Avalonian island on Bala Lake, is, in the metaphor of glass, "seen then unseen" as the light of human perception passes, more often than not, unheedingly through it. So it was that Merlin called there upon Gwendydd to build him an "observatory"; that is, of course, a tower with celestial emphasis. A note in the Peniarth manuscripts tells us that when this structure was complete Merlin collected the Thirteen Treasures of Britain and took them there.

That said, the majority of Neolithic and more especially Bronze Age ritual sites and burials were surrounded by a ditch, most of which are silted up now. However at times of rain/fertility these would presumably have filled with water, giving the burial mound the intentional and symbolic appearance of an island.

Islands had a special place in the Brythonic mysteries. The excavation of a late Bronze Age ritual complex at *Fengate* near Peterborough showed the deliberate construction of an avenue over eight hundred metres long and an artificial island some hundred and forty metres wide ... the whole utilising about four million pieces of timber in its construction! Surrounding this, along with human and animal sacrificial remains and jewellery, were such items as deliberately broken swords, bringing to mind the votive lake of *Llyn Cerrig Bach* on Anglesey.

Our most obvious example of an artifical island (at Glastonbury it would have been natural) is *Silbury Hill* sited in the most impressive Neolithic/Bronze Age area of Britain … the complex of *Avebury/West Kennet/Stonehenge* and other important monuments. Whether Silbury Hill contained a burial or was simply a ritual site has yet to be proved archaeologically, but what is certain is that a great deal of trouble was taken to construct a synthetic island, a proto-Avalon. It was built at the end of the Neolithic era or beginning of the Bronze Age and was in effect a massive model (it is forty metres high and covers some five and a half acres!) of the round barrows which were subsequently to be constructed through the Bronze Age … though not on anything like this scale! It is estimated that it would have taken some five hundred men something like ten years to construct it.

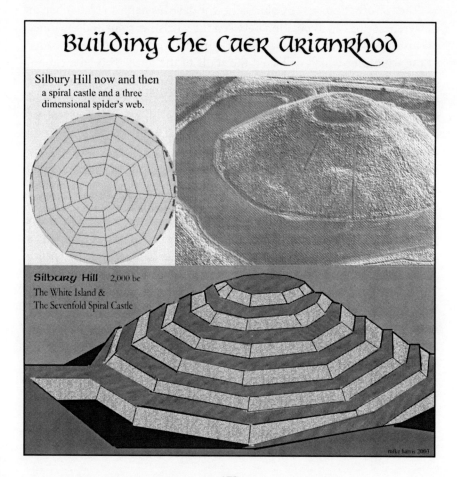

Building the Caer Arianrhod

Silbury Hill now and then
a spiral castle and a three
dimensional spider's web.

Silbury Hill 2,000 bc
The White Island &
The Sevenfold Spiral Castle

mike harris 2001

Whilst the 'natural' island of Glastonbury has the construction of a spiralling path/maze leading up the evocatively shaped Tor, Silbury had the same sevenfold steps to its flat summit.

This made it a "spiral castle" and an island, both elements enabling Silbury Hill, like the Tor and indeed Bardsey Island, to meet the appropriate Avalonian/Otherworld criteria. As at Silbury however, there seems to be no evidence on the Tor of an important prehistoric burial. A couple of south facing, and therefore presumably pre-Christian, burials were found but archaeology (on the summit at least) does not seem to have found any marked mortuary or ritual evidence. The indications are that through the ages there seems to have been fairly mundane occupation with some metal working being undertaken (not that the mythology of metalworking doesn't have Underworld significance!) Legend however gives the Tor great significance as an entrance to Annwn.

The *Life of St Collen*, the Celtic saint who gave his name to Llangollen in Powys, describes an altercation between the Christian saint and the inner occupant of the Tor, *Gwyn ap Nudd*, king of Annwn/Faery and leader of the wild hunt which collected the souls of the dead. This 'altercation' may however be a later interpolation of Christian orthodoxy. A number of good Christians, even clerics, have enjoyed cordial relations with and experience in the Underworld, not least the Scottish seer the Rev. Robert Kirk. Gwyn ap Nudd also appears in the *Culwch ac Olwen* Mabinogi tale as a knight of Arthur's court! It may be that we will find little on the summit of the Tor to do with the Underworld, because as Taliesin's puns constantly remind us, it is *beneath* the mounds and thus deep inside the earth that we find his *Caers*.

St Collen (having presumably moved south from Powys into Somerset) is, however, said to have established his solitary cell at what is known as the *White Spring* at the foot of the Tor, and it is here, where the spring issues from the rock into a brick chamber, that an entrance beneath the Tor exists. I am reliably informed that this entrance and others, though now inaccessible, constitute a substantial cave system, which would have been a much more likely place for burial and Underworld ingress and ritual. The Elizabethan Magus Dr. John Dee, astrologer and advisor to Elizabeth I (who was, according to Spenser, a *Faery Queen* ... if in name only!) and exponent of the *Enochian* magical system, is said to have used caves beneath the Tor to do "star magic", and as we shall see there are considerable stellar allusions in this and other Taliesin poems, confirmed, as we shall see in our next chapter, by actual star maps upon the landscape. In this connection, it is interesting that the *Triads* cite

Gwyn ap Nudd, the Faery King of Glastonbury Tor, as being one of the three great astronomers of Britain!

Be that as it may, the Tor seems to have been, not surprisingly, a sacred place from a very long time ago. Its pre-Christian dedication to the Underworld powers seems to have been implicit in the later erection of the Christian church dedicated to St Michael (archangelic commander of the armies of light) at the summit, of which only the tower now remains. The remainder of the church collapsed in a mediaeval earthquake, perhaps implying that the shadowy Underworld powers refused to be suppressed! It is also interesting to speculate upon the St Collen connection, in that Llangollen, Collen's other location, is dominated by a similar Tor-like feature, the hill called *Dinas Bran*, dedicated to Bran. Again, there seems room to speculate upon St Collen's interpretation of Christian orthodoxy!

Whilst the initial Underworld Arthurian connection with Glastonbury may be implied in Arthur's association with Gwyn ap Nudd mentioned in *Culwch ac Olwen*, the weight of Arthurian legend relies not on the Tor but on the Abbey ruins at its foot, where a Celtic Christian wattle church is said to have stood. Henry II (father of Richard the Lionheart and husband of the remarkable Eleanor of Aquitaine the queen who inspired, as we saw, something of a bardic revival in the form of the Trouvères or troubadours) is said to have learned from a Welsh "Druid" (in as much as they then existed!) that Arthur and Guinevere were buried at Glastonbury. We have touched upon King Henry's motives in seizing the opportunity to mortalise the immortal Arthur, and lay him to rest along with Welsh aspirations of nationhood! But not surprisingly, when a fire destroyed Abbey buildings shortly afterwards and money needed to be raised, the monks got digging and soon reported that they had found the grave of Arthur and Guinevere. From this it is easy to see how the connection between Arthurian legend, Brigid legend, the Grail (with the Joseph of Arimathea story) and Glastonbury as Avalon (incorporating the Gwyn/St Collen myth) developed.

Whatever the factual truth of any of the Glastonbury legends, the fact that our Taliesin poem cites Glastonbury, and the fact that it has (especially in recent years) become a national shrine, tends to make the location self-authenticating.

The books associating Arthur, Merlin and even Taliesin with Glastonbury would doubtless, if collected together, reach the height of the Tor itself, and it is not our place to add to them. Suffice to say that in our context, Taliesin says *"beyond Caer Wydyr they behold not the prowess of Arthur"* which seems to suggest that he knew exactly what Arthur was and only the ignorant would be taken in by Henry's ruse to unearth an historical but very dead Arthur! We are reminded again of the Welsh poet's assertion *"anoeth bid bedd y arthur"* meaning that there is no location for the grave of Arthur … even if the weight of legendary material tends to drown such poetic assertions.

In addition to the Arthur legend, there was the St Joseph legend, that placed the founding of British Christianity at Glastonbury. This coupled with legends that Joseph had brought the Grail (the 'new cauldron') to Glastonbury, added to the inevitable (though not necessarily too fantastical) legend that he had also brought Christ there as a child, gave tremendous mythological momentum to the place. Added to this the legend that Brigid, the rumoured foster mother of the divine child, had spent time in Glastonbury, completed this mythological tour de force. The power of such projection of the racial psyche upon a place with this weight of mythological, archetypal significance tends to 'validate' the location in a way which makes historical verification irrelevant. Belief makes the place what it is. The marriage of William Blake's words ("And did those feet in ancient time" etc) to Parry's music in the hymn *Jerusalem*, which has since become a second, unofficial, English national anthem, seems to prove the point!

5. *Caer Golur* is the gloomy castle … a fairly obvious observation to make about a burial chamber or indeed any of the Caers of death to which many go and only a few return! However, as we shall see in our next chapter, the pun may conceal a reference to Gwydion.

6. *Caer Fandwy* is translated by Graves and Davies as "the castle on high". This would seem to refer not simply to a mound but the stellar allusions of "star prisons". These are both high in the night sky and, to Bronze Age thinking at least, at the same time deep in the Underworld. The point being that whilst we are in spatial description travelling 'down' into the darkness of inner earth, we are also being invited to see this equally as the deep darkness of interstellar space. In this the Glastonbury pun which we have just discussed, about "glass" castles and the Welsh word *glas* meaning "blue" is expanded. The twinkling slivers of "glass" in the deep "glas"/blue of the night sky are the stars and star prisons of the goddess Arianrhod. Whilst this is something that we shall expand upon shortly, we might also note that *Fandwy* in spoken Welsh may be taken appropriately to mean "the castle of/in two places". We may be able to see why in our next chapter.

John Matthews, in his book *Taliesin*, suspects that *Fandwy* is a corruption of *Manddwy* and from this makes the Caer sacred to the sea god *Manawydan*. Whilst there may be some justification in aligning such symbolism with the "deep blue" and the imagery of the "sea of space", I am not personally convinced that this was the bard's intention.

7. *Caer Ochren*. Matthews's assertion that Caer Ochren may be a pun on (*Caer*) *Achren* from the *Cad Goddeu* (Battle of the Trees) poem is more convincing. It is however clear that the Welsh word *Ochr* means "side", from which Graves assumes "sloping side" which whilst not being technically accurate, nonetheless fits the continued imagery of a burial mound. Davies translates it as "the side which produces life", seeing the *en* as an abbreviation of the Welsh word for "life force" or "soul", *enaid*. There may be something in this, in that the mound is the entrance to the deep places of the cauldron – and the cauldron gave, transformed and restored life.

But let us see how Taliesin's remaining riddles fall into place:

The journey

Before Taliesin takes us on his tour of the Caers he arranges a theological safety net for himself by prefacing his inner travelogue with praise to the Almighty as *"supreme ruler of the heavens who has extended his kingdom to the shores of the world."* Whilst the allusions of the poem are extremely archaic, this Taliesin was writing at a time when Christianity was established to the extent that the old Celtic Church had long since been doomed by the Synod of Whitby in 663 AD. Wales was therefore by this poet's time very much a Roman Catholic country, and heresy was not something to court lightly for the good of one's body or one's soul! It may even be that, Templar allusions aside, our "Taliesin" was a cleric like so many of his bardic predecessors, and thus only too aware of the need for such a dogmatically correct preface; cleric or not, he doubtless was a Christian. Experience shows that the assumption that Christian belief and occult practice (rightly understood) are mutually exclusive is erroneous. Certain Christian clerics, as we have already said, have enjoyed cordial relations with the Underworld. John Dee is one example of a devout Christian and one time cleric who was actively engaged in occultism in the sixteenth century. We have also cited the instance in the seventeenth century of the Rev. Robert Kirk, a translator of the Bible into Gaelic, and author of *The Secret Commonwealth of Elves, Fauns and Fairies* who is said to have passed into Annwn. There were also countless others who, before the grip of the inaptly named Holy Inquisition was weakened by the Renaissance, were a little more reticent about their Underworld activities.

Gwair in Caer Sidi

Having, by the grace of God, taken us to *"the shores of the world"*, Taliesin invites us to dive into the murky deeps of Annwn where we encounter the legend of the imprisonment of *Gwair*. We must beware of the distracted copyist here and the possibility that *Gwair* may have been *Gweir*. If such were the case, *Gweir* would be Gwydion … hence Lundy Island was sacred to Gwydion and was called as we have already observed *Ynys Weir* (the G is dropped in the mutation of the phrase). The Taliesin cult had always seen Gwydion as the archetypal bard. He was, so the Mabinogi romance of *Math fab Mathonwy* tells us, "the greatest storyteller", a master magician, and more significantly, the brother/lover of the star goddess Arianrhod, who presides over a "prison" in Caer Sidi. Hence the *"spite of Pwyll and Pryderi"* both of whom, father and son, were keepers of the cauldron and guardians of Annwn. Gwydion, as we have told, tricked Pryderi and stole the sacred swine from the Underworld and subsequently exacerbated a war in which Pryderi was killed. This tale outlined in *Math* is structured on some half-remembered star myth which we shall attempt to reconstruct in our next chapter. In this, it seems that Arianrhod probably tricked her youthful brother Gwydion into becoming her lover. Whilst the original myth is lost in its entirety it may have been perpetuated in the later tale of Morgan le Fey seducing her youthful half-brother Arthur. The trickery/imprisonment/seduction theme is also reiterated in the tale of Merlin and Nimué. Of these Gwydion would, however, certainly have been *"the first to go there"*. As to the *"heavy blue chain"* that held him, we have already seen that on one level of interpretation these are the waters surrounding the Underworld island. In Gwydion's case this watery "chain" had the onomastic outer location of Lundy Island, from which only the seven-fold company of the Blessed head of Bran were to eventually return. On the other hand if Gwydion represented the new cult "from overseas" that overthrew the indigenous Bran cult, then his incursion into these islands may for a time have been held by the "heavy blue chain" of the sea.

Alternatively, if the copyist is correct and the poet means *Gwair*, we are talking about a vague figure from some other fragmented myth. Matthews, taking his lead from the notoriously unreliable *Triads of Britain*, seems to go along with Professor Malcolm Smith's view that *Gwair* is the *Gair ap Geirion* (of Triad 61) who was heir to a continuing period of family imprisonment that lasted for three generations. He echoes Smith's view that this Gwair is rather like *Mabon* the abducted youth/child liberated by Arthur in *Culwch ac Olwen*. The possibility that Taliesin is deliberately misleading *all* of us here should not of course be overlooked!

Bedwyr, the cauldron and Caer Pedryfan

When Taliesin takes us to Caer Pedryfan, we are no longer in the star/ island/prisons of the goddess Arianrhod but in the depths of a Bronze Age burial mound leading down into the deep inner earth and the precincts of Ceridwen's kingdom where the cauldron of transformation and rebirth is to be found. This is the castle of those who are remade and transformed into the bardic paradisal ideal in the goddess's cauldron. As to the cauldron having "pearls" about its rim, it seems likely, as we shall later see, that these pearls represent the circlet of stars which form the Pleiades. The nine maidens whose breath warms the cauldron would be the nine planets. The ancients frequently talked of *nine planets* in that they included the lunar nodes, approximately and mythologically at either end of Draco, in their scheme of the solar system. Malory indicates this practice when he writes about Uther (Pendragon!) on his way to meet the Saxons in battle. Uther and his men see a great star ... *"stretching forth one ray whereon was a ball of fire spreading forth in the likeness of a dragon and from the mouth of the dragon issued forth two rays, whereof the one was of such length as it did seem to reach beyond the region of Gaul, and the other, verging toward the Irish sea did end in seven lesser rays"*. We shall be meeting these two additional "rays" in the solar scheme in our next chapter. Meanwhile we shall return to the cauldron and the *awen* (and bardic mystification!) which rises from it.

"The first word from the cauldron, when was it spoken?" is another bit of bardic double talk, because those warriors who were brought back to life in Bran's cauldron had lost the power of speech. This parallels the Thomas the Rhymer Underworld experience where Thomas on his return is unable to speak of the things which he saw in the Underworld/Faery realm. This is because a fallen world cannot accept the truths enshrined in an area/mode of being which holds the paradisal/Edenic patterns of being which would restore humanity to unfallen perfection.

This Edenic idea is hammered home by the image of the place being guarded by a flashing sword. The sword however is not wielded by the traditional Cherubim of Genesis, but by *Bedwyr*, or as later Arthurian legend called him, *Sir Bedivere*. In the original poem he is called *Llyminawg* which means one of severe, not to say 'sharp' aspect, a suitable aphorism for a swordsman! But it is certainly Bedwyr who is being referred to, for it was Bedwyr who was the one who was charged with the final brief stewardship of Excalibur (or *Caledfwlch* as the weapon was originally called) and who eventually returned the sword to the Lady of the Lake ... the *Gwraig Annwn* of so many Welsh legends. It is therefore Bedwyr, the one who stands at the edge of Annwn holding the sword of destiny, the sole survivor of the last battle at Camlan, and the one who saw "Arthur of mournful memory" go into Avalon/Annwn, who has earned the honour to guard the gates to the Underworld.

Bedivere's Welsh name probably derives from *Bedw*, the word which means birch. In an old folk song *The Wife of Ushers Well*, the wife has three sons return from the dead at midwinter, with their hats of birch bark from the tree which grows at the gates of paradise. The birch tree in Graves's Tree alphabet/calendar interpretations is assigned to midwinter. It will also be noted that witches traditionally find their Underworld powers of flight with the aid of birch brooms and that *Bran mac Febhail* received his invitation to the Underworld by receiving a silver branch, presumably of silver birch. Bedwyr the "birch hero" is therefore an apt choice for the one to guard the gates of Annwn. It is interesting that this seems to have been archaeologically borne out in the Hochdorf burial of the Celtic chieftain, where the dead man was laid to rest with a birch bark hat!

The Royal Caer

Taliesin then takes us on to a place between twilight and *"black night"*, an apt description of entering a burial mound, and thence to Caer Rigor the Royal Caer. In that *"blood red wine was the drink of our host"* this would seem to have allusions to the bloody cult of sacred kings that we have described. Despite the obvious Eucharistic interpretation, of this being the Mass of *the* Sacred King, we should also note that bread and wine were elements of the sacred feast of Mithras and other pre-Christian deities. If *Rigor* is, however, a pun for *Rigel* the "star of death" in Orion, then the "host" of Caer Rigor/Rigel would probably have been drinking wine red blood, rather than as quoted "blood red wine". This may well be the case in view of the mention of a "four cornered enclosure" which would again seem to refer to a Bronze Age burial cist, with all the gory attendant rites of sacrifice that we have previously detailed. The fact that these rites and the Celtic syntheses of them which came after were very much to do (as Bran shows us) with the defence of the realm would prompt the mention of "The Island of the strong door" in that this has generally been taken to mean Britain. We must however, by now, be alerted to any mention of "islands". Annwn is so obviously an island (albeit between the worlds) and the bards were, as we have seen, very concerned that the door to that inner island was strong and well guarded.

Caer Wydyr

The experience in Caer Wydr is again reminiscent of episodes in *Culhwch ac Olwen*, which is interesting in view of the fact that some prominence is given in this story to Gwyn ap Nudd the Underworld/Faery king reputed to have lived under Glastonbury Tor; except that in *Culhwch* he is one of Arthur's war band, albeit with supernatural powers. In *Culhwch ac Olwen* Arthur and his men have to confront various sentinels and gatekeepers in their mission to help Arthur's nephew *Culhwch* achieve a number of seemingly impossible tasks so that he may win the hand of *Olwen*, the daughter of the chief giant *Ysbaddaden*. This story from the *Red Book of Hergest* is, of all the later Mabinogi romances, the one least touched by the Anglo Norman influences on Welsh bardism. It again offers a possible insight into the conflict between the cult of Arthur and the cult of the (giant) Bran. The Underworld theme is emphasised in that Culhwch is found in a pig pen ... hence his name. "Hwch" was a type of pig, the animal sacred to Ceridwen, and *Olwen* means *"(she of the) white track"*, a peculiar evocation of the Annwn/white metaphor and of the Milky Way. Culhwch is also described as riding forth with a square purple cloak that has an apple of red gold at each corner ... reminiscent of the cloth of invisibility in the supernatural *Gwyddbwyll* game that Arthur plays with his other nephew Owein in the *Dream of Rhonabwy*.

An apple cut open reveals a five pointed star at its heart. This would of course give the association between the five-fold Hercules rites and the golden apples of the Hesperides and/or Avalon, the inner island where the dead king journeyed towards the stars. The sacred king theme seems to be hinted at in *Culhwch*'s cloak not only having an apple motif at each corner but also being of regal purple. That the gory sequence of the Hercules rites made any sacred king 'invisible', both by virtue of the breaking apart and disposal of his body and his departure to "another place", would seem to confirm this. Moving through death to the paradisal state would also mark the apple as the appropriate paradisal fruit, as in the biblical Genesis story, where, conversely, by eating the fruit Adam and Eve come to know death. As we shall see, this association is carried forward in the Gwyddbwyll game of sovereignty, the game that the king, or his bard, must play with the inner powers to bring the paradisal ideals into outer reality in his kingdom.

There are more practical hints here too perhaps, which take us into the realms of "sleeves up" magic! The fact that we are dealing with Caer Wydyr, a "glass island", and the fact that it was "difficult to speak with their sentinel", seems to carry through the idea of Gwyddbwyll and invisibility. That Gwyddbwyll may have been played with glass or quartz crystal pieces, and that it conferred invisibility and entry into realms not normally perceptible to mortal sight, is interesting. Human sight operates on the electromagnetic frequency of visible light, and the material required to view the spectrum, showing the constituent colours of white light, is glass. Higher electromagnetic frequencies beyond the wavelength of light require other materials, not least quartz crystal which enables the spectrum of the ultra violet frequency "on the edge of visible light" to be perceived. Old legends suggest that Faeries become invisible by turning sideways … i.e. to the edge of light. Many burials in North Wales in the period we are considering were covered with quartz crystal. This may have been simply for decoration or to give the "white" metaphor of Annwn, but one is tempted to wonder if there was an awareness that quartz was a means to perceive other realms beyond visible light. The implications of such "weird physics" will be discussed in our final chapter. We may only conclude our considerations of Caer Wydyr, the glass castle, by noting the way that the poet's mind was working when he came to consider this Caer. At face value *"Further than Caer Wydyr they can never see Arthur"* is understandable enough in view of King Henry's supposed exhumation of the Bear king, but the wording that the poet uses suggests that his mind is working along the lines of "how far can one see?" … an interesting thought in view of our latter speculations.

The white ship and the triple goddess

From Caer Wydyr, Arthur and his band set sail again in *Prydwen,* Arthur's ship. The name simply means "of white aspect", the standard Underworld metaphor as we have already seen. It may also suggest invisibility. Malory also gives *Prydwen* as the name of Arthur's shield and there were countless mythological examples of shields which conferred invisibility.

We must also consider that a shield and a *coracle* (the small saucer shaped boat which may still be seen in Carmarthenshire) would not have been dissimilar and the Round Table/shield arrangement may refer to other more esoteric modes of moving between states of being, practiced *in the round* within henges, and the stone circles which frequently formed the perimeters of Bronze Age burials. *"Three times the capacity of Prydwen"* is a way of saying that journeys to the Underworld, whilst seeming to be in seven phases, have a three fold/triple aspect. This is because such journeys inevitably result in an encounter with what Graves termed the "triple goddess". This feminine power, whose essence and paradisal pattern is mediated to the kings of humankind by the Faery women of Annwn, is, as we have repeatedly seen, the bestower

THE SPOILS OF ANNWN

and empowerer of sovereignty. Graves also described her as the "white goddess" (again we see this encapsulated in the "white ship" *Prydwen*, and the use of the adjective "white" to describe her underworld realm) whose triple persona can be met with in various of the Mabinogi myths. The story of *Math fab Mathonwy* showed us these three aspects, in *Arianrhod*, the (seemingly) virgin star goddess, *Blodeuwedd* the woman made from flowers, and *Ceridwen* the goddess symbolised by a flesh-eating sow. It will be seen that, events in this story notwithstanding, these three variously represent archetypal functions of a Mother goddess of an Underworld which encompasses respectively the stars, the paradisal garden and the deep earth. It should be emphasised that these are however intended to illustrate three archetypal functions of *one* goddess.

The oxen, the plough and the furrow

Passing through Caer Golur the gloomy castle, Taliesin urges courage in the gloom ... not least the gloom of a lost Wales, at the time this poem was written. He says "*I won't praise men with trailing shields*" adding that they don't know the day of *Cwy's* birth. *Cwy* has posed something of a puzzle for scholars and esoteric interpreters alike. The Welsh word *cwys* means *furrow*, and because a furrow is scribed by a *plough*, it may seem that this is again some fragment of lost star lore ... not least in that the Plough stars are the stars of the Great Bear, with apposite Arthur connotations.

The furrow occurs in a number of legends which apply to the "*brindled ox*" (mentioned in the next line of the poem) who is used to draw the plough in a number of Welsh folk tales, notably that of the *Ychen Bannog* ("oxen-long horned") of Llandewi Brefi and as the animals of the *gwraig annwn*/lady of the lake of Llyn y Fan Fach. Ychen Bannog are reckoned to have been a particular type of long-horned brindled cattle which were prized in Wales from the Iron Age and through the Dark Age. The ploughing and furrow motif is applicable to both the plough and the bear as we have seen. Indeed a bear will plough the earth with its claws to expose grubs and other things to eat. The imagery also suits the internment of a sacred king in that, like a plough, he enters the earth, penetrating the land to make it fertile ... a good metaphor for the consummation of his marriage to the goddess/earth mother.

But *Cwy* here may be a person, and the day of his birth and the fact that he was prevented from going down to Devwy dale obviously has considerable significance. *Devwy/Defwy* may be *Dyfrdwy* the Welsh name for the River Dee and certainly the vale of Dee encompassing the Bala/Corwen area has, as we have seen, much ancient and mythological significance, and seems to have been the focus of a number of Bronze Age mortuary/ritual sites. We can only assume that Cwy was some star hero who was onomastically associated with that area and that his failure to fulfil some destiny there had great esoteric implications. But Taliesin won't let us get away that easily, he hasn't finished with his plough/furrow riddles.

"*They don't know the brindled ox with the thick headband and seven jewels on his collar*" … and here we can be much more sure of what Taliesin is talking about. The brindled ox is a creature of Annwn who makes an appearance in the Mabinogi myth of *Culhwch and Olwen,* and in various myths about the long-horned *Ychen Bannog.* It may also of course represent the constellation of Taurus, the Bull, and the "*seven jewels on his collar*" are the stars called the Pleiades or *seven sisters,* which sit upon the bull's shoulder.

Che pleiades and the Great Year

To the naked eye the Pleiades circle of what appear to be seven stars (there are in fact many more) sit upon the shoulder of the constellation of Taurus the Bull. These "*seven sisters*" rose in November at *Samhain,* announcing the start of the Celtic year. This was when the ploughman broke up the frozen earth and, in that opening up of the earth, the long dead sacred kings came out from under the mountain, leading the dead to feast with the living – at the time that our children still, ghoulishly, celebrate as *Halloween.* The Pleiades set again in May at *Beltane* when the sun was beginning to get hotter, the days longer and everything was beginning to bloom. So the rising of the Pleiades announced the nearness of winter, but when they set it could be seen that summer wouldn't be long in coming. The associations of the Pleiades with obvious cycles like birth, fertility and death will be clear. For this and other reasons, the rising and setting of the Pleiades were of considerable importance to the Celts and to other ancient peoples in the northern hemisphere, and no less so to our Taliesin initiate.

As we recall from our earlier chapter and perhaps our schooldays, the seasonal cycles of the year are created by the tilt of the Earth's axis at twenty-three and a half degrees to the orbital plane. To briefly recap and expand upon our axis theme, we may imagine the earth as an apple with a pencil stuck through it to represent this axis. The pencil will always be inclined at twenty-three and a half degrees, with the Earth/apple spinning around it, and the whole arrangement with the rest of the planets revolving around the sun making a complete orbit in a year. The earth's angle, relative to its orbital plane around the sun, the *ecliptic*, defines the seasonal points of solstices and equinoxes. In other words, the relative position of the sun to the axial angle of the Earth, offering greater or lesser heat and light to either the northern hemisphere or southern hemisphere, provides climatic seasonal variations. The equinoxes which announce the onset of spring and autumn are the points where the earth is at such an angle to the sun that day and night are of equal length. The solstices marking summer and winter are when the earth is at such an angle that we have the longest day (summer solstice) or the longest night (winter solstice). As our solar system plunges through space with this cycle recurring year on year, however, there is a further variable.

For thousands of years the axis of the earth has appeared to point to Polaris, the North Star in the constellation of the Little Bear. Consequently we can look at this star and see that whilst the constellations revolve, and some (those that are not *circumpolar*) disappear and reappear, the Pole Star holds its position, because in terms of our illustration of the apple, it's the star that the pencil always points to. Well almost.

In fact, due to the gravitational struggle between the sun, moon and planets and the earth's gyroscopical inertia, the pencil point, whilst retaining its twenty-three and a half degree angle, is scribing a very gradual circle of its own. This means that every year the relationship of the Earth's axis to the stars moves a little, which also means that the orientation of the earth to the sun at the vernal equinox isn't quite the same each year. Whilst the movement of the direction of the Earth's axis from one Pole Star to another star takes many thousands of years, the effect on our viewing of the zodiacal belt of constellations around us does have a slightly shorter term effect. Whilst, for example, we are now experiencing the vernal equinox point as corresponding to the constellation of Pisces, it is on the verge of moving into the constellation of Aquarius (hence all the hullabaloo about the "age of Aquarius"). This apparent *precession* westwards through the constellations of the zodiac is known, in its twelve-fold totality, as the *Great Year of the Pleiades,* or a *Platonic Year.* Each *Platonic Year* is some twenty-six thousand solar years long!

The Egyptians were aware of this cycle, as were the Greeks, the Celts and other ancient civilisations. In terms of the equinoctial cycle of the seasons and the earth's fertility it is interesting to note that the Incas held the Pleiades in especial reverence to protect cereal crops. The fact that the cycle of the precession of the equinoxes was seen to be governed by the Pleiades can be seen in their naming from Greek mythology.

The Pleiades were the daughters of Atlas and Pleoine. Atlas is essentially remembered for being the Titan who was sentenced by Zeus to hold the axle of the Earth in place and support the Earth and heavens. In this of course we see the mythological concern over the astronomical fact of the movement of the Earth's axial relationship to the heavens. This also recalls that ancient, universal idea of the tower and the "tentpole of the heavens" ... the Celts were afraid that the sky might fall. In Greek mythology, the Pleiades or seven sisters came to be in the heavens after being pursued by the lustful Orion, having invoked Zeus who foiled Orion by turning them into doves. The Egyptians on the other hand saw the action of the Pleiades in marking out this cosmic cycle as that of the goddess *Neith* weaving the web of the heavens with the axis as her shuttle.

This, as we shall see, is a theme which also held good in Celtic mythology. In fact this symbolism would be known to our Taliesin initiate, particularly as associated with Arianrhod. Her spinning/weaving symbolism resulted, so he tells us, in this spider-like goddess incarcerating him in her starry web/prison on three occassions!

In terms of the Greek myths, Arianrhod's counterpart is Ariadne, the spinner of the thread by which the hero Theseus found his way out of the labyrinth, having killed the bull-like Minotaur (which provides the connection with Taurus and to some degree with the Persian/Roman Mithraic mysteries). The whole object of Theseus's Underworld journey was to rescue Persephone, which he did with the help of Hercules, the archetypal sacrificed hero king who as we have seen was subjected to a five-fold death as a sacred king.

Various mythologies and prophecies have not unnaturally associated the Pleiades as cosmic milestones for the coming and going of epochs in the evolution of the world. The Manicheans held that at the end of time, Atlas, father of the seven sisters, would walk away from the Earth and allow the sky to tumble. Geoffrey of Monmouth's *Prophecies of Merlin* also invoke the Pleiades at the closing of the age. To early peoples, such holocaust would be largely symbolised by agricultural failure. And again Taliesin provides clues to the appropriate images by invoking the plough, the furrow and the oxen in the scribing of this great cosmic circle. Again we have to consider the word *cwys* meaning a furrow.

We have already mentioned the practice of a ploughman using his oxen to scribe a circular furrow from a central, sacred point to mark out the consecrated ground of early Celtic churchyards ... "God's little acre". We gave as an example of this the church dedicated to St Illtyd at Llanelltyd near Dolgellau, situated curiously within a stone's throw from the place where the manuscript material which was to comprise the Mabinogi was brought together many centuries later. Dominating the view from here is the great ridge of Cadair Idris, Taliesin's "uneasy chair". That our Taliesin was familiar with this landscape now seems to be implicit in this poem because the Pleiades were called in Welsh *Twr Tewdws* ... the "tower of Theodosius". Presumably this was the first Roman emperor of that name, Theodosius the Great – the other, second Theodosius was rather unnoteworthy and ineffectual! Theodosius the Great would have been pretty much the last of the Romans to take the defence of Britain seriously, which would have stood him in good stead, except for the fact that in real history he killed one of the heroes of the Mabinogi, Macsen Wledig! He was in fact the Roman emperor of the Eastern Empire who historically put down Macsen's attempt to take the imperial crown. The Mabinogi romance *The Dream of Macsen Wledig* tells, erroneously, of Macsen using the native cunning of his Brythonic in-laws to take Rome and become emperor. This would all be completely irrelevant were it not for the legend that one of Theodosius's soldiers was reputed to be a certain *Illtyd*.

This is of course the great St Illtyd, teacher of Maelgwyn Gwynedd, who exchanged sword for sackcloth to become one of the celebrated fathers of the Celtic church. It is to him that this little church of St Illtyd at Llanelltyd, with its ploughed/rounded enclosure, is dedicated. The agricultural metaphor is emphasised when we turn to the (albeit not very reliable) *Triads*. Triad 56 tells us of "*Hu Gadarn who taught the Cambrians how to plough when they were in the Summer country, before they came to the isle of Britain*" and of "*Elltud (Illtyd) the holy knight of Theodosius, who improved the mode of ploughing land.*" Illtyd, it seems, in addition to being a celebrated father of the Celtic church, had also turned his sword into a ploughshare. We are tempted to wonder what he told Maelgwyn about ploughing ... or the mythology associated with it!

This Triad hasn't finished with us yet though! It has mentioned *Hu Gadarn* ... "Hu the Mighty" as he is usually known. As the Triad implies, Hu was the character who Geoffrey called "Brutus". It was Hu who brought the Britons from "the Summer country" where he'd taught them how to plough. He becomes in this the founding father of the Welsh Celts, although he makes scant appearance among the gods that we know the pre-Christian Celts to have worshipped. In his mention of him Graves makes the unassociated and peculiar statement that "*Hu*" means "dove" in Sumerian. This would be completely spurious were it not for our consideration of the *doves* of the Pleiades! A further peculiarity here is that the correct translation of Hu's second name, *Gadarn*, would seem in fact not to mean *mighty* so much as *warrior!* We thus have a name embodying the contrast of a warrior and a dove!

As ever, it is doubtful that such subtleties escaped Taliesin, who, it will be remembered, was reputed to have harangued Maelgwyn's ignorant bards for their lack of esoteric understanding. Taliesin would also know that doves had been associated with the oak god/Hercules/sacrificed king cult which we have already discussed in terms of making *the king and the land one* ... that the land may be fertile and the tribe prosper. Furthermore, Hercules in his quest to secure the golden apples of the Hesperides (with their Avalonian, paradisal associations) enlisted the aid of Atlas!

The connections begin to become clear. Although the *Preiddu Annwn* was written down perhaps eight hundred years after the time of Maelgwyn, the Taliesin tradition shows us how, where and why it planted the roots of its starry Arthur tradition. In doing so it transplanted the ploughing metaphor with the bull, or oxen, and especially the furrow, from the cult of sacred kings as it was symbolised in the earlier Bronze Age culture. In this planting, St Illtyd, as Maelgwyn's mentor, becomes seen as a reincarnation of Hu Gadarn, the original father of Celtic nationhood. The association with Illtyd and the Roman army, if not with Theodosius as such, seems to be historically correct because Illtyd did set up his abbey of Llantwit Major on what had been a considerable Roman estate. He seems, in this, to have returned to a place that he had once known and it may be that, like Myrddin, he had known tragedy and inner transformation at that place. This may be surmised from the fact that the archaeological evidence indicates that the Roman occupation of the Llantwit Major site ended in a massacre, a good enough reason to make the young Illtyd, as a survivor of such, lay down his sword and take up his cross.

Like Myrddin he seems to have taken up something else as well, for Illtyd was reputed to have the gift of prophecy, as well as great learning. Illtyd's monastery at Llantwit Major on the old Roman site seems to have had none of the austerity of the sites of the other great Celtic saints, like David. Indeed many of the great saints were actually pupils of Illtyd at this Avalonian haven in South Wales. His pupils may have been men of God, but they were not by any means meek and mild. There are a number of accounts of how they rallied and organised the local people as militia and fought alongside them to resist raiders. St Illtyd never, it seems, entirely forgot his Roman military roots.

In all this we again see the suspicious shadow of the concept of Arthur. Illtyd had the knowledge, the foresight and the authority to put across the vision of Arthur. Maelgwyn Gywnedd on the one hand, and the bards of the Taliesin ilk on the other, had the various means to turn the vision into a practical proposition.

It was probably Illtyd who named the Pleiades as the "tower of Theodosius". We can see that he might want to honour the emperor that he had served under, one of the last protectors of Britain; also, in his father of the Celtic church hat, to honour Theodosius as the first Roman emperor to legislate against paganism. But why should he tie all this up with the Pleiades?

There wouldn't have been a problem with knowing star lore, having the gift of prophecy and being a pillar of Christian Britain. We know from Gildas that it was quite acceptable to dabble in stellar mythology, and there were biblical precedents. The prophet Amos in the Old Testament had, after all, invoked the Pleiades as the instrument of God against ungodly Israel. We must also see that in their weaving symbolism the Pleiades could have been cited in connection with the apocryphal story of the Virgin Mary (of seven sorrows) being a weaver of the veil between manifestation and the unmanifest. Then there was also Mary Magdalene, Mary of Magdala, the place of doves, from whom Jesus had driven out "seven devils". And there was also of course St Brigid, who among other things was a patron of weavers. In a Celtic church working with a racial consciousness still steeped in goddess symbolism, the Pleiades could be not only validly, but usefully, invoked!

St Illtyd seems to have been a man of many talents and many parts, and all of them geared to getting a job done. His wisdom and knowledge, not to mention his down to earth, soldier-like common sense, soon placed him in a position of unassailable authority. One gets the impression that as the 'golden boy' of British Christendom, he was therefore in a position to do and say as he pleased, and it pleased him to be the prime mover in events where other churchmen, even other statesmen, may well have faltered. To what extent he discreetly stepped outside of the parameters of Christian orthodoxy in his dealings with, say, the Taliesin cult, we may never know. That they had the same objectives and were brothers in the experience of prophecy would certainly have drawn them together. Like them he had tasted awen, and the threads of awen lead back through that pre-Christian maze to the bloody rites of a people who had known and cherished the land of Britain two thousand years before.

This harking back to the origins of the Celtic mysteries in the Bronze Age becomes startlingly clear by the obvious understanding/tradition that during the early Bronze Age the precession actually passed through the Pleiades (in the constellation of Taurus). At this time, the time of the Beaker people, the Pleiades themselves were magnificently across the Vernal equinox. This was the time that Silbury Hill was built ... that great proto Isle of Avalon. To be such an "island" it was circumscribed by the massive ditch, the most impressive of "furrows" that the oxen of Hu Gadarn had ever ploughed! If Silbury is sacred to any god we can name, the name of that god must be Hu Gadarn!

The myths of Hu's Ychen Bannog were however invoked to go back to even more ancient Neolithic times, when the Pole Star would have been in the eye of the Bull ... that great red star Aldebaran. As ever, myth and folktale provide their own commentary.

The Llandewi Brefi and Llyn yr Afanc legends, whilst being onomastic, both seem to use the Ychen Bannog (long-horned oxen) to retain this same Pleiadean/Taurean star lore. In the Llandewi Brefi legend a lake called Llyn Llion that reputedly once flooded all of Britain was stopped from ever doing so again. The one who stopped this happening was, predictably, Hu Gadarn who enlisted the help of the Ychen Bannog to drag the cause of the trouble, a great *afanc,* or water monster, from the lake. These same oxen also, whilst helping to move stones for Llandewi Brefi church, opened a great furrow in the mountain (still known as *Cwys yr Ychen Bannog*) but in the effort one of them dropped dead. The other ox then died too, but before doing so gave nine bellows (the number of the goddess – 3x3) which caused a great rock to split open. A pair of Ychen Bannog were also used to extract another afanc, this time on the river Conwy, and in doing so the strain caused the eye of one of the oxen to fall out.

Here, in this latter tale, we have the more obvious fragments of star lore, where the ox's eye is obviously an allusion to the star Aldebaran, "the eye of the Bull", in the constellation of Taurus. Yet here the lake between Avalon and the mortal world, between the remains of the sacred king in his burial chamber and the world he has left, are still defended by some mighty ploughman whose oxen drag away anything that infests that pure lake between the worlds .

The fact that the Ychen Bannog are always in pairs, and that in the second Llandewi Brefi story, when one died the other followed suit in sympathy, may suggest that the constellation Gemini was also associated with these great cattle, who have since been identified as the *Bos primogenius* species who were in Wales up until the pre-Roman era. In stellar terms Gemini is adjacent to Taurus ... but that takes us further back again!

The upshot of all this is that Taliesin is describing the circle of the Sidi or in the Irish *Sidhe*. Eventually, having gone through that seven-fold initiatory journey, he came to the high bardic chair in Arianrhod's starry Caer. He sat where the sacred kings of old sat, the ancestors who had stood for Bran, and Math, and Hercules, the heroes who had preserved the sovereignty of Britain from a time when the Celts were but a gleam in the eye of the goddess. He sat with them and looked to a paradisal Wales that his Arthur of mournful memory had been unable to achieve.

Che Chief, the Owner of names and the Silver headed Beast

After another shot across the bows of those who would try to unravel these mysteries at intellectual arm's length, our Taliesin initiate finally drops his three last clues (or red herrings) into place.

"They don't know what day the chief arose
They don't know the hour of that splendid day that the owner was born
Or what silver headed animal they keep."

Chief, in the sense of chieftain, is *Pennaf* in Welsh, which gives a play or words/sounds between *Pennaf* and *Pen arth*. The latter being taken to mean *the chieftain of the bear,* who was of course Arthur. Again we are faced with the old "So you think that you can pin down Arthur" riddle. *Perchen* is the Welsh for owner, but *perchi* is the verb which implies reverence. Here we may look, as we did in chapter five, at the Gnostic Taliesin, well versed in Middle Eastern apocrypha. In the apocryphal gospel of pseudo-Matthew we find *"Then that which was spoken through the prophet Isiah was fulfilled. The ox knows his owner and the donkey his lord's manger"*. The owner of the ox is the Ploughman ... but who does this make the Ploughman – Jesus Christ or Arthur ... or even Mithras? Again the old Arthur riddle presents itself, but of course the one who named, armed and empowered Arthur in true Celtic fashion, and hence owned the name, was the goddess, even as Mary named her Son.

There are plenty of candidates for the silver headed animal, not least the hell hounds of Gwyn ap Nudd collecting the souls of the dead, but experience will by now have shown that conventional answers are not what are called for in this mythological crossword puzzle. By now we know Taliesin well enough to know that he can't stop himself if there is the chance of a pun and it would be too good to be true to think that he would get to the end of this poem (if indeed the version we have is complete!) without finishing with some deliciously witty riddle.

Every poet knows the feeling of getting to the end of a poem and the temptation to stamp his own lessons of life into its final lines as a kind of trademark. The Taliesin initiate's whole life experience was (and is) built upon his trials at the hands of the goddess who "breaks to make" her initiates. Like the most frantic of love affairs it's a bit of a love/loathe relationship. Because he wants to love her, praise her and adore her she puts him through hell. As Ceridwen to his Gwion she tries to kill him, as Blodeuwedd to his Llew she is unfaithful to him and plots his death, and as Arianrhod she denies him and incarcerates him three times. Yet through all this he becomes her bard, the rainbow-browed, star-crowned. She is Arian-rhod (silver-circlet) like the tiara of seven silver stars that are her home in the Corona Borealis, and she has placed her mark upon him. In fact he probably wore a silver fillet around his head (in addition to the corona shaped torc around his neck) in honour of her and is thus her silver headed creature … and creature in her name he had certainly been. He had been a silver greyhound, a silver salmon, a white stag whose shining head is silver, and a bard, a man of wisdom, a silver headed sage. She is the goddess, the land, the barrow and the bear cave and she owns Arth the bear, the name of Arthur and Math, and she owns Taliesin. Nobody knows when she was born because she is without beginning and end. She is Alpha and Omega, as Taliesin in one poem also (as her son) claims to be. But what of Arthur of "mournful memory"?

"Arthur", as we have seen, is what the Welsh, the true Brythons, once hoped for. He is the archetype of Brythonic sovereignty, empowered by the goddess who makes *the king and the land one*. But he was (certainly by the time that this poem was written) the dream that had died. He had become a memory at sleep under the goddess's mountain, on the island of ancient dreams across the lake of time, and for the time being his days of quest and raid were done.

CHAPTER NINE

Caer Idris

ARTHUR DID NOT of course die ... he was transformed. With him, Welsh aspirations were also transformed, and as Arthur, Merlin and Taliesin now reassert themselves in countless recent outpourings of books, workshops and films in a more universal sense, so Welsh aspirations have also transformed themselves to take on a more pragmatic and universal stance. At the time of writing this book, a Welsh assembly was being established, and a parliament, unknown since the brief ambitions of Owain Glyndŵr six hundred years ago, seems to be a very real possibility. At the same time Scotland has achieved its own parliament, albeit with limited powers. So now Celtic nationalism sees itself as a state which takes its place in a wider world, where its archetypal heroes sit on every bookshelf from Santa Fe to Shanghai! It is almost as if the patterns laid down by those bards of old are now resolving themselves, and as the Brythonic mysteries have survived for something like five thousand years, there is no reason to believe that the bardic magic they entailed should not have looked to the longer term for its resolution. There were however, certain victories in the meantime.

A Question of Patterns

One wonders whether the Taliesin initiate who wrote the *Preiddu Annwn* would have foreseen that within less than two hundred years a Welshman would sit upon the throne of England and found perhaps the greatest dynasty that these islands have ever seen. Would he have known that such a Tudor dynasty would furnish England and Wales with a queen more powerful and capable than any monarch before or since? Would he have foreseen that the same "Faery Queen" would look to the defence of the realm as readily as Bran, yet with all the cunning of Gwydion ... not to mention the bleak single-mindedness of Arianrhod? The patterns that the bards had set down in the racial psyche, the Brythonic folksoul, have always seemed, sooner or later, to have found their resolution in history.

The place where those patterns of destiny were woven so long ago by the Taliesin tradition, and the nature of their weaving, may still be seen. The patterns which *awen* forms and transforms in Annwn are, as we have already recognised, presented not only in a mythopoeic code of stars, goddesses and heroes, but also by sacred places upon the landscape.

There are places across every landscape, but particularly the Celtic landscape, where folk have instinctively realised down the ages that inner and outer worlds overlap. One of the more spectacular places where this occurs is Cadair Idris in South Gwynedd, the long ridge which starts up from the sea meadows of Cae Ddu and runs inland along the southern egde of the Mawddach estuary.

Above the village of Arthog the ridge soars up in the first sheer bastion of Craig y Llyn, overhanging lonely Cyri lake, then on and up at Craig Las, and on to the high wind-lashed rocks of Craig Llwyd before it soars up the sheer wall of Cyfry's faery castle. At Pen y Gader, *the head of the chair,* the ridge reaches its highest point of almost three thousand feet above the level of the sea, beneath which, geologists tell us, it had its beginnings. This is the highest continuous ridge in the Isles of Britain, a fragment of a once great volcano that thrust up from the primordial sea hundreds of millions of years ago to form a feature which geologists call the Harlech Dome. In some distant time the central part of this great dome, covering some thousand square miles, collapsed so that only the northern escarpment, which is Snowdon, and the southern escarpment, which is Cadair Idris, remained. Then the Ice Ages came, scouring the precipitous cliffs and cutting huge corries to hold the deep, dark lakes.

When the Bronze Age folk began making their way into Wales, one of the many places that they seem to have made landfall was where this ridge has it beginnings, around the Dysynni estuary. The much later missions of the seafaring Celtic saints Cadfan and Celynin to the same area would seem to indicate that this was a good, time-honoured place to come ashore.

From this coastal bridgehead, in the approximate area of the present day Rhoslefain, the Bronze Age folk established a trackway following the Cadair Idris ridge inland along its west-east flank. Their standing stones and burials still mark the route now known as the Ffordd Ddu, *the dark road,* that crosses the high moorland above the sea and the Mawddach estuary under the shadow of the Cadair ridge. The trackway is still in sporadic use, more than three thousand years later, and Iron

Age (Celtic) and mediaeval settlements, as well as the more recent farms, which the road connects with the old drovers' roads to the market town of Dolgellau, attest to this continuity of use. The ever rising bulk of Cadair Idris dominates the road, and one tends to feel that the many standing stones and barrows are by no means spiritually incidental to the shadow of this mountain which is as shrouded in mythology as it frequently is in cloud.

The name Cadair Idris literally means *the chair of Idris* and, inevitably, Idris was a giant. Along with Gwydion son of Dôn, and Gwyn son of Nudd, the *Triads* cite Idris as being one of the *three great astronomers of Britain* and it is said that from his heady chair on the fortress (Caer) of this great ridge, Idris not only mapped the heavens but was able to "*prognosticate whatever was wished to be known until the day of doom*". These qualities of astronomer and astrologer, of all-knowing, all-seeing star mage, whilst subject to the doubtful scholarship of Iolo Morganwg (compiler of the *Triads,* and romantic eighteenth century "improver" of early Celtic material) seem to have forgone the treatment of Iolo's florid imagination and to be based upon actual Brythonic mystery practice. As Robert Graves pointed out, Taliesin's initiatory experience in an "*uneasy chair above Caer Sidi*" described in the thirteenth century *Hanes Taliesin* would seem to refer to the *Cadair/chair* of Cadair Idris.

The Taliesin initiate who described this "uneasy chair" was talking about a chair of mythopoeic bardic knowledge ... the mythological power and complexity of which will by now have become apparent. The knowledge that he applied and the consequent power at his disposal were absolutely directed towards the concept of sovereignty. The signatures of that sovereignty were to be seen in the shape of the land and the patterns of the stars, and from the summit of Cadair Idris both were mythologically and actually apparent. This was, after all, where Idris the star mage had set his Caer, long before the coming of the Celts, when the land was ruled by Geoffrey of Monmouth's "giants". Indeed the mountain is shaped in great scooped out corries like a series of giant chairs, and there is a chair-like excavation in the rock at the summit. In the *Hanes Taliesin* (story of Taliesin) we have the boast of astronomical knowledge "*I know the names of the stars from North to South*", which, as the Idris legend indicates, we may assume to be part of Taliesin's initiatory experience.

A gold torc found some years ago on the precipitous Fox's Path approach to the summit of Cadair (known as Pen y Gadair, the "head of" *or highest/most esteemed chair*) may or may not prove the mountain to have been "Taliesin's chair". Yet when one stands at the old church of St Illtyd at Llanelltyd and looks across to this great natural fortress with its precipitous cliffs raking the sky, the question becomes not so much *if* Cadair Idris was the place of that chair, but rather *how could it not have been?*

Star patterns on the land

By some peculiar chance, of which the cult of Taliesin and their predecessors were well aware, a number of the high buttress/crag configurations upon Cadair Idris, together with its general shape, do mean that it can – almost exactly – represent the plan of the constellation Ursa Major, the Great Bear, upon the landscape. An ancient awareness of this is apparent in the naming of *Arthog* on one side of the mountain and *Peniarth* on the other. *Arth,* as we have seen, is the Welsh word for a bear. Arthog may therefore be the combination of two words … *arth* and *ogof.* Ogof means a cave, so we have on one side of the Cadair Idris ridge a bear's cave, associated with the stars of the Corona Borealis which the Welsh called the *Caer Arianrhod.* As if any further confirmation were needed, Arthog church, though not the original building, is dedicated to St Catherine, who with her associations with the wheel can be considered to be the Christian successor of Arianrhod ("Silver wheel"). On the other side of the ridge lies Peniarth … *the head of (or Chief of) the bear.* Peniarth would therefore seem to relate to the constellation of Boötes, sometimes known as the "bear ward".

In addition to this, the circular churchyard at Llanelltyd to the North, with its associations with St Illtyd and hence with the Plough, Hu Gadarn and the Pleiades, gives a further fit. Thus Llanelltyd becomes the pivotal point of this terrestial representation of the turning heavens, its *Pole Star,* the stationary point from which the ploughman/sacred king "scribes his furrow" and places himself at the centre of this microcosmic representation of an idealised kingdom shown in the stars. There is a stone, perhaps once a standing stone, preserved in Llanelltyd church. It is a "footprint stone" with the outline of a foot purposely carved upon it. One is reminded of Math and his sacred feet placed in the lap of a virgin, and his axial position at the centre of his kingdom, aligned to this Pole Star. This stone probably came from the burial mound just across

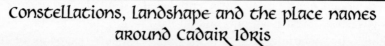
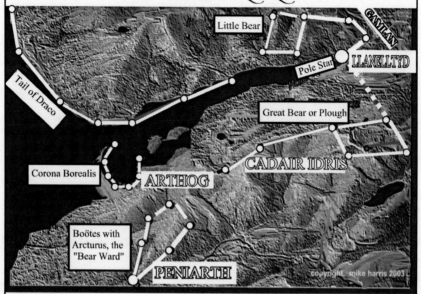

constellations, landshape and the place names around Cadair Idris

Constellations shown are in their relative positions to Cadair Idris as the Great Bear at mid-evening Vernal Equinox in 500 AD, which relate to the Arthurian/Taliesin mythology. Place names relate to constellations at Arth-og, the "Bear Cave" for the Corona Borealis, and Arcturus in Boötes, the so-called Bear Ward at Peniarth, which means chief of, or one in charge of, the bear. I have also included the Afon Gamlan in the top right hand corner, which is the River Camlan, the supposed site of Arthur's last battle.

the river from Llanelltyd church, which gave the spot its ancient pre-Christian sanctity.

These extraordinary representations of Celtic mythology upon the landscape are, however, continued in the accurate alignment of terrestrial features to stellar positions. The "pointers" – the two Great Bear stars *Merak* and *Dubhe,* used from time out of mind to give a stellar fix on the Pole Star, are also apparent upon this landscape. The terrestrial Cadair Idris equivalents of Merak and Dubhe are the crags of Moelfre and Mynydd Moel, which do actually provide an alignment to Llanelltyd church, the Pole Star's landscape equivalent! We may now see a physical metaphor for that enigmatic verse (though they are all pretty enigmatic!) in the *Hanes Taliesin,* which translates:

"I have been in an uneasy chair above Caer Sidi
whirling around without motion
In between three elements."

Positioned upon Cadair Idris, enthroned within the parameters of this terrestrial Great Bear, our Taliesin bard would therefore have been symbolically "whirling around"! The *three elements* (elements of the sovereignty of the Bear) which can be identified upon the landscape are the Little Bear constellation centred upon the Polaris star position at Llanelltyd, the Caer Arianrhod/Corona Borealis "Bear Cave" constellation corresponding to Arthog, and the Boötes "Bear Ward" constellation corresponding to Peniarth. All these, in addition to the Great Bear, the seat or vantage point of the uneasy chair, form the relevant "Bear" constellations fundamental to the Math/Arthur cult of sovereignty.

From nearly three thousand feet (900 metres) up on Pen Y Gadair, the constellations would be vivid in a clear May sky above, and laid out onomastically upon the landscape below – marked in the darkness by the Beltane fires, which on this day, the date of Taliesin's emergence as a bard, purged away the old Gwion so that the new Taliesin could come to birth. But our Taliesin initiate did not sit on the throne of a king, as such. The king's position was the Little Bear, and Taliesin sat upon the throne of the Great Mother Bear who circled protectively about her kingly cub, just as Merlin had made his magical circumambulations around the life of the young Arthur. This was after all what the office of Pen Beirdd, chief bard, entailed. Yet in some senses this throne of the Taliesin Pen Beirdd was that special throne brought for Arthur in the *Dream of Rhonabwy,* so that the king, or in this case the one who stood for that sacral kingship,could play the sacred chess game of sovereignty called Gwyddbwyll. In this, as we shall see, the board represented the kingdom and the moves upon the board were moves of talismanic magic which adjusted the king's relationship to the powers of Annwn, in which his right to rule that kingdom was vested. At the summit of Cadair Idris, the Taliesin cult were laying down magical patterns as a basis to play the sacred chess game of Gwyddbwyll ... and play it on a very grand scale indeed !

The game was a five-fold game, just as those bloody Bronze Age rites had been, with the surrogate king standing at the precincts of Annwn to mediate for his tribe. Now it was the initiate bard who represented the archetypal priest king, and like Hercules, he took charge of the axis of the world in Atlas's stead. He took the four essential "bear" constellations and orchestrated them into harmony with the four elements, seasons and directions of the king's earthly rule, apparent in the kingdom laid out around and below him. He became the surrogate priest king, the archetypal Melchizadek, whom St Paul likened to Jesus Christ, bringing the unbalanced forces of four Kings of Edom into balance and setting the Abraham of his particular tribe on his way to the promised land. This was, in essence, the job of every Taliesin initiate who sat in the windswept, uneasy chair three thousand feet above the kingdom of Gwynedd, and waited for the stars to come out.

The Chair of Idris ... and Taliesin

"I have been in an uneasy chair, turning around between three elements"

He was enthroned above Caer Sidi, the sacred furrow of his jurisdiction, with the round of the seven-fold stars above him. Far below and to every side, laid out before him, the kingdom mimicked the heavens as he looked out to the four quarters across the four turnings of seasons and saw and felt the elements of the natural world ... the water, the wind, the hard rock, with the Beltane fires glimmering far below. From here on this high ridge, he sat in Annwn – surrounded by the cauldron-like, lake-filled scoops of Idris's mountain, in that place between the kingdom of the natural world below and the heavens above. This was the place where the patterns were woven, the dreams dreamed, the awen known. This was the place where the screaming hag of the wind seemed on some nights to wrench soul from body and where the cloud billowed up from the cauldron lakes to make a man blind. And in that blindness and fear he might get up and start to run and plunge to his death, or be driven mad by the isolation and the shapes and voices which come in the cloying mist. Even now, seven and more centuries later, it is said that no man may spend the night upon this Chair of Idris without being either driven to madness, meeting his death, or becoming a bard. These were all part of the initiation process ... the Merlin madness, the 'death in life' of initiation, and from this the emergence of bardic insight. These were (and are) the very real trials of the Cadair, the chair from which the bard played his magical game.

His uneasy chair between heaven and earth was the pivotal point of the *now*. The future was in the stars above, and what had come to pass was apparent in the kingdom spread out below. He was on the unchanging, paradisal battlement of the Caer of Idris, where in contrast to what was both above and below him, nothing would seem to have changed or moved for hundreds of thousands of years, since the mountain's birth. In the world below folk came and went, and in the heavens above the stars turned, but in this place between, time and space would eventually become still within him. Then he could look down and see the goddess's weaving of the past resonated in the world of men, and of the ethereal future formed in the patterns of the stars above. And between the warp and weft of these two were woven the patterns of his nation's dreams.

Like all Celts he dreamed the old dreams, but he also dreamed the new dreams in the stars, he "remembered the future". In this he was able, like Idris, who had stood on this mountain before him in primordial time, to *"prognosticate what was wished to be known until the day of doom."*

We have indicated how the Taliesin bards were so profoundly influenced by the past, but we should never marginalise the element of prophecy in the endeavours of these *awenyddion* who were able to perceive (and hoped to mould!) the patterns of the future. Geoffrey of Monmouth's *Prophecies of Merlin*, written as part of his *History of the Kings of Britain*, indicates the popularity of prophetic works at the time of the Taliesin bards, and perhaps goes some way to implicating Geoffrey as one of them. The work is couched from end to end in star lore ... some of it quite obscure. R.J. Stewart's commentary *Prophecies of Merlin* (Arkana 1986) does a great deal to clarify these obscurities.

Whilst the Taliesin bards were in some measure able to shape events, they could not of course, for all their magical prowess, shape the landscape to the extent that natural features conveniently aligned to the relative positions of the stars! The fact that Cadair Idris happened to be shaped like the Great Bear would have been the starting point – and the establishment of Llanelltyd as a Pole Star, Arthog as the Corona Borealis and so on, became synthetic terrestrial markers, with suitable mythological/onomastic backing to confirm the associations. We could possibly add to Taliesin's pattern however by including the Aran Fawddwy ridge to represent Orion, Arenig Fawr to represent Taurus and Arenig Fach to represent the Pleiades, all of which do happen to hold the correct relative positions.

Interestingly, the name *Arenig* means "reins" in Welsh, so the concept of the ox pulling the Plough of the Great Bear and being controlled by the reins of the Ploughman is maintained. The reins are attached, of course,

to the yoke about the shoulders of the ox … the yoke of the Pleiades …
and the holder of those reins is Hu Gadarn (who was in some senses
also Idris) and whose sacred stars were the constellation of Orion. The
task of the Ploughman was to steer the stars and the stars were steered
by the precession marked by the cycle of the Pleiades. To guide that
precession was to guide the gradual movement of the terrestrial axis, to
guide Orion's own rampant axial libido in pursuit of the Pleiades, from
dynasty to dynasty across the sky.

For the other additional 'synthetic' features of the terrestrial star map,
the burial and ritual complexes around Dyffryn Ardudwy would provide
both an accurate and appropriate location for *Ercwlf*/Hercules. Indeed
the square and additional features of the constellation of Hercules can be
easily constructed between any number of the many sites in that area.

The Celts of course had not invented this idea of transposing starscape
upon landscape; they had, in its rudiments at least, inherited it from the
Bronze Age culture. Where a mountain, lake or other feature stood in the
appropriate position it was drawn into the star map. Where one didn't
exist the 'synthetic mountain' of a burial mound or the corona (a *torc* in
stone) of a stone circle was inserted. There is, for example, a large tumulus
near to Llanelltyd church for the Pole Star position. What is however
extraordinary is that such 'synthetic' sites and the 'ley lines' which
connect them are by no means simply monuments, placed to conform to
an astronomical map. There is ample evidence that such places were sited
and constructed to take advantage of geophysical factors and many still
betray high concentrations of electromagnetic and other energies.

Whilst such factors have become the lynch pin of much colourful
speculation since the early 1970s, a lot of serious research has nonetheless
been undertaken in this field. The semi-conclusions of such research have
indicated that the Bronze Age culture had not only a profound knowledge
of astronomy, but also of some of the laws of astrophysics and geophysics
– including, one uneasily suspects, laws which savants of both the New
Age and the new physics have yet to fathom! But these are matters which
we shall set aside until our next chapter when we consider the practical
implications of all this.

In the meantime, we might however reflect that the bards and their
predecessors were people of great intellectual subtlety who lived in times
which demanded that intellect was directed to precise practical ends.
Mythology was something more than a diverting fantasy to provide, as
some would assume, escapism from – or even spurious 'reasons' for – a
harsh life. We have seen how the initiate bards of the latter Celtic era
laid out patterns in the racial psyche to achieve sociopolitical objectives

of sovereignty. We have also seen how these were a refinement of the earlier Bronze Age patterns which had stemmed from environmental and thus survival objectives from which the concept of the sacred king and thus of sovereignty arose. The means to these ends were sometimes, to our way of thinking at least, decidedly bestial, and the world is seen to have moved on from such origins. Having said that, we live in an age which has by no means forsaken such bestiality, but happily provides the cultural and technological means of insulation. In past ages when the consciousness of human beings was more collective and tribal it was not so. They would never (if questioned now) choose to excuse themselves and there is no reason why they should. They may however have made the observation that they could not ignore nature, and especially human nature, "red in tooth and claw", whereas we have the means, and generally the inclination, to do so!

Such things would have not been the preoccupation of our Taliesin initiate, sat upon his uneasy chair on Cadair Idris. He would look about him on a clear night noting the features that we have described representing the Bear Cave, The Bear Ward, the Little Bear and of course the Great Bear on which he sat "whirling around" in the lap of the goddess, and call upon the powers that confirmed sovereignty to be directed through him. The focus of those powers was the focus of desire implicit in his love affair with the goddess. Thus he became the phallic axis between the heavens and the earth and the pivotal point for transmitting and transforming the paradisal patterns of right sovereignty to his people and their king.

In the Lap of the Goddess

In the *Math fab Mathonwy* romance we saw that the sacred king Math always had to rest his feet in the lap of virgin, so that in effect such a virgin was "the king's chair". As Faery Queen, his virgin footholder was from Annwn and was the representative of the goddess, the validation of sovereignty. Thus the lap of the great goddess, the constellation of the Great Mother Bear, became the priest king's throne … he rode the plough of the heavens. The sexual overtones of this are implicit in the old ideas of sovereignty and of the sacred king mating with the goddess.

We should perhaps pause here to emphasise that our prehistoric ancestors' apparent preoccupation with sex cannot for a moment be thought of in the context of our own times and culture. Our far ancestors were not 'sexually obsessed', because sex had not become associated with any of the prudery or vulgarisation which we have, in spite of so-called "sixties liberation", set upon it. St Augustine of Hippo and British saints like St Cuthbert still loom in the deep places of our racial psyche and have much to answer for. Had they lived in an age where good psychotherapy had been as prevalent as bad dogma, our attitude to sex may have been a good deal healthier. We also have to appreciate that sex has, in the main, ceased to be considered as an essential facet of survival and more of a recreation.

To our ancestors it was not so. They faced death and famine in a very direct and personal way rather than through the second hand, dissociated medium of a television screen. A death in the tribe wasn't something which happened to "the other guy", it was something felt very acutely in the corporate psyche of the tribe. Survival depended upon fertility, and fertility so obviously depended upon virility. Healthy children were *needed* to provide workers, warriors and mates. Fertility was fertility – whether in people, animals or crops – and the obvious gates of life were also the obvious gates of death and transformation. What did die, rotted down and produced new life, or died and produced food. The cycles of life would have seemed to revolve around that single act which was symbolised by an erect phallus and the power that stemmed from it, the powers which give rise to the cycles of life: arousal, conception, birth and setting out on a path which would end in the womb of the earth in death. But it didn't end. After death came transformation, just as it did in other branches of nature … as the stubble of one crop was ploughed back in and rotted down, another sprung up to provide food, life and seeding.

Annwn was seen as the place where these erratic cycles originated and where they thus worked perfectly. It was the paradisal place "in between" where the archetypal powers came to regulate and maintain creation and seed their wishes in the Celtic folksoul. They came from the stars which Idris had mapped, for the stars were rents in the dark veil which separated their heaven worlds from less perfect worlds. Thus the stars, those dots of the heaven worlds' light, showed the patterns of their divine ingress into creation and gave some clue as to what they might implement in that "place between" which was Annwn.

The stuff of the stars was then the light of heaven, the stuff of archetypal ideas, the stuff of awen, which was streamed like potent semen across the dark open void of the sky. Annwn was in a sense behind the mysteries of sex and death, and if it could be tapped then the erratic cycles of life could not so much be laid aside, but rather, set to function to the perfect archetypal pattern. The gods and goddesses hadn't abandoned sex, conception and birth, they just knew how to do it better! We should not therefore deride the imagery of myth as being crude, primitive and trivial simply because of its sexual nature, neither should we shrug it off as simple, honest and earthy. As we shall see, the ancients, for all their straightforward imagery, were aware of a range of sexual dynamics far beyond simple reproduction or physical gratification. To treat this as "crude, rude paganism" and as a primitive, superficial cultism based upon physical sexuality is to completely misunderstand. On the other hand, to describe it in the clinical jargon of theoretical magic as "energy exchange" or "polarity" is equally misleading and dehumanising. What is being described is a full blooded love affair between the initiate bard and the goddess, a love affair which consumed him body, mind and soul.

In this totality of expression our Celtic ancestors were unhindered by the conditioning which may warp our view of such things. The story of Taliesin (even though the version we have is twelfth century) is about this love affair with the goddess who is of course of three aspects. This is why in the *Hanes Taliesin,* young Gwion (prior to becoming Taliesin) has his finger touched by three drops of the stuff of awen from her "cauldron". The symbolism is basic, direct, and honest. It describes in earthy terms the approach of the lover to his beloved and potentially fruitful mate. The dampness of the drops of awen from her cauldron upon his finger signifies that he has stimulated her and in that sovereign mating between humanity and the goddess and potential mother of us all, she is aroused. The cleaving of that cauldron and the great cry which accompanies it, after Gwion's initial advances, continue the sexual imagery of the goddess opening herself to him and the ecstatic cry of orgasm. Awen, as the female ejaculation of the goddess, is what subsequently flows from the cauldron of her being, and awen provides that rainbow bridge between the archetypal and natural worlds. The stuff of awen becomes, in biblical terms, the waters which flow out of Eden.

The cauldron of the goddess is therefore many things. It is a chair of knowing, it is her lap, so that bardic 'knowing' is every bit as 'biblical' a knowing, and as earthy, as it is intellectual or intuitive. For without the fire of desire there is no knowing in any magical, poetical or mystical perceptive sense. The goddess's cauldron may therefore be seen as that heavenly circlet which is the bear cave in the stars, but equally it may be a cave or lake or burial chamber. As a bear cave, however, it is the place of hibernation, where the bear mother brings her cubs into being: it is a womb. So it is into this womb that our bardic initiate must enter to be reborn, so that he, the rest of humanity and the natural world may be reborn to inherit the genetic patterns of paradise.

Before the bards it had been the sacred kings who had entered her, never again to be seen alive, and whilst their lot was to be reborn, it was never again as tangible flesh and blood. What we see in the later Celtic epoch is, however, an initiate bard becoming in effect a surrogate for securing the principle of sovereignty … and living to (inasmuch as he can) tell the tale.

The spawn of Gwydion

The archetypal bard was Gwydion. In which prehistoric culture he originated to take his place among the Bronze Age/Celtic labyrinth of Brythonic gods and goddesses is uncertain. The Mabinogi describes him as a *son of Dôn,* and Dôn has been identified with the Irish goddess *Danu.* What is however likely is that Gwydion marked that period during or following the incursion of a people who were more advanced than the incumbent inhabitants of these islands, and was the focus of a new cultism based upon sovereignty under the axial alignment to Ursa Minor, rather than to the old axial order of Draco. The battle for that new order is shown in the poem *Cad Goddeu* or "Battle of the Trees", a battle fought, via various species of tree, between Gwydion and the lord of the "old" underworld *Arawn.* This theme of Gwydion's wars with, and victories over, the old Underworld is reiterated in his war with *Pwyll,* the subsequent Underworld ruler of the old order – an order which had found its mythological focus in *Bran.*

Robert Graves's *The White Goddess* confirmed that the "new" bardic skills exemplified in Gwydion and concealed in the *Cad Goddeu* poem embodied a Druidic tree/calendar alphabet, whose codex was used and alluded to down many centuries by the Taliesin cult. Gwydion, as we have noted previously, became the alter ego of each Taliesin bard, a fact which has no small bearing upon what our Taliesin was doing playing Gwyddbwyll on the top of Cadair Idris.

Gwydion's name appears from the Triads to have had an alternative version ... *Gwyddon Ganhebon,* which is interesting to the extent that we can be sure that the root of his name was *Gwydd,* the Welsh word (the falling diphthongs of modern Welsh notwithstanding) for both *Plough* and *Loom,* which could allude to the constellations of the Great Bear and the Pleiades respectively. In fact, Gwydion is in some senses responsible for persuading the goddess to fulfil the functions signified by each of these constellations and so establish sovereignty. This persuasion, which the Taliesin bards were also attempting to emulate, may be summed up as *Gwyddbwyll,* and in the name of this game played in the intermediary confines of Annwn, we have of course Gwydion's name. *Gwydd,* a plough or loom or, interestingly, in the *Cad Goddeu* context, "trees". *Bwyll* is probably in this instance a mutation of the noun *Gwyll,* meaning *gloom.* We have come across this idea of ancient and potentially magical things being dark or black, not least the Ogham/Tree speech used by bards, as well as in the names of various ancient sites. As an aside to this we might note how bardic technique for ingress into Annwn appears to be dark (not least in nocturnal star gazing!) whilst everyone and everything that comes out of Annwn appears to be white! We might also recall Caer Golur, the "gloomy castle" found in the *Preiddu Annwn.*

The new cult which focused on Gwydion needed a new creation myth based on the new stellar emphasis of the Bear. By finding what this was we can get some idea of the cosmology that the Taliesin/Gwydion cult were using, and clarify and perhaps expand upon what they were doing and why ... not least on their excursions to the summit of Cadair Idris!

The star belt of the Milky Way was, as we have observed before, the *Caer Gwydion.* This in effect marks Gwydion as a prime creator god figure, for in many ancient cultures the creator was seen to betray the path of his creative impetus by the "track" left by the Milky Way. In treading out this starry path, Gwydion also became the archetypal priest magician, the Hermes of the Celts, a facet all too easily seen in his mythological role of divine, even devious, "fixer"! From the fragmented star myths that we have in the *Math* tale it is obvious that Arianrhod and Gwydion were not only brother and sister but also lovers. In another sense Gwydion came to be Hu Gadarn himself, who was a Celtic version of Orion, romantically chasing those seven sisters of the Pleiades across the turning heavens to bring some new era to birth.

Seen in the night sky, flung across space, the Milky Way, Gwydion's Caer, represented his sperm, the initial seed of creation. But this was not to be merely a patriarchal creation story. In certain Egyptian mythological illustrations which never reach those respectable coffee table tomes on

Ancient Egypt, one can see graphic illustrations of creation originating from a divine brother and sister, when the brother god is aroused and masturbated by his sister goddess. This appears also to have been the case with Gwydion and Arianrhod.

Having induced Gwydion's ejaculation, Arianrhod took the mucous threads of her brother's sperm and like Arachne the spider goddess, she spun them on her wheel into star threads. The spinner was, however, only the instigator in this scheme of creation – it was not for her to bring that thread of destiny into form. Thus we see her denying her pregnancy until, at Gwydion's instigation, she takes that fateful step over Math's wand. In the *Math* story, both Math and Gwydion are presented as wizards and thus much is made of their use of "wands." Then Llew of course becomes the famed spear-thrower, equivalent to the Irish *Lugh*. All these embody the phallic/axial symbolism that we have discussed, apparent in the Bear stars and the alignment of the Pole Star to the Little Bear.

So the step that Arianrhod takes in stellar terms is from the Corona Borealis, over the Pole Star (to which the high king's wand/axis is aligned) and into the Pleiades. The mythology again fits the astronomy perfectly. In the night sky the Corona Borealis can align to the Pleiades on the other side of the sky *through* the Pole Star. What is more, Arianrhod would have been stepping from one circlet of seven stars to another circlet of seven stars, a veritable *Caer Fandwy*, a starry Caer in two places. Whilst however the coronet of the Corona Borealis is open, the circle of the Pleiades appears to the naked eye to be complete. She is thus, reluctantly, taking a step from an unfinished seven-fold circle into a complete seven-fold circle ... from spun yarn to finished weaving. She is also taking a step over the Pole Star/axis to extend her mythological creative role, for whilst the Corona Borealis, the crown behind the north wind, may be the province of the spinner of threads, the Pleiades are traditionally the constellation of weaving goddesses.

The step from spinner to weaver which Arianrhod has taken is the step from the archetypal insubstantiality of a heaven world into the world of pre-formation, the world of Annwn. Thus she has moved, via the potent axis of Math's "wand", from her accustomed constellation where she spins the archetypal thread to the area where those threads of awen are woven into proto-creation. Her reluctance to name, arm and allow for Llew's validation in taking a wife is a reluctance to become a mother goddess and allow archetypal ideas to take root in Annwn and subsequently in the material world. The Taliesin bards, however, had the same remedy that Gwydion had for her reluctance ... magic!

When the Taliesin initiate who wrote the *Preiddu Annwn* taunted the court bards as being men of "drooping courage" who knew not on what day the "chief arose", he was perhaps taunting them for their lack of manliness in their love affair with the goddess, for their lack of potency through which the magic was empowered. He is using almost locker room jargon to accuse the so called *chief* (bard) of loss of phallic potency (drooping courage) implicit in the role of a Taliesin *pen beirdd*, but that he didn't know when (on what day) in astronomical terms this had to happen. He could therefore provide no phallic wand for Arianrhod to step over to bring the magic into being.

For the magic to be brought to earth, however, it had to be talismanically appropriate to the mundane world that it was intended to transform. When we look at the mythology being worked out by the bard, we soon see that this was the case.

For many people now, the image of a woman using a spinning wheel is an obscure one, relegated to postcards of a traditional tourist Wales with the stereotypical Welsh woman with tall black hat. Not too long ago it was however a central feature of Welsh rural life, wherever sheep were raised and wool fibre needed to be spun into yarn ready for knitting or weaving.

Rural life in the Celtic lands hadn't, until very recently, changed much since Taliesin's time, in the essential practices of virtual self-sufficiency, of which the making of clothing was of course fundamental. If we were to look into any Welsh hut, cottage or Caer down the centuries we would see an archetypal family group, as archetypal as any family of gods and goddesses. The image of the matriarch sat at her spinning wheel was central to this; she clothed the family, she placed the plaid upon the son of the family and named him, and in more noble families, armed her boy. A daughter would have held the distaff, the stick on which the yarn was wound, and a further daughter might have been employed in cooking and the care of the domesticated animals close to the house, like geese and pigs. In this we have the archetypal three goddess figures. The matriarch at her spinning wheel, the prettiest and most marriageable of the daughters holding the distaff and assisting her mother to spin and keep house. Then there may have been a second daughter managing the cauldron over the fire, or delegating this task to a little brother whilst she busied herself in the farmyard, where she would be responsible for feeding the animals, keeping the pigs and collecting eggs and so on. Nor in rural life would it be unusual for the mother and father of this family to be brother and sister … the inroads of Christianity and the risk of genetic defect notwithstanding. Such situations were not unknown when I first came to rural Gwynedd some thirty years ago! The fact that there was however a taboo on such things is shown in the way that the fragmented star myth of Gwydion and Arianrhod was presented in *Math* by the time that it came to be written down in the Middle Ages. Arianrhod's shame at carrying and giving birth to a child that she will not acknowledge, and Gwydion's actions in taking his son away and hiding him in a bed chest are reflections of this. The contrast between the wit of Gwydion and the obvious lack of wit of his son Llew may also reflect hints of idiocy, coupled with Arianrhod's *geasa*/curse to prevent Llew from having a mortal wife and thus extending the idiocy further in the clan bloodline! This may also account for myths which suggest that the sexual relationship between brother and sister consisted of mutual masturbation rather than full, and potentially fruitful, sexual union!

No Freudian leaps of imagination are required to identify the distaff or spinning stick from which the pretty daughter, the May maiden, who is Blodeuwedd of the flower-like countenance, teases out the fibres.

Che Sword of Kingship

As mythology began to embrace the distinction between the king as the mundane figurehead of sovereignty and the bard as his surrogate mediator with the goddess, their respective symbols of axial office diverged. The bard's 'weapon' and symbol of his potency was his magic wand or bardic staff, through which symbolically the patterns of sovereignty were translated. The king's symbol of such axial potency was, however, more appropriate to achieving and retaining sovereignty in more practical terms. At the time when the Math mythology was prevalent the essential weapon of the warrior king had been the spear, which carried all the phallic/axial symbolism that we have described. Thus Llew, the epitome of the virile warrior and thus a suitably Herculean prospective sacred king, was a spearman of unerring aim. He symbolised axial accuracy, and this central axial position is seen in his being further portrayed as a solar hero ... the sun at the centre of the round of the Celtic solar system. Llew in this guise was the centrally placed sovereign piece in Gwydion's chess game of Gwyddbwyll, surrounded by the empowering yet vacillating powers of the goddess and her Faery maidens, for it is impossible to consider the axial symbolism of either a king or his bard without considering the theme of Underworld feminine empowerment, the paradisal empowerment of Annwn.

By the time the Math mythology found its revival in the bardic creation of Arthur, the weapon of kingship had ceased to be the spear and had become the sword. Everybody knows that Arthur's sword was called *Excalibur*, few know that his spear was called *Ron*. Notwithstanding, the bardic romancers could not resist reverting to the weaponry of the older legend at the climax of the Arthurian tale. It is with the spear that Arthur despatches Mordred, his bastard son and disrupter of the paradisal pattern, just as Llew had similarly despatched Gronw with a spear at the climax of the Math tale.

Geoffrey calls Excalibur *Caliburn*, but the sword's original name was *Caledfwlch*. Caledfwlch expresses this seeming dichotomy of paradise sought through warfare in that its name probably meant "hard/wet" or possibly was a play on the word *celanedd* which means "slaughter". Yet this weapon that was named with such practical, gruesome expediency had to have its origins in that ethereal, paradisal world of Faery.

It was said that Caledfwlch had not been wrought with human hands, and as we know, the sword which was to become the most famous of all mythological weapons came into Arthur's hand with the contrivance of the old powers. Yet, as the Celtic weapon of all weapons it must have embodied the triumph of Celtic technology over previous races and have had a blade of iron rather than bronze. But tradition tells us that Faeries fear iron. Whilst this may well record the defeat of the bronze-weaponed indigenous population by the iron-wielding Celts, it seems to contradict the Faery origins of the sword at the hands of the Lady of the Lake. Other evidence suggests, however, that whilst it may have been made of iron this was probably meteorite iron, so in effect its origin was in the stars. The stars and the Underworld, the deeps of Annwn, were considered to be one location. Certainly gazing into the surface of Llyn Tegid or one of the other great glacial lakes of Gwynedd on a still, clear night would show a view into Annwn (the deep), patterned with stars. Stone circles and sacred mounds/mountains orientated to star patterns seem, as we have seen, to have acted as a catalyst between these "stars above" and the "stars below". If by implication Caledfwlch was made from meteoric iron its origins would be in "the depths of rock and the stars".

The "sword from the stone" tradition has, in one version, the sword turning up in a miraculously floating rock ... which brings in both the lake and stone symbolism. In this account of Caledfwlch/Excalibur's origins one version has Arthur's father Uther Pendraig (Pendragon) placing the wondrous sword in the stone from which his unknown bastard son, the boy king Arthur, later draws it to become king. This is after Arthur's foster brother Kay's initial duplicity in claiming that he was the one, not Arthur, who drew the sword. When the sword is drawn it ushers in a new epoch. This is prefigured, as we have seen, in the precessional movement of the axis from Draco into Ursa Minor, from the stars of the Pendragon to the stars of the Bear. Under the old symbolism of the standing stones of the Bronze Age, Caledfwlch is essentially a star sword – *seren cledd.*

In this axially heralded shift in sovereignty, and the patterns of belief underpinning it, we are aware that *Bran* and *Uther Ben* are one and the same. As *Uther Ben*, Bran is *Uther of the head* ... and Arthur's father. In that Gwynhyfwr is of the old Faery order and the daughter of Bran, this would of course make Gwynhyfwr Arthur's sister and his wife, which is an interpolation of the Arianrhod/Gwydion relationship ... not an uncommon state of affairs in ancient sacred dynasties, where despite the inbreeding risks, it was seen as essential to restrict and preserve the sacral bloodline. This sister/mate relationship is again echoed in the Arthuriad, in Arthur's illicit relationship with his half sister Morgan le Fey.

Much is made of the right to wield the sword being implicit in its scabbard. The sexual symbolism of this, of the male king's sword having to be enclosed in the female queen's scabbard brings us yet again to the idea of the validation of the king's axial sovereignty being implicit in his relationship with the goddess through a Faery Queen surrogate. This is emphasised in the Arthuriad when Morgan, in the guise of Gwynhyfwr, seduces Arthur (thus exacting appropriate vengeance for Arthur's own fraudulent conception on her mother Ygraine by Uther). This theme is repeated when the powers of Arthur's sword (and thus sovereignty) are blighted because Morgan "steals the scabbard". In all this we may see, as noted before, the retelling of the Math story in the Arthuriad. Morgan is as determined to thwart Arthur's sovereignty as Arianrhod was to thwart the proposed sacral kingship of Llew, and Merlin was as frustrated as Gwydion in trying to counter her schemes. Myrddin, the bard/monk whom Geoffrey made into Merlin, found himself fighting shy of the incestuous threads of the old myth. An awareness of the axial phallic symbolism of the sword, and the relationship between the archetypal god magician and his sister the goddess, reflected in the relationship between the king and queen, would be well enough known. As, however, such ideas were unthinkable in Christian terms, we find a faltering in the Christian bardic interpretations of Myrddin's relationship with Gwendydd, who alternates between being his sister and his lover ... but never, heaven forefend, both at once!

Caledfwlch's delivery into the hands of Arthur from either an ancient sacred stone or from the deep dark waters of Llyn Tegid, less than twenty miles from Cadair Idris, are both equally valid assumptions. Either way the potent weapon is withdrawn from the secret dark places where it, phallically, has been inserted into the goddess/womb of the landscape by the previous sacred king, rather in the way that a bee inserts and surrenders its sting … and dies in the act.

The ancient stone symbolism of the origin of the sword speaks of sacred sites, of which there are many in the area, or a chunk, as we have said, of meteorite iron. Failing this, a sword in a stone image can equally point to the new technology of casting metals from stone moulds. The images of a sword in a rock also prefigured the sword and scabbard and spear and Grail symbolism that was to come later. We should for a moment, however, consider the more popular version, of Arthur obtaining the sword from the Lady of the Lake.

Welsh folklore places many a Faery woman at places where water wells up from the underground depths, and all springs and lakes were potentially gateways to the Faery Underworld, to the deeps of Annwn. Again, without wishing to stress the sexual symbolism to exhaustion, sacred trees, springs and lakes were seen as the rising sap/fertility force of the good Earth and were therefore quite naturally seen as representations of climatic female ejaculations of the goddess in anticipation of, or through stimulation by, her mortal sacred king at such points where Middle Earth and Otherworld met.

The Lady of the Lake is a type of Faery well known in Welsh folklore as one of the *Gwragedd Annwn* (the wives of the deep) who frequent lakes and sometimes, like the famous lady of Llyn y Fan Fach, became the wives of mortals. But it is Arthur's Lady of the Lake from Llyn Tegid (which visitors know as Bala Lake) who was able to make the cultural leap into the more universal, mediaeval Arthuriad.

Though nowhere near the size of Scotland's Loch Ness, Llyn Tegid has its monster legend, as well as its flooded town legend, and in places plummets to very considerable depth. As the lake upon which the Underworld Goddess Ceridwen also had her island home with the great cauldron which contained *Awen* … inspiration, which was to be the instrument of Taliesin's original initiation, it is an Underworld precinct par excellence.

Llyn Tegid is within the ambit of the Cadair Idris ridge, for the ridge running on into the area called Camlan (a name of no little Arthurian import) effectively continues on in the Aran and then Berwyn Mountains which encircle the south eastern side of Bala and the upper Dee valley, including the lake. This Bala/Corwen area is littered with Bronze Age, Iron Age, Roman and Dark Age remains including the superb Bronze Age stone circle and burial complex of *Moel Ty Uchaf,* which we have visited already. There is another long complex of cairns on the other very isolated flank of the mountain, two of which are named as *Cadair Berwyn* and *Cadair Bronwen* respectively, seeming to continue the theme of sacred, high mountain "chairs". Bronwen is of course *Branwen,* the sister of Bran. Another cairn in the same group as *Cadair Bronwen* however is called, predictably, *Bwrdd Arthur* (Arthur's Table). It goes without saying that it is by no means the only prehistoric cairn in Britain to carry this name! It is, however, this concentration of prehistoric sacred sites around and about Llyn Tegid, as well as a cave near Llanuwchllyn at the south west end of the lake associated with Arthur, which indicates that Caledfwlch was placed to emerge at the centre of a complex of ancient esoteric activity. Further evidence of this area as an "Arthurian setting" is the old Roman fort of *Caer Gai* near the south western end of the lake.

Most folk are familiar with Arthur's childhood companion, and subsequent lieutenant, Sir Kay. Kay is a Normanisation from his original Welsh name in the Mabinogi, *Cei,* and in the phrase *Caer Gai, Cei* has simply mutated to *Gai,* just as the Welsh word for Wales, *Cymru,* when used with other words can, for ease of pronunciation, mutate to <u>*Gymru*</u>.

From this we see that this old Roman fort, like *Tomen y Mur* just across the moors at Trawsfynydd, and so many other Roman sites, came to the aid of myth. Whilst there were Iron Age/Celtic hill forts in the upper Dee valley (*Caer Euni, Caer Caradog, Caer Drewyn, Moel Caws*) this site of a Roman cavalry fort at Caer Gai was, as far as can be ascertained, only ever built upon and occupied by the imperial army. A small shrine to Hercules was found there with the information that detachments of the First Cohort of Nervii used the fort. It was abandoned in about 130 AD. As was generally the case, however, most of the occupying force consisted of northern European auxiliaries under Roman commanders. The first Cohort of Nervii were in fact Celts from Northern Gaul.

It is easy to see from this how some particularly outstanding Romano Celtic cavalryman at the fort easily became the model for the Arthurian warrior (and later knight) *Cei,* though Cei may have already been a mythical warrior waiting for a flesh and blood hero to fill his archetypal sandals. As one of the rough and ready original Celtic characters that became absorbed into the later Arthuriad, Kay became written up as something of a loudmouth with a tendency towards duplicity. He is said to have initially claimed that he, not his young foster brother Arthur, took the sword from the stone, but this at least places the Kay of the sword/

stone incident with Kay/Cei beside the lake where the other version of Caledfwlch/Excalibur's origin is sited.

Gwynhyfwr's Table

Just as the themes of the validation of sovereignty in the axis symbolism made their transference from Math into the Arthuriad in the shape of Excalibur, or Caliburn as Geoffrey has it, so the symbol of the furrow in the heavens, the turning of the Great Plough/Bear became resurrected in the shape of the Table Round. By now the importance of the turnings of the heavens to the Taliesin cult's preoccupations with Welsh sovereignty will be clear. The various versions of the Arthuriad credit Merlin with bringing both the Table Round and the Giant's Dance (the stones of Stonehenge) to Arthur and Uther respectively. In this we see terrestrial symbols of the turn of the heavens, symbolising the archetypal and paradisal pattern, being represented to the incumbent king. Such a plan is therefore in some senses the board or basic gameplan for the sovereignty game of Gwyddbwyll. The role of the Taliesin bards in this provision of the archetypal paradisal pattern to which the king, and by extension the kingdom, should aspire, is implicit in the romance that has Merlin bringing the Table from the stars of the Great Bear. The implication is that the bard should come from the mountain which represented the Great Bear upon the landscape and deliver this star plan, the plan of Idris and Gwydion, to the king. As we have seen this was precisely the role which the Taliesin bards on Cadair Idris saw themselves fulfilling.

As with the sword however, the validation of this Table Round is vested in the feminine empowerment of sovereignty. Hence in the Arthuriad, when Merlin brings the Table (from the stars of the Great Bear) he is only the intermediary. The Table itself is said to be "Guinevere's dowry", so Merlin, or the bardic order that he represents, is acting as the catalyst for a paradisal pattern which originates in the goddess and which is held in the gift of the Faery Queen who represents her.

Again the mundane origins in which this great stellar symbolism is couched become plain. That a piece of land delineated by the round furrow might be a daughter's dowry would be natural enough in the bucolic setting that we have described. That the dowry of the goddess in her "marriage" to the sacrificed sacred king might also be the burial mound delineated by the furrow ditch, would also fit with mythology and what we know of mystery practice.

Gwynhyfwr's father, as we have seen, was considered to be Bran. The guardian of the Table Round was later called *Leo de Grance*, the great lion, by the Norman French romancers of the Arthuriad, hinting at his sacral kingship under the lion totem of Hercules from that earlier Bronze Age epoch. The name Leodegrance has, however, as we have already noted, been shown to derive from the Welsh *Ogyr Fran ... Bran*. The Celts, as will by now be obvious, looked to patterns of the past and to the previous Underworld cult to empower and inspire their present. But again those past patterns were not ancient and dusty, but ancient and dynamic. The Celts did not think of the past as 'dead' in the sense that we might. The feast of Samhain, when the Pleiades rose, was the time when the ancestors came to visit their incarnate successors, but they came not from some ghoulish backwater of Hades but from a living co-existing world which was more vibrant and dynamic than the material world they had long since left behind.

This world was the archetypal one, the paradisal world that was in the process of becoming in earth. It was the Table Round of the great feast, once the feast of each cannibalised village Hercules, but soon to be the feast where all humanity as sacred kings and queens sat with other representatives of creation. When all were gathered, the cauldron of *awen*, the Grail of love, manifested among them, to feed each and every one their heart's desire.

That such a table of the Grail was to be identified with the Table of the Last Supper, and the Holy Chalice with the twelve disciples as the embodiment of the sacred king's presence (the body of Christ), was a natural progression of the mythology into virtual biblical history at the hands of the initiate bards.

Much may be said about the stellar associations of this, not least of the twelve disciples as the zodiacal points indicating the precession of the equinoxes, the sacred cycle, the twelve labours of the sacrificed Hercules. This Hercules, lion of Judah, the sacred king of all sacred kings, *Crist mab Mair*, son of the virgin mother, had instituted a new phase, a Great Platonic Year which would see the restoration of the paradisal ideal of heaven brought to earth in the New Jerusalem. All the symbolic elements of the ancient beliefs were in the biblical mythos, which appeared to have been witnessed as actual history. There was the sacrifice of this sacred king, impaled five-fold upon the tree of the cross. There was the sharing of his body among his initiates in the feast, with its chalice/cauldron symbolism. There was the burial chamber after death, though unlike the sacred kings of old, his body would not, as was foretold by the prophets, be broken. Subsequently he passed through the Underworld to be taken up into the heavens. In all this, all the old longings for it to be *real* upon the land, for this particular sacred king and the land to become one, seemed to have been fulfilled in real history.

By mediaeval times this ancient pattern would have seemed more vital, more urgent to the initiate bards of Wales. The dogma of Rome and the power politics of England must have seemed to have uprooted that whole entwined knotwork of Welsh national identity, national spirituality, national history and a national sense of sovereignty and belonging.

The late Taliesin poetry like the *Preiddu Annwn*, whilst looking to this new revelation, still sought to emphasise what it believed were its ancient roots. Everything that had happened among those other oppressed people in Palestine so long ago had been a fulfilment of these ancient things that the Brythons had known.

Arthur, the faery women and the Spoils of Annwn

The pattern had been lost somewhere, way back before the ancestors who now slept in the deeps beneath their lonely burial mounds among the stars. The pattern belonged to another time when the shining ones had walked the earth openly. So very long ago when mythical Troia had been inhabited by giants, just as the new earth of Genesis had been walked by the great *Nephelim*. That was back where it all began, that was where the pattern of paradise, the garden East of Eden had its origins, when the great ones gave the first names to things, when Gwydion's desire issued forth as the starseed of the Milky Way and ancient Idris named the stars, and knew their pattern and purpose.

The realm of Idris the star mage was always associated with the old pre-human race, the shining ones, the Faeries, the *Tylwyth Teg*, or fair folk. We have established that an innate chain of association between primeval, paradisal patterns, ancient, supposedly pre-human races, the land, its sovereignty and the stars, was etched into the Celtic psyche and landscape. Special values were attached to the far past and the peoples of that past, and the Bronze Age inhabitants of Britain, the main builders of Stonehenge upon Neolithic foundations, had obviously possessed certain peculiar technologies and artifacts which the Celts would have valued. As we have seen from the *Spoils of Annwn*, anything that was of value, materially or esoterically, became legitimate *Spoils* for the Celts.

In terms of the great table, Gwynhyfwr's dowry, the Celts could see that the Bronze Age people had made the great meeting 'tables' in the round ... the henges of stone, often with a flat topped capstone (like a vast table top) over a burial cist at the centre. As to the cauldron of *awen*, of inspiration and regeneration, the Holy Grail that was later to miraculously appear at such Tables in Arthurian legend, these too were found in the past.

If we can then imagine that the landscape surrounding Cadair Idris, which even today is dotted with standing stones, trackways and burials of the Bronze Age epoch, was known by the Celts as the last bastion of these ancient people, we can see its esoteric attraction to the Celts of Taliesin's time. Here was a place where the people who had had contact with the paradisal realms, the Faery realms, had last been seen to walk the earth.

Taliesin's Chair in Paradise

When our Taliesin bard wrote of this as the place which represented knowledge of a paradisal state, however, he was able draw upon parallels beyond his native Britain. He tells us in the *Hanes Taliesin* that *"I was in Canaan when Absalom was slain"* and *"I was in the ark with Noah and Alpha"* and generally makes a number of other claims to having witnessed major events not only in Celtic and pre-Celtic British mythology but also in Hebrew/biblical mythology, including *"I was with my Lord in the highest sphere when Lucifer fell..."* and *"My accustomed country is the land of the Cherubim."*

We have already observed that such utterances may have stemmed from visits to the biblical lands as a Crusader, even a Templar. It would, in any case, come as no surprise that writing in the sixth century in a (by then) Christian country, this Taliesin should know his scripture, and based on his calling, that he should be given to prophetic vision. We must, however, become alerted by his extensive use of biblical material and particularly to his reference to the fall from a paradisal state, when he claims to having been *"with my Lord in the highest sphere when Lucifer fell"*. Again this is a reversion to the theme of having known the paradisal creation before what we call the angelic Fall, but which theology knows as the *Prime Deviation.*

So sitting in his chair on this paradisal mountain he felt at one with God, able to transcend time and space, and aware of a paradisal pre-Fall state. This is by no means a case (as many a neo-pagan would have us believe) of the material being given a biblical gloss to escape the disapproval of Christian orthodoxy. Taliesin's references are for the most part to the Old Testament and temple-based Judaism rather than the 'new' Christian faith invented by St Paul! However, Taliesin's esoteric cosmopolitanism indicates that a lot of what he seems to present to us as the "Celtic Mysteries" is not in fact home grown. Having said that, it is only fair to note that most mystery systems are an amalgam of practice and belief drawn from an array of cultural overlays. The classical mysteries of the Mediterranean being a case in point. Taliesin does what pretty much any practitioner of magic does, he borrows material from all sorts of sources, with the one proviso … that it works. In this case it does!

The Celtic world of Taliesin's time was very much part of the larger world; Greek and Phonecian traders coming up the Atlantic seaboard, followed by the Roman invasion and occupation, had seen to that. Caractacus had gone to Rome and now this was the age of the Celtic saints who made their pilgrimages across the sea. Maelgwyn the king of Gwynedd, at whose court Taliesin disputed with the bards, was a cultured man who spoke Greek. St Gildas wrote in Latin and likened himself to one of the Old Testament prophets of Israel. Middle eastern philosophy and metaphysics were imported as readily as wine and other goods. Furthermore the Celtic church had strong links with the original Coptic church of the Desert Fathers, the church of North Africa, an area which had long been a repository of esoteric lore.

Taliesin's quick and fertile mind would have made metaphysical connections, even if they hadn't been made already. There were other sacred mountains which represented the paradisal state and which had sacred chairs upon them, and one in particular had its seat in the *"country of the cherubim"*.

The Jerusalem temple had finally been razed to the ground some four hundred years before the first Taliesin's time but the Romans who occupied Britain had been at great pains to write about it. Britain also had, even in the sixth century, a complement of Jews – and Jews also came and went from these shores in the course of trade. The traditions of Judaism, perhaps better realised then among the educated than they are now, would have meant that Celtic bards would have been well aware of the traditions and symbolism of the Jerusalem temple.

The temple rock was (and is) the absolute centre of Jewish belief. It was the place where the Lord appeared to David, "*the threshing floor of Ornan the Jesubite*" as the first book of Chronicles describes the site. David was unable to build the temple because he had blood on his hands, so it fell to his son Solomon to build the first of the three temples which were to stand in Jerusalem (if not as tradition has it, on the same site) until the final destruction of the third in 70 AD.

The Jerusalem temple was the place in Earth where the door to heaven was left ajar. It represented the centre of the paradisal kingdom upon the mountain of God, the Garden of Eden before the Fall, and the point of contact between God and his people. How this contact occurred and how this paradisal image was implemented varied throughout Jewish history. The Deuteronomists, who were effectively the Puritans of Judaism, said that God could only be heard and not seen, and it is largely their reforms which we inherit in Old Testament scripture with its severe monotheism. Anything that smacked of polytheism or blatant mythology was excised from their scripture, and consequently we lose sight of a good deal of the earlier temple practices and beliefs. However, we do know that Hezekiah removed much of the mythological trapping from the temple, especially the *Asherah*, the symbol of the Goddess. Thanks to the Deuteronomists much is also lost about the Veil and the Chariot Throne within the sanctuary, but it is a constant of temple worship that the door represented by the Veil of the innermost temple sanctuary (the *Debir)* was entered by the High Priest, and only the High Priest. This happened but once a year, on the day of Atonement, when the High Priest would don simple white robes and enter that room which was a perfect cube, to encounter the *Shekinah*, the tangible presence of God in Earth. This was the place of the *Cherubim;* indeed the *Mercy Seat* where the Shekinah manifested was a "chariot throne" formed by the Ark of the Covenant and mirror statues of two Cherubim who faced each other with outstretched wings over the Ark, prompting Isiah's assertion "O Lord of Hosts, God of Israel, thou art enthroned above the Cherubim" (Isiah 37:16).

The Holy of Holies, the *Debir* in which the Shekinah manifested, was the holiest and (physically as well as metaphorically) the highest point in the temple. It was the "pinnacle of the temple" described in the gospel temptation stories of Christ and whilst it wasn't some soaring Minaret as the gospels make us assume, it was in spiritual terms the 'highest' place and thus gave Satan a lofty vista of the world to roll out before the Christ.

The Debir also represented the pre-Fall garden of Eden, so that the High Priest, coming through the *Hekal,* traversing the great curtains of the Veil which were embroidered with images of lush vegetation, was in effect symbolising the unfallen Adam walking in the garden to meet and speak with God. What we have, therefore, in the Taliesin intiate going up on the mountain of Cadair Idris to mediate the paradisal pattern, has direct and deliberate correspondence with the High Priests of the first Jerusalem temple. The chair upon which he is sitting is the mercy seat. He has entered the high place of the Holy of Holies, to mediate the Shekinah, the essentially feminine presence of God in earth, on behalf of the king and his people. On this basis our initiate bard would be able to deny to himself and to the Christian dogma of his times any dichotomy between Christian and pre-Christian belief, in the exercise of his bardic, poetic and priestly duty.

Theology was not in any case his job. His task, his destiny, was to operate effectively in that place between heaven and earth which is called Annwn and there to mediate the essentials of sovereignty in the Celtic lands. To do so, as he saw it, was to preserve and empower the very lifeblood of his race so that they may make that long journey through the desert of human ignorance to arrive in the promised land. If he were asked whose promise that was, he would have given an enigmatic smile and pointed to the stars.

CHAPTER TEN

Gwyddbwyll

We have covered, albeit in a very general way, the lineaments and development of material that comprises the Mysteries. We must now tussle with a number of matters which will try the credulity of some readers and excite the speculations of others. That a corps of bardic initiates of outstanding ability and intelligence should, over so great a span of time, have gone to so much trouble in the origination and preservation of the material we have considered, simply in the cause of either literature, pseudo-history or superstition is unthinkable. We have seen that the bards of the sixth and succeeding centuries *believed* in what they were transmitting and the way they present the material suggests that their minds were incisive enough to require something more for their pains than a round of applause and a good meal. That they were subject to the romanticism that pervades the Celtic soul cannot be doubted, but they were practical people too.

A Question of Magic

As we have seen, they deliberately worked upon the Brythonic folk soul and applied mythological patterns which resonate, even now, the principles of Brythonic identity and sovereignty. The enduring tradition of their King Arthur indicates that the principles they planted have grown to be an integral part of the British psyche. Whilst it may be argued that much the same job is continued, albeit for more cynical motives, by the establishment propaganda machinery of our own times, the distinctions are absolutely clear in terms of motive, depth and perspective. Propaganda certainly knows which buttons to press in the collective unconscious but it does this in a detached, superficial and often cynical way. It touches the unconscious mind rather than the soul, and these are by no means one and the same. The bards whom we have cited as belonging to a mystery 'Taliesin cult' believed in the material they were transmitting and were consciously part of it, rather than being detached from it. They were poets and prophets rather than mere spin doctors, who very much practiced what they preached. The changes in consciousness that they implemented were primarily changes in their own consciousness. They were, in every sense of the word, magicians – and the buttons that they found to press in the Brythonic psyche were buttons that they crafted through their own inner experience. They lived in times when practicality and survival were synonymous and drew from that inner experience lessons which produced not only long term results in collective consciousness and action, but more individual and immediate results.

What results? This is where we must part company with the literary and cultural aficionado and look at the texts as the magical (and mystical) treatises they were meant to be. We have already examined what the initiate bards who composed them hoped to achieve in the universal context of the folksoul. If, however, we are to understand this as something more than an historical curio, we must look to the practicalities of their magic.

Poetry and magic are one and the same discipline. Both seek to wedge themselves into those crannies of being where intellect can't reach. Their technique therefore is to throw the gears of consciousness so that it may operate at entirely different frequencies to those required for the more mundane pursuits of life. This is by no means a matter of letting the mind slide into idleness and daydream, but rather the construction of precise and effective connections with the soul of oneself and the soul of nature, and other areas of consciousness that we share creation with. Magic is the use of the imagination in a very precise way attended by a battery of technique applied as purposefully as a surgical procedure. The late Dion Fortune defined magic as "The art of making changes in consciousness in conformity with will" and such procedures are by no means those of the dreamer.

Poetry in its truest sense has an equally demanding task, and can only be written through the exercise of highly tuned intuition externalised in disciplined technique. As Graves and Lewis and the bards knew, to be true poetry, it can only adopt the single theme assigned to the poet by his or her muse. All else may be verse … but can never be poetry.

Whether that muse is an integral part of our own being, some Jungian Anima or Animus, or some Holy Guardian angel or other being of distinct independence from us has been a matter of long standing argument. As to the inner world of Annwn, is this simply a collective psychological state, or an inner world which exists on its own terms, with or without the support of the human imagination?

Magic works on the basis of belief. As an exercise to (by Dion Fortune's definition) "make changes in consciousness", any unbelief or denial in conscious would obviously be self defeating. It is also a discipline which works from desire. To get results you have to want results ... even if the results end up being not quite what you envisaged at the outset! Belief and desire are powerful sources of energy and originators of action, but the question remains whether other *conscious* sources of energy, of non-human, independent existence are available to participate in the process. The Celts and their predecessors believed that they were.

That we share our human lives with other non-human forms of consciousness is readily apparent to those of us who have household pets. The readiness of Celtic mystery practice to participate in the world of animal consciousness appears, as we have seen, in many of the Taliesin writings including the core mythology of the Taliesin cult itself. Most Celtic mythological literature is structured on the basis of a journey or series of journeys. Other states of consciousness are experienced in progressive, linear terms, with changes in what we might call the frequencies of consciousness being made as the protagonist crosses a landscape or (particularly in Arthurian myth) explores the environs of a castle or, in Taliesin's terminology, a series of Caers. The progression of Taliesin as Gwion, for example, is a rapid one, across an island and into the waters of Llyn Tegid, then into the sky beyond, as he goes through various frequencies of animal consciousness while being pursued by Ceridwen. The essential feature of this pursuit is that it provides initial contact with the goddess. Ceridwen, in effect, imitates Gwion's progression of consciousness, matching the frequency of her own consciousness to his by adopting animal forms which correspond to those which Gwion is experiencing. The lesson here is quite clear – that Gwion's desire to experience other modes of consciousness actually stimulates a response from another higher/wider order of consciousness. What we may describe as a proto-human order of consciousness meets human consciousness on the neutral ground of animal consciousness, and in doing so impels Gwion into the radical transformation of consciousness which comprises the initiatory experience which makes him "Taliesin" or "radiant brow". That this radiance of illumination had subsequent practical application in the world of Celtic politics is shown as the myth concludes with Taliesin arriving at the court of Maelgwyn Gwynedd to obtain the release of Prince Elphin. This is reminiscent, as it was no doubt meant to be, of the apocryphal New Testament tale of the risen Christ releasing Joseph of Arimathea from jail.

Magic and miracles were part of the spirit of the age of course, but we certainly do have claims of the efficacy of the day to day practical magic of the bards, not least the rather questionable magic of being able to produce, by sarcasm, boils upon the face of a bardic opponent. In quasi-scientific terms this implies the use of the voice at particular pitch to induce physical effects, or perhaps effects in consciousness upon the opponent which would give a psychosomatic reaction. As we have noted in an earlier chapter, the use of sound waves pitched at particular frequencies to give material effects is well known enough in such medical techniques as ultrasound. Viewed from this standpoint we may suspect that bardic magic employed the use of some "weird physics", where extended uses of consciousness were able to tap into and employ a wider range of energy frequencies. Yogis, shamen and medicine men in a plethora of supposedly underdeveloped cultures across the world still demonstrate this ability, and experiments in parapsychology, particularly in the former Soviet Union, demonstrate that these abilities are no less dormant in more technologically and rationally minded societies.

Magic is all about patterns and their synchronisation. These may be patterns in form or consciousness, but the objective is to harmonise the patterns of a number of energies and gain an interaction. Physics and chemistry can agree with this in principle but would traditionally cite other technologies to achieve it. When fledgling science still held to a pan-psychism which saw the same life force or fundamental energy running through all matter, human or otherwise, and endowed everything with a fundamental basis of consciousness, it was of course a universally more digestible proposition. But perhaps the pendulum is swinging slightly towards this universal view once more with the cautious and abstract assertions of quantum mechanics.

A few years ago, Jungian psychology became the hook of respectability on which many a magician hoped to hang his or her work. Now quantum theory has become the latest lynchpin for magical respectability, in that it opens itself to interpretation as a conservative pan-physicism. This particularly arises from the quantum notion that human observation, by its nature, intrudes human consciousness into subatomic matter, causing an interaction which collapses the wave function of the matter under observation. Here we have what appears to be a synchronisation, or collision, between the proto-conscious patterns of wave and particle in subatomic matter and human consciousness. Ironically, 'under laboratory conditions' this raises that age old dilemma of whether the magician is an equitable partner in the inner workings of nature or an unwelcome intruder. Whilst being dismayed by this latter interpretation, our

Taliesin bard would perhaps have gained some crumb of comfort from the revelation that human beings are made from the same elementary particles as the stars. This would have seemed to validate his notion of magical synchronisations between the archetypal behavioural patterns of stars and the behaviour of flesh and blood human beings. In seeing the quantum soup of 'probabilities' he would have found himself seeing the Awen, bubbling with potential in the cauldron womb of the goddess. In quantum terms, his work of Gwyddbwyll would become a consideration of the many paths and patterns which are potentially available to proto-consciousness and pre-matter. A difficulty would arise, of course, in that further factor of personalised contact with powers which are beyond and independent of the process, the goddesses and their Faery women envoys.

weird physics

This does not however invalidate the processes themselves. Whilst magic derives its operational power from belief, the processes which complete the operations as such must be subject to the same laws of physics when they emerge in the material world. This leads us, however, to the embarrassing conclusion that the ancients had a ready understanding of certain laws of physics which we have only just "discovered" ... or are yet to discover!

That our ancestors were well aware of the precession of the equinoxes, a cycle which takes some twenty-six thousand years, has already been cited; as has the fact that in this they were readily aware of the earth's tilt, and the ecliptic, and other matters which show a sound grasp of astronomy. What is more extraordinary is the vindication of their five-fold rites and Taliesin's later "five chief trees" as assimilation devices between the human senses and a perception of a Great Bear goddess, whose constellation appears to be of seven stars. Could they have possibly known that only five of the stars of the Great Bear belong to the same *moving group?* Could they, in other words, have known that the Great Bear is in effect a group of *only five* truly related stars which had their origin from the same 'mother' cloud of interstellar gas and thus share the same motion? In establishing relationships between Ursa Major and other heavenly bodies, could they also have known that Alpha Corona Borealis is another refugee from that same original group and that this group originated at about the same time as the Pleiades? Whether these particular perceptions were merely coincidental or intuitive, the reader will be aware that many other instances of ancient astronomical and scientific competence have been published elsewhere. Not least among these being the astronomical knowledge of the African Dogon culture, who have been aware for centuries of astronomical phenomena that the civilised world was blind to until the recent advent of radio astronomy. Other instances of ancient scientific and technological knowledge have been cited in thousands of books, covering everything from Egyptian sacred geometry to the two thousand-year-old electrical battery found in Iraq. The fact that most of these scientific achievements were encoded in the mythologies of the cultures concerned seems for some reason to give rise to further modern embarrassment, as if indicating that the science which we take so seriously was in some way trivialised by incidental mention in quaint stories and utilisation in primitive ritual. That the galactic marvel of the Milky Way should be understood as the ejaculation of a god or the covering of a tent whose pole is the axis of the Earth seems to imply that any serious understanding of the underlying astrophysics is impossible. And yet this appears not to have been the case. It is all of course a question of perception, and the language which derives from it. The Taliesin cult has shown us that even when that language emerges there is also a science (or a magic) in its very utterance. The magical technologies/weird physics described in such utterances may however be slightly glimpsed if we are prepared to suspend the prejudices of our own perceptive language.

The priest/magicians of Bronze Age Britain seem to have attempted to reconcile factors of astrophysics and geophysics to bring their beliefs to fruition. To do this they attempted perhaps to synchronise the electromagnetic frequencies operative at particular locations in sympathetic patterns, which would open doors between the natural world and the causative pre-natural world of Annwn. The employment of stone circles for this purpose prompted legends of "revolving doors" and "turning castles" as catalysts for such endeavours. Other legends of trees aflame, and of lightning at places where they sought to enable doors between the worlds, may be more than metaphorical. The generation and utilisation of considerable amounts of electromagnetic energy could certainly give such physical effects. Certainly the components of a physics, albeit a *weird physics* may be found in the composition of Bronze Age sites.

The large amounts of milky quartz (with which Newgrange was once covered, just as the Great Pyramid was encased in white limestone) and the use of standing stones with a high proportion of quartz crystal at British Bronze Age sacred sites may, however, possess something of the physics that we do know. The material for a prism for the electromagnetic wavelength of visible light is glass. Mythologically speaking, this means that if you want a rainbow bridge you must have it leading to or from a glass castle! However in the less visible realm of the ultraviolet wavelength, the material used for prisms is quartz. A number of modern magicians have independently found that in entering what they supposed to be the inner world of Faery they found the area to be bathed in ultraviolet light. Legends of Faeries becoming invisible by "turning sideways" to achieve invisibility, and suggestions that they are in some sense "on the edge of light" (at least as far as human perception is concerned) would seem to enforce this idea of a 'Faery' consciousness operative upon the electromagnetic frequency which we know as ultraviolet.

The current craze for crystals, the prisms of that ultraviolet frequency, has brought up odd bits of science liberally laced with New Age fantastica, not least concerning the piezoelectric properties of crystals. Claims that arrangements of crystals in wands prepared in a particular way can act as particle accelerators seem, however, to have some credence. The writer knows of an instance where such a wand, 'charged up' by the consciousness of its operator, was carelessly placed upon a table pointing towards a cut glass bowl. Within a matter of seconds the bowl was cleaved neatly in two along the axis indicated by the wand! The owner of the wand and onlookers were mightily impressed, except of course the onlooker whose bowl it was. Certainly a radiation with the "tingle" of electricity can be felt emanating from the end of such a wand.

The writer can also vouch for an occurrence at the conclusion of a particular magical ceremony where a number of the participants were invited to take pieces of 'charged up' roseate quartz. This 'charging' had been through the focused used of the imaginations of those involved, in which various mythological patterns had been invoked. Each of us took our piece of crystal as an assumed symbol of the archetypal ideas that had been invoked, and left the place of this working, assuming that to be the end of the matter. The crystals were, as far as we were concerned, just symbolic bits of inanimate rock, slightly cold to the touch. Absently clutching these we dispersed to our various individual rooms.

When we gathered together to eat some half an hour later, however, a number of us almost simultaneously related the experience of having picked up our bits of crystal to put them away and being shocked to find that our hands had been all but burned. The crystals which had been cold and inert at the conclusion of the ceremony had become extremely hot when dispersed to differing locations some twenty minutes later.

Crystal technology in a more conventional mode may of course be seen in the microprocessors used in computers, but the fact that the construction of patterns in consciousness can be focused to raise the energy frequencies in crystal to give rise to physical effects seems to give some weight to the assumptions of a weird physics being employed by our ancestors.

If indeed a primitive, or at least unrecognisable, means of generating electromagnetism was used by the Bronze Age circle and barrow builders, whose sacred kings were said to have been at times five-fold bound to a "lightning struck tree", we are tempted to look at the construction of these sites in more detail. The use of quartz in some form of 'particle accelerator' tempts us to compare stone circles with cyclotrons, and stone rows (alignments) with linear accelerators. Curiously enough physicists have found that some standing stones *do* emit electromagnetic radiation and that in a number of instances radioactive hot spots can be found on the periphery of stone circles. Far fetched as this may seem, there seems to be little doubt that these were constructed both to utilise and modulate the Earth's energy field in some way.

Such stone rows and their extensions into ley lines (which also occur as circular as well as the more commonly noted linear relationship between ancient sites) assume some of the assertions of the Chinese art of *Feng Shui* which is currently enjoying something of a vogue in the West, as is the art of dowsing. Both of these arcane arts emphasise the notion that some modes of human consciousness have an awareness, as animals do, of patterns of obscure geophysical frequencies operating in the earth's electromagnetic energy field. The ability of animal consciousness to be attuned to such frequencies may account for the enthusiasm of our Taliesin bards not only to tap into animal modes of consciousness, but also to be enthused by patterns upon the landscape and to utilise the symbolism of the Bronze Age sacred sites which often delineated these patterns. A similar magical technique may be seen in the ancient Egyptian priestly inclination to portray gods and goddesses in animal forms. We may imagine that particular totem forms were appropriate to the energy frequencies through which 'divine' archetypal energies could be contacted. This too was allied to a sacred geometry.

The extension of that geometry to correspond terrestrial features to certain stars, which represented the pure archetypal essences of those energies, seems to have been expressed in much the same way by the ancient

Egyptians as it was by our Bronze Age ancestors and subsequently by our Taliesin bards. The fact that the spectroscopy of modern astrophysics is able to ascertain the types of energy manifested by far flung constellations, by deducing the frequencies that they emit on the electromagnetic spectrum, gives unwitting credence to such ideas. One is tempted to suggest that the ancients followed much the same procedure, substituting the focusing of a telescope with the focusing of a mode of consciousness and using the prismatic properties of quartz and other minerals in stone circles to translate that archetypal stellar energy frequency into its corresponding frequency within the earth's magnetic field.

The holistic idea that the electromagnetic energy field of the earth may exist in miniature in the aura of the human body provides a further correlation for the Bronze Age and some time Celtic penchant for human sacrifice in these rites. As has often been pointed out by 'Earth magic' enthusiasts, the placing of Bronze Age sacred sites and the rites which took place at them seem to have been a kind of acupuncture performed upon the body of the Earth. Acupuncture of course recognises *meridians* or frequencies that are operative within the body's energy field and places needles at the appropriate points on these meridians to regulate and correct the energy flows. The related Chinese art of *Feng Shui* utilises much the same theory in respect of the earth's energy field and suggests the most beneficial places for the siting of particular human activities within terrestrial energy patterns. This again emphasises the relationship between the individual human energy complex and the energy patterns of environment.

The fact that the bioelectrical energy generated by brain activity may influence the individual energy field/aura and that this may have physiological effects is pretty much accepted now. Meditation and visualisation techniques to alleviate the psychosomatic effects of stress is the most obvious of the techniques which arise from this. More specific techniques, such as the use of visualisation to regulate blood pressure and suppress malignant cell growth, indicate the synchronisation in consciousness of more specific energy frequencies. The use of 'healing' crystals and other seemingly inert substances use, in effect, the crystal as a catalyst to achieve this synchronisation and to regulate the frequencies in the energy field that underpins human physiology. Such holistic correspondence between the human energy field and that of the earth give a new meaning to that Arthurian affirmation of sovereignty "The king and the land are one".

The fact that this oneness becomes expressed in a sexual relationship between the king and the goddess, or her Faery surrogate, may now be seen as something more than the most obvious expression of synchronisation. What is occurring in this is a synchronisation upon an intermediate frequency of consciousness just beyond the edge of human perception, on what we may know as the ultraviolet frequency. This is not, however, in any way to de-humanise this encounter into a mere 'energy exchange'. Tantric magic has nonetheless long been aware of the fact that sexual and emotional arousal accelerates the energies in the human aura to very high frequencies. Again, the acceleration of human energy and perception to synchronise with energy patterns of higher frequencies is implicit in our discussions of the overtly sexual symbolism used in the mythology and philosophy of our ancestors. The potency of the king, and later his surrogate bard, were intended as practical means towards bringing sovereignty to a point of synchronisation with the land, and the land to a synchronisation with the paradisal archetypal energies found in the stars. The personalisation of this was not however incidental; such archetypal energies were seen and may still be seen to have their own order of consciousness, for all were permeated, then as now, by the Divine mind, the ultimate 'pattern' of energy that is expressed in love.

The king and the falling sky

We now find ourselves able in some measure to anticipate Taliesin's magical activities of Gwyddbwyll, by seeing that this was based in practical terms upon an ancient holistic science which appreciated the synchronisation of energy fields. In having already stated that the practicalities of that time were synonymous with survival we may find reasons beyond those of terrestrial sovereignty for Taliesin's stellar preoccupations. What were the Taliesin bards afraid of?

The fear of the disaster of planetary collision or other cataclysm "from above" has been embedded into pretty much every race memory across the world (along with the accompanying flood fear) from a very long time ago. The Celts were afraid (in as far as they were ever afraid of anything!) that the sky may fall, which would seem to lend further importance to the Celtic and pre-Celtic ideas of the king's responsibility to uphold the axial "tent pole" of the earth. That we are dealing with a corps of bards who were intelligent men, living in times when it would not have paid to be frightened of one's own shadow, such a fear seems absurd. We may however see from Taliesin's poetry, confirmed in the theories of the extraordinary Immanuel Velikovsky that this fear may not have been entirely groundless.

The Hermetic philosophy which underpinned a Renaissance magic which was to flourish after the decline of the Taliesin bards was nonetheless based upon the same premise of ensuring the correlation between the archetypal world of the heavens and the good earth. Its essential dictum was "*as above, so below*", and at the heart of its mythology was the Holy Grail. The Hermetic myth told how an emerald which fell to Earth from the crown of the doomed lightbearer Lucifer became the Grail. All this placed an emphasis on the now familiar paradisal ideal, an ideal connected, as we have seen, to the supposed races of Faery who had occupied the world in times before the Edenic fall. Legends that the lightbearer himself fell to earth and that the Grail/cauldron or emerald – or even the fallen lightbearer himself – were incarcerated in the deeps of the Earth, in Annwn, are variations of one theme. The emerald was associated with the planet Venus and as we shall see the Taliesin poetry has things to say about Venus which are consistent with the 'falling sky' and planetary catastrophe.

Dr. Immanuel Velikovsky's *Worlds in Collision* appeared in 1950 and committed massive scientific heresy by suggesting that Venus had spun from its orbit and had a near collision with the Earth during the late Bronze Age. This seems to have been contemporary to the destruction and consequent cultural upheavals that we have described as having occurred in this period. Many archaeologists concur that this upheaval does not appear to have originated through any human agency. The 'falling sky' is generally attributed to the eruption of an Icelandic volcano, whose dust enveloped northern Britain. This seems to have initiated the abandonment of many Bronze Age sacred sites and effectually an end to the Bronze Age as a theocratic era. A poem of Taliesin's concerning the flooding of Cantref Gwaelod, the legendary land that is said now to be below the waters of Cardigan Bay, says:

"*Accursed be the damsel who after the wailing, let loose the fountains, of Venus, the raging deep.*"

And

"*Accursed be the maiden, who after the conflict let loose the fountains of Venus, the desolating, raging sea.*"

Are we to assume from this that the speculations of Velikovsky were correct? If this were the case, a case remembered over a thousand years later in the Taliesin poem, we may start to understand this almost obsessive preoccupation with the relative position of the stars to the earth and the earth's correct axial tilt. We may also place further interpretation upon the cauldron deep within the earth in Annwn, which had to be warmed by the breath of nine maidens. While not discounting the appropriateness of this to signify the gestation cycle and the obvious gestation analogy of Annwn, this would account in this instance for the fall of the lightbearer from the sky and the nine-fold planetary order which fell with him. That the arrangement may be nine-fold rather than seven-fold to include the lunar nodes (as it frequently was in the ancient world) is of no little importance in this. Of no less importance is the preoccupation with the earth's magnetic field which seems to have reversed at about this time, consistent with the near approach of another heavenly body. Such magnetic upheavals would have caused the extensive floods which Taliesin, and indeed many other mythographers around the world, describe. Ancient literature frequently describes Venus as adopting comet-like characteristics. The Old Testament has fire and dust falling from the sky and the advent of pestilence, all of which would of course be consistent with such a near miss.

Perhaps the incident which Geoffrey of Monmouth describes in the *History of the Kings of Britain* during the upheavals just prior to Uther Pendragon's ascent to the kingship of Britain is a further folk memory of this. As Lewis Thorpe's translation describes:

"There appeared a star of great magnitude and brilliance with a single beam shining from it. At the end of this beam was a ball of fire, spread out in the shape of a dragon".

It is interesting to note that Geoffrey places this incident just after the construction (by Merlin) of what we can assume to be the late Bronze Age phase of Stonehenge (the Giant's Dance) incorporating the bluestones into the central elliptical arrangement (mythologically from Ireland … actually from Pembrokeshire). He also associates this change in cosmic order to the change in British sovereignty, passing from Aurelius to Uther Pendragon. He makes sure that Merlin emphasises the connection when he has him say to Uther *"the star signifies you in person, so does the fiery dragon beneath the star."* In this we seem to have the precession and the near collision with Venus all parcelled up in one incident and laid out as a new pattern of sovereignty.

It is only fair to say that whilst Velikovsky's speculations were considered to be scientific heresy at the time of their publication, Velikovsky was a scientist of some eminence and many of his more specialised speculations about the character of planets have since been scientifically proved beyond doubt. If then his theory is correct we may anticipate a late Bronze Age preoccupation with the modification of the Earth's magnetic field. We may also begin to understand why elliptical "circles" were adopted (as in the later phases of Stonehenge) when we look at Velikovsky's supposition of the elongated and exaggerated elliptical orbit of his recalcitrant Venus during the Bronze Age. Was the building of these elliptical circles in imitation of the Venusian orbit an attempt at a sympathetic magic to influence the orbit of Venus during her catastrophic meanderings?

What then of Taliesin's sympathetic magic, his Gwyddbwyll, to preserve sovereignty and prosperity for a king who had to be at one with the land, and a land, an earth, that needed to be secure in its destined relationship to the other heavenly bodies?

Gwyddbwyll

We come across Gwyddbwyll on a number of occasions in the Mabinogi, as a game played five-fold between the king and the supernatural powers which empower his sovereignty. It appears that in Celtic, or more probably pre-Celtic, Britain and Ireland it was a talismanic magical rite in which the king set out his kingdom in a symbolic arrangement upon a board or cloth under the direction of his chief bard. As such it would have been something of a simulation of what went on in the ritual circles of the late Bronze Age. At the end of the Celtic era it had probably degenerated into a form of (almost) mundane chess played by the nobility, even though the initiate bards like those of the Taliesin cult would have continued to exercise the magical principles of the game out on the landscape under a starlit sky. The golden throne which was brought for Arthur to play Gwyddbwyll in the *Dream of Rhonabwy* seems therefore to have been superceded by Taliesin's "uneasy chair" upon the heights of Cadair Idris.

A modern magical equivalent of Gwyddbwyll might be seen in the Hermetic Order of the Golden Dawn's *Enochian Chess*, which was synthesised from Dr. Dee's Enochian magic, which again called for the initiate to establish his relationship to the supernatural powers by setting

Gwyddbwyll

The Gwyddbwyll Board on the mantle Gwen

The mantle is the white of Annwn and is secured by an "Avalon" apple at each corner. The board is of 13 x 13 alternating red and white squares. The Gwen conferred invisibility, but would tolerate no other colour upon it than its own (white). This stipulation, which would of course obviate the red/gold apples, is yet another bardic conundrum.

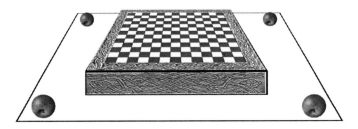

The Three Dimensional Board as the Seven-fold Mountain

out their representations on a board. Gwyddbwyll, or *Brandubh,* or *Fidchell* as it was variously called in the Gaelic traditions, occurs in the Mabinogi in a number of the tales.

In *Peredur*, the knight witnesses the game playing itself without human assistance, and in consternation throws the board and pieces into (significantly) a lake. He is admonished by a maiden who tells him *"Thou hast made the Empress lose her board and she would not wish that for her empire."* We have already seen Arthur playing Gwyddbwyll upon the cloth of invisibility in the *Dream of Rhonabwy* and the supernatural upheavals that attend that game. In the *Dream of Macsen Wledig,* Macsen, based upon the historical Roman Maximus who was killed by Theodosius in his attempt to take the imperial crown, has a dream. In the dream he encounters a beautiful woman upon a paradisal island playing Gwyddbwyll. He eventually finds that the island is Britain and gets to meet his dream girl, Elen, at Caernarfon, where she is again playing Gwyddbwyll. It is interesting that this is again a tale of sovereignty and that Elen, the Faery muse of dream and vision, appears elsewhere as "Elen of the Roads". In fact an ancient trackway in south Gwynedd, the *Sarn Elen,* is named after her. In this we have an association between the game of Gwyddbwyll, the Faery realm of aspiration and empowerment which is Annwn, and the 'roads' of the ley line structure which delineates the energy field of the earth. Elen and her roads therefore represent the archetypal, paradisal pattern of the kingdom. It is interesting that elsewhere an "Elen" also appears as Myrddin's wife!

The basic Gwyddbwyll pattern of the kingdom is always five-fold. The Irish *Book of Invasions* describes the division of the land into five parts with the sovereignty in the central position of Tara. Of the thirty-three Irish heroes, we are told that there are five "chief heroes". Indeed the weight of five-fold symbolism that stands behind the operation of Gwyddbwyll will by now be plain. Primarily we have the five-fold bloody rites of Bronze Age sovereignty and the five-fold circles, alignments and polygonal chambers of Bronze Age times that a Gwyddbwyll board was originally meant to synthesise. As extensions of this we have the five fingers/letters of Ogham communication and their corresponding vowel sounds, and also of course the five senses of human perception, even the five-fold core of the paradisal apple.

We may even cite the psychological analogy of the Jungian mandala ("magic circle") of the 'sovereign' integrated self standing at the centre of its mandalic kingdom of four-fold consciousness, just a king stands at the centre of his kingdom and turns to survey his domain spread out across the four directions of the compass and the four seasons of the turning year. Such symbolism still provides the basic format for ceremonial magic.

Parallels to the magical exercise of Gwyddbwyll also appear in other mystery traditions. We have already cited the practices of the Jerusalem temple in that same priestly endeavour to synchronise archetypal paradisal patterns with those of the material and natural world. In this we may imagine the high priest entering the Debir to mediate before the enthroned and essentially feminine aspect of Godhead, the Shekinah. He

GLASTONBURY – Gwyddbwyll on the Landscape

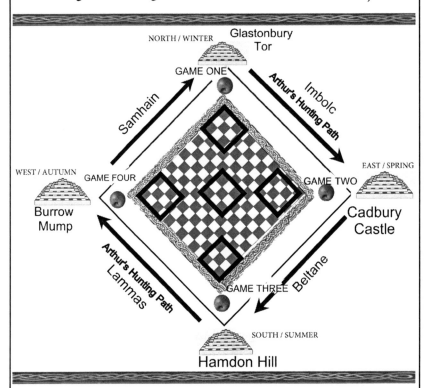

The Bronze Age "Glastonbury diamond" metaphorically provided a five-fold Avalon and a geographically accurate 'Gwen' upon an actual sacred landscape. The diamond, as well as being set to the four sacred sites with their seven-fold terracing, also happens, weirdly, to form an even-sided parallelogram. Two sides of this parallelogram are aligned to significant solar/lunar events. Each of the four locations has its own "Grail story" (Gwyddbwyll is, after all, a Grail Quest). The fifth 'caer' or 'terraced hill' is in effect the central Gwyddbwyll board itself.

In thinking of the ascent of the Gwyddbwyll board through seven terraces or levels to its summit/centre as a journey through the seven Caers, we must think of their collective name, Caer Sidi, the "turning castle". The castle of Caer Sidi/Annwn therefore "turns" with the seasons, obliging Arthur and his companions to approach it from *four* directions – thus his 'hunting path' around the four sides of the board. In the *Dream of Rhonabwy*, perhaps the most complete account we have of Gwyddbwyll, Arthur and Owein play a 'set' of *four* games. Caer Sidi, the turning castle represented by the Gwyddbwyll board, is also therefore Caer Pedryfan, the four-sided, foursquare Caer of the *Preiddu Annwn*. Another way of saying this is Caer Bannog, from which we get *Carbonek*, the Grail Castle of later Arthurian romance.

would wear the square golden breastplate of the Urimm and Thummin with the Logion jewels set out upon it to represent the twelve tribes as the archetypal arrangement of the kingdom of Israel, as a manifestation of the twelve constellations of the zodiac. It was said that this device had divination properties and in it we may assume something of similar purpose to the original conception of the Gwyddbwyll board.

playing the game

We may choose to consign all this mythology, albeit coupled to a weird physics, to the dustbin of history ... and prehistory. We may however choose to pause in this sorting of the dusty attic of our Celtic folksoul and wonder if these ancient things still have any further use. Is there anything in what the Taliesin bards knew which can enrich lives which are already obese with information?

The poet and magician will find things here, if he or she has not already done so, which may be of use. Even the Gestalt psychologist may see echoes of his technique in the integration of patterns of consciousness, and the Jungian will see archetypes of the unconscious in mandalic array as echoes of the more academic work of the father of that tradition. Enthusiasts of the new magic of N.L.P. (Neuro-Linguistic Programming) will confirm some of the inner processes cited. The collation of experience through the five windows of perception, its processing and programming in a personal Annwn and the consequent five-fold expression in a life which demands and gets results, will be a familiar theme. These and many other contemporary philosophies will be able to take their selective pickings from the Brythonic mysteries.

The Brythonic mysteries however survive and evolve as a living holism and that holism is encapsulated in spiritual integrity. The ultimate cloak which is laid out upon the land to play Gwyddbwyll is that same cloak which Faery Brigid wove and placed upon the shoulders of the Christ whom she had fostered and nurtured with the milk of the stars. The starlight which showed Taliesin the unifying patterns for a paradisal world were, and are, the same light of heaven which fell from the grasp of the Son of the Morning, before time and its anxieties formed their cancer on the body of Evermore. Like that Son of the Morning, we hold in our grasp the substance of *Awen,* of *becoming* ... and of choice.

AWEN

Glossary

As this is essentially a work based upon a mythology originally set down in the Brythonic and Welsh languages, some of the words and names may not be familiar to readers. Whilst these are explained throughout the text, a brief ready reference of terms used and the major dramatis personae featured is given here. Other expressions, including those in the general currency of the mysteries, are also included. The latter is essential as the terminology of the mysteries in general is in hopeless confusion and certain words hold differing meaning and significance to the adherents of different schools and traditions. All these are defined here essentially in the context of the material of this book. This does not necessarily invalidate other definitions.

Annwn *(pr. "An-noon")* Literally "The Deep", but referring to the Welsh Celtic Underworld *(cf)*. An interactive, overlapping area between the archetypal *(cf)* heaven worlds and the material world.

Archetype/archetypal An original and unblemished pattern, or power; the ideal primal representation. Particularly used in this book in association with the 'ideal' patterns and energy matrices of heaven worlds, shown in the patterns of the stars. Used in Jungian psychology to denote primary universal images within the collective unconscious.

Arianrhod *(pr. "Ah-re-an-rod")* Literally "silver round" representing a goddess, or the aspect of one triple goddess, whose nature is of the stars. Sister of Gwydion *(cf)* in the Mabinogi romance of *Math fab Mathonwy* *(cf)*.

Arthur Name of mythological sacred king, originating from the Welsh word "Arth" meaning "bear". A bardic resurrection of a similar more ancient archetypal sacred king, Math fab Mathonwy *(cf)*, "bear son of bearlike". Arthur is considered (in this book) to have no historical standing.

Arthuriad The corpus of mediaeval writings which describe King Arthur and his adventures.

Avalon/Afallon *(pr. "Av-ath-on")* Derived from Welsh for apple, "afal", denoting an inner, paradisal realm … a Celtic Eden. See also **Annwn**.

Awen *(pr. "Ah-when")* May be inadequately translated into English as "inspiration", but inspiration which also gives certain formative and transformative powers. The stuff/liquid which came from the cauldron of the goddess Ceridwen *(cf)*.

Awenyddion *(pr. "Ah-wen-ith-ee-on")* Those inspired by the awen. Typically wandering bards beyond the rules and confines of court bardship, who entered into trance and spoke prophecy.

Axis/axial/axis mundi The axial tilt of the earth, on an axis which points to the current Pole Star and thus towards the centre of the heavens as perceived from Earth.

Bard General term for initiates/loremasters/poets who effectively succeeded the Druids *(cf)*. Not, in the context of this work, connected (except in exceptional individuals) with the modern bards as known by the Welsh "Gorsedd", or members of present day neo-Druidic societies.

Barrow Generic term for burial mound. See also **Cairn, Cist, Passage Graves**.

Blodeuedd/Bloudewedd *(pr. "Blod-e-eth/Blaw-de-weth")* Derived from the the Welsh word "Blodau", flowers, as befitting the goddess conjured from flowers by Math and Gwydion to be a wife for Lleu *(cf)*. When Gwydion later turns her into an owl, for being unfaithful to Lleu, she retains the stamp of her floral origins, in that an owl has a dished face like an open flower.

Bound souls Used in this work to describe souls that were set 'in limbo' at an ancient burial or other sacred sites, by ritual slaughter, to protect it with their 'ghostly' presence. A practice generally attributed to Bronze Age sacred king/Hercules *(cf)* rites.

Bran The Welsh word for raven, applied to an early Celtic god, probably of Bronze Age origin, found in both Welsh and Irish mythology. In the

Welsh tradition a primitive, giant, sacred king archetype, who was later to become a god of the Underworld.

Branwen. Sister of Bran in the Welsh mythology, whose name means white raven, but whose "wen/white" suffix to her name indicates that she is a being from Annwn.

Brighid/Brigid/Bride/Ffraed A goddess of Irish origin whose name means "high one". Most Irish mythologies have her as the daughter, or one of three daughters (all called Brighid), of the Dagda *(cf)*, the chief of the immortal Tuatha dé Danann *(cf)*. Her role became expanded down the years and she made the easy transition to Christian sainthood – so much so that in Irish Celtic Christianity she all but supplanted the Virgin Mary as "Mary of the Gael" and is still much revered in Roman Catholic Ireland. Her cult extended to the British mainland, with cult centres at Glastonbury and throughout Wales, where she was known as Ffraed.

Bronze Age The period in prehistoric Britain after the Neolithic period, which marked the rise of the first metal-using peoples. The Beaker people (so known because of their characteristic pottery) started to use copper and bronze (an alloy of copper and tin) from about 2,400 BC. This mix of bronze-using indigenous and immigrant peoples were, it is assumed, gradually displaced by the influx of the iron-using Celts from about 600 BC.

Brythonic Of the Brythons/Britons – pertaining to the British mainland, as distinct from Ireland, and its peoples. The so-called Celtic Mystery Tradition of the British mainland may more properly be defined as the Brythonic Mystery Tradition, as many of its essential elements were indigenous and predated the arrival of the Celts in Britain. Brythonic is also, however, used to identify the Celts of England, Wales and Brittany in respect of their branch of the Celtic language – Brythonic – which preceded early Welsh, Cornish and Breton, and was spoken and written (as "late Brythonic") until about the ninth century AD.

Caer *(pr. "Car")* Welsh word for a defensive earth mound, but used by the Taliesin bards as a pun for burial mounds, and thus underworld bastions. See also **Sidhe**.

Cairn Heaped rough stones covering/marking a prehistoric burial chamber, much as Barrow *(cf)*. Frequently used to qualify shape and style of such a burial, i.e. "long cairn", "round cairn", etc.

Canu Aneirin *(pr. Can-ee An-err-in)* "The song of Aneiren". The earliest extant writing in the "British" language, thought from its late Brythonic orthography to date from the time just after the battle of Catreath (600 AD), which a section of the text (*Y Gododdin*) describes. The existing document is a copy made in about 1265 AD. It is particularly notable for being the document which carries the earliest mentions of Arthur, Myrddin (Merlin) and Taliesin.

Capstone Huge flat stone used to cover a burial chamber, usually used as a single flat slab covering a burial **cist** *(cf)*.

Celt/Celtic *(pr. Kelt/Keltick)* The conglomeration of tribes identified by the Greeks as "Keltoi", as sharing a particular language and culture. The Celts originated in eastern Europe and moved westwards, covering most of the northern European mainland by about 600 BC. It is now thought that the Celtic peoples did not actually invade Britain and Ireland (as previously supposed) but that the native British had begun to adopt and adapt their own indigenous "Celtic" culture from about 600 BC. A universal Celtic language was thought to have been in use a century or so before this, synonymous with the British Iron Age. This Celtic language later divided into two forms, 'P' Celtic and 'Q' Celtic. Areas which may still be identified as retaining Celtic language and culture include Wales, Ireland, Brittany and north western Scotland, although the Isle of Man, Cornwall, North western Spain and the Languedoc in southern France also retain some traces of their Celtic heritage. Small Celtic enclaves exist across the world, not least the New World, as the result of modern migration. Welsh speaking communities survive in both North and South America, notably in the latter case in Patagonia. A Welshman is credited with having fired the first shot of the American Civil War.

Celyddon *(pr. Kell-ee-thon)* The forests of lowland Scotland to which Myrddin *(cf)* was reputed to have fled, suffering from what we would call post traumatic stress disorder after the battle of Arfderydd. Following on from this, it is here that Myrddin receives his illumination, and this "wild wood" seems also to serve as a metaphor for what Jungian psychology calls the collective unconscious. Charles Williams called this same place and state of consciousness Broceliande.

Ceridwen *(pr. "Ker-id-when")* The goddess of the cauldron who was responsible, among other things, for the transformation of the boy Gwion into the illuminated bard Taliesin *(cf)*. Ceridwen tends to represent the "earth mother" aspect of the triple goddess, but is also very much an initiatrix. She is frequently represented by the totem animal of a white sow and appears in this guise in the *Math fab Mathonwy* tale in the Mabinogion *(cf)*. Her 'Caer' or dwelling place was said to be the rainbow.

Cist *(pr. "Kist")* Usually encountered in individual burials of the Bronze Age, being a square stone box set in a round mound to contain a single corpse or cremated remains and covered with a capstone *(cf)*.

Clas *(pr. "Klaz")* The loose organisational structure of Celtic monasticism, which allowed for collectives of Christian solitaries and hermits, before the adoption of the more unifying and formalised Benedictine rule.

Cyfarwydd *(pr. "Cuv-ar-with")* A class of bard, a wandering storyteller, typified by the guise which Gwydion and Lleu (or Llew) take to get into the court of Arianrhod. Gwydion *(cf)* was "the best storyteller in the world".

Dark Ages Simplistic term used to describe the period of British history between the departure of the Romans in 410 AD and the start of the Middle Ages. Generally the term refers to the 'darkness' or paucity of historical information about this period, which was a time when the Romano British Celts fought both amongst themselves and against Viking and Saxon incursion. The period was not entirely however one of barbarity, as the name might imply!

Debir The Holy of Holies, beyond the veil of the Jerusalem temple where the Ark of the Covenant and the **Kapporeth** (mercy seat) formed by the Ark and the wings of the Kerubim were situated. The Debir was only entered by the High Priest and then only once a year, being represenative of Adam speaking with God in Eden. In the pre-exilic temple, the Divine Presence or **Shekinah** was thought to manifest upon the mercy seat.

Druids The initiate loremasters of the pre-Christian Celts. Their teaching was largely conveyed by oral instruction, so little of their lore is factually available from original and unbiased sources. Because of this, modern orders of supposed "Druids" (while representing a commendable spirit of Druidism) should not be assumed to be a reflection in any practical sense of the original Druids. The name seems to have derived from "Derydd" meaning "oak seer". The role of the Druid was largely taken on in Celtic Christian times by the Bards *(cf)*.

Echtrai Mythological adventure stories of the Otherworld in the Irish tradition.

Englyn *(pr. "En-glin")* Welsh term for poetic incantation. An example would be the *englyn* sung by Gwydion to persuade the eagle form of Lleu to come to him in the *Math fab Mathonwy* story in the Mabinogi.

Faery The term which describes the situation and state of pre-human races, who traditionally occupy the Underworld, or **Annwn** *(cf)*, as it is described in the Welsh mythologies. See also **Tuatha dé Danann, Tír nan Óg.**

Fidchell Irish version of quasi magical chess game called **Gwyddbwyll** *(cf)* in Welsh.

Folksoul Also Group soul/Racial Soul. The soul (or in Jungian psycho-logical terms the collective unconscious) of a racial or composite multi-racial grouping, usually attached to or originating from a particular environment or territory. A folksoul is typified as sharing within its collective psyche its own unique versions of universal archetypes *(cf)* which are reflected in its mythology.

Fortune, Dion Non de plume/magical name of Violet Mary Firth (later Evans). Influential occultist and magical publicist who left the Hermetic Order of the Golden Dawn to found her own mystery school, the Society of the Inner Light, in 1922, which still thrives today.

Geasa Welsh. A prohibition, restriction, or magical curse. Arianrhod set a geasa upon Lleu that he may never marry a mortal woman, etc.

Gnostic From the Greek "gnosis", knowledge. Heretical strains of belief in early Christianity – though one early church father, Clement of Alexandria, used the term to describe a Christian who had penetrated deeper into the mysteries of faith than had the ordinary Christian believer. Gnosticism was not however exclusively Christian and its concepts may be found in earlier Persian and Mithraic philosophy and in pre-Christian Judaism. It became characterised, among other things, by its belief in salvation through esoteric knowledge. It has therefore become linked by association with much mystery school activity from the time of the classical mysteries up to the present day. The Templars and Cathars *(cf)* are assumed to have held to broadly "Gnostic" beliefs.

Gwendydd *(pr. "Gwen-deeth")* Welsh. In some legends the wife and/or sister of Merlin and in some also his collaborator in magical endeavour.

Gwenwawd *(pr. "Gwen-wowd")* Welsh. A religious eulogy. For example *Y Gododdin* in the *Canu Aneirin*, sung by the priestly Aneirin for his fallen comrades.

Gwraig Annwn Welsh. Literally "wife of the deep". A Faery woman who sometimes mates with a mortal and typically appears from deep lakes, e.g. the Lady of the Lake.

Gwyddbwyll *(pr. "Gweeth-buth")* Welsh. Quasi-magical chess game, mentioned in several instances in the Mabinogi. It appears to have originally been seen as a ritualised setting out of (usually five) tokens on a board to reach an equitable balance and interaction between innerworld and outerworld powers to establish sovereignty. Called Fidchell or Brandubh in Ireland.

Gwydion *(pr. "Gwid-ee-on")* Welsh. Son of Dôn, brother and lover of Arianrhod, apparent father of Lleu and nephew of Math. Gwydion is the Welsh Hermes in many respects. A master of magic who it was said brought writing and other cultural advances to the Welsh. In this he seems to have replaced the earlier Bran and may therefore be a personalisation of a folk memory when a 'primitive' culture was superseded or overrun by a more advanced one. Also known as the "greatest storyteller in the world". He was the archetypal Druid and Bard who provided the mythological format for magician/bards like those who called themselves "Taliesin" *(cf)*.

Gwyllion *(pr. "Gwith-e-on")* Mountain "faeries" of north Wales. "Faeries" in this instance may be seen as either nature spirits or proto-human beings from Annwn … depending on your point of view … and experience!

Gwynhyfwr/Guinevere Welsh/English. The original name may mean "white phantom" and the Gwyn/white prefix indicates that she is a being from Annwn *(cf)*. Queen of Arthur.

Hekal Sanctuary of the Jerusalem temple, leading to the Debir *(cf)*.

Henge Circular sacred enclosure, usually made by the digging of a ditch and embankment, sometimes with occasional standing stones in

Neolithic *(cf)* times, starting to appear in about 2,800 BC. Many such sites were elaborated upon in the last days of the Neolithic era and into the later Bronze Age *(cf)* from about 2,000 BC by the erection of stone circles and/or the placing of burial mounds and chambers within them.

Hercules Cults Cult practices of sacrificial rites of "sacred kings"*(cf)* and heroes, who appear to be in the mould of the mythological Hercules/ Greek Heracles.

Hermetic Order of the Golden Dawn The influential magical fraternity/ mystery school founded in England in 1887 by S.L. Macgregor Mathers and Drs. Woodford and Westcott. The Order is said to have taken its mandate from an (unknown) German Rosicrucian fraternity. The Golden Dawn is notable for reviving, and in some measure bringing to public awareness (albeit unintentionally) a synthesis of the magical practices of the mystery schools of ancient times (including some Celtic mystery practice) plus a number of modern and Far Eastern innovations. Most modern mystery schools in Western Europe, North America, Australia and New Zealand have at some time or another owed their structure, philosophy and practice to the Golden Dawn model. The Order and its various schismatic offshoots included such celebrated members as W.B. Yeats, Arthur Machen, Charles Williams and Florence Farr. After various schisms down the years it effectively ceased to exist by the late 1930s. Two or three mystery schools which exist today may be said to have tangential lineage from it (including the school which trained this writer!) and a number of revivalist groups have latterly sprung up (presumptuously using its name!) in the United States.

Hiraeth *(pr. "Here-eyeth")* Welsh word which describes a melancholic longing for the land of one's birth.

History – actual-factual-virtual *Actual history,* as seen and recorded by a direct eye witness. *Factual History:* "Facts", recorded with varying accuracy and bias by those who collate actual histories at a later time. *Virtual History:* Commentaries which, rather than relating "history" use factual history on a selective basis, usually embellished to pursue a particular agenda. Geoffrey of Monmouth's *History of the Kings of Britain* would be a good example of *virtual history.*

Hwyl *(pr. "Hoy-ell")* Welsh word which describes the upsurge of feeling in the Welsh folksoul.

Initiate Generally, one who has gone through a radical transformation of consciousness which enables illumination. In modern day terms one who has gone through the regime of a mystery system and thus experienced transformation of consciousness. Initiation is however considered to be a 'beginning' which sows the seed for mediative work between one mode of being and another.

Inklings The group of writers and scholars based in Oxford and essentially comprising J.R.R. Tolkien, C.S. Lewis, Charles Williams and Owen Barfield. E.R. Eddison was also an "honorary Inkling". Tolkien and Lewis in particular agreed to undertake the purposeful writing of "mythopoeic" material. Others belonged to the group over the years and the name Inklings wasn't coined until 1931, but the Inklings are generally considered to be this group of men who had such a profound effect upon the modern shaping of British mythology through their association between 1922 and 1945.

Lleu/Llew Welsh. Light/Lion. The hero of the Mabinogi romance *Math fab Mathonwy (cf)*. The nephew and presumed son of Gwydion *(cf)* and of Arianrhod. Gwydion tricked Arianrhod into acknowledging her son by getting her to name and arm him in accordance with Matriarchal Celtic custom. She named the boy *Lleu Llaw Gyffes*, which is translated as "lion with the steady hand". He has a mythological counterpart in the Irish *Lugh*.

Ley lines The rediscovery of the ley line concept may be attributed to the late Alfred Watkins, who noted that certain ancient sites were aligned across the landscape, and published his findings in *The Old Straight Track*, proposing these alignments as prehistoric trackways. Later commentators, particularly in the last forty years, expanded Watkins' concept after research of their own, which included dowsing, to demonstrate that these "leys" were geophysical "energy lines". Ideas were subsequently muted to the effect that such leys were rather like the *meridians* that acupuncture believes mark the flow lines in the human body's energy field. This analogy was then extended to suppose that the earth had a comparable energy field and that our prehistoric ancestors realised this. In doing so it was believed that they had set standing stones and other monuments upon the earth's surface in the same way that an acupuncturist places needles into a patient's skin to modulate energy flows. Myriad ley lines may be found by tracing ancient site alignments upon maps, sometimes over many hundreds of miles, but few people realise that such alignments do not only occur as straight lines. Many, for example, occur in circular configurations with a number of widely distributed sites sitting upon the circumference of vast circles upon the landscape; many also trace stellar configurations. The ley line/geophysical energies theory has lately been given some weight in the western adoption of Chinese *Feng Shui*, a theory of geophysical energy flow which has official credence in the Far East.

Mab Darogan Welsh. Literally "the prophesied son", a theme of a number of the Mabinogi (and indeed universal) myths.

Mabinogi/Mabinogion Welsh. Literally meaning "youth tales", a name coined by Lady Charlotte Guest to collectively describe the bulk of Welsh myth still extant in written form, notably the *Red Book of Hergest,* the *White Book of Rhydderch* and certain of the *Peniarth* manuscripts. Whilst many of the tales seem to hold traces of very ancient custom and belief and had obviously been around in oral form since ancient times, the actual written forms date from between about 1200-1400 AD.

Magic Defined by the late Dion Fortune *(cf)* as "the making of changes in consciousness in conformity with will". Generally done by inciting the imagination in a disciplined way. Myth is a very potent device for doing this.

Manu Far Eastern/Theosophical term which denotes an *avatar,* one who comes from another realm of being, generally of virgin birth, to show humanity the way that it should evolve. Examples would be *Jesus Christ*, from the New Testament, *Melchizadek* from the old Testament and such figures as the mythological versions of *Merlin* (as distinct from the historical Myrddin) and indeed J.R.R. Tolkien's *Gandalf.* Jesus Christ however has the distinction of being an historically verifiable figure ... "a myth made real".

Math fab Mathonwy *(pr. "Maath-vab-Math-on-wee")* Welsh. Title of one of the Mabinogi romances and name of the sacred king of that myth, meaning *"Bear son of bearlike".* Uncle of Gwydion and Arianrhod and husband of Goewin.

Merlin/Myrddin/Mirdyn *Myrddin/Mirdin* was an historically verifiable figure who survived the battle of Arfderydd (573 AD) and seems to have later become a monk at Carmarthen. *Merlin* arose from Geoffrey of Monmouth's inflation of this historical figure (adjusting the name to make it suitable for his Anglo-Norman audience). Further inflation occurred in later myth/legend to give Merlin the archetypal standing of a semi-divine Manu *(cf)*.

Mithraism Dualist mystery religion practised by the Roman legions and drawn originally from Persian myth.

Morgan le Fey Half sister of Arthur. Depicted in late myth as being a malevolent witch and protagonist of Merlin, who magically assumed the guise of Arthur's queen Guinevere to get Arthur to sleep with her. The result of this union was Mordred, the bastard son who becomes Arthur's protagonist. Had Morgan done this, she would only have been avenging the same deceit inflicted upon her mother Ygraine. (Arthur's father Uther had slept with Ygraine using a similar magical deception of Merlin's magical contrivance so that Arthur could be conceived). Morgan's name may be related in earlier myth to the Irish war goddess the *Morrigan* and she also appears to be either a direct reflection or priestess of the Welsh goddess *Ceridwen*.

Mysteries (the) Originally from the Greek *mysterion,* which specifically described sacred rites, as distinct from later and current usage to simply mean secrets which have no explanation. In the former sense most mystery systems agree that particular knowledge is attained through the *experience of* initiation *(cf)*. They further agree that in view of this, their 'esoteric' knowledge may not be devulged to, or indeed comprehended by, those who have not undergone such initiative experiences. Mystery religions appear to be as old as humanity, but what scholars consider to be the "classical mysteries" of the Mediterranean world flourished from about the seventh century BC until the fifth century AD. These were however influenced by the much earlier mysteries practised principally in Egypt and Persia. Mystery systems also appear to have thrived in north western Europe from Neolithic times on through the British Bronze Age and into Celtic times (as this book is at pains to point out) … and indeed beyond and into the present day!

Mysticism A much abused word which is frequently confused with its equally abused bedfellow "magic". Mysticism, properly understood, seeks direct experience of and union with the divine … the ultimate creator. Magic, by contrast, seeks to work with the inner side of creation … which is itself within that ultimate creator.

Mythopoeic The term coined by the Inklings *(cf)* to describe poetically inspired myth.

Neolithic The "new stone" age. Taken by archaeologists to be from about 4000-2000 BC in the British Isles.

Onomastic Myth which refers to a particular place, generally to explain how it was established and named.

Passage graves Neolithic *(cf)* and early Bronze Age *(cf)* tombs which developed the idea of entry into "mother earth" through vagina-like passages of drystone construction within a burial mound. *Bryn Celli Ddu* on Anglesey (see page 136) would be a good example.

Pencerdd/Penkerdd *(pr. "Pen-care-thh")* Welsh, meaning 'chief' or 'supreme' bard.

Polarity A word frequently used in practical magic to imply the purposeful use of the flow of sexual magnetism between male and female participants. Contrary to popular beliefs about "sex magic", however, this 'polarity' is, or at least should be, utilised as a starting point from which to raise energies to impersonal archetypal levels (beyond human sexuality). If the energies evoked merely become focused towards sexual gratification then the resultant consummation prematurely neutralises or 'earths' the energies and defeats the magical raison d'etre of the operation ... and frequently causes no little personal complication for those involved! Magical polarity, still utilising sexual energies as a starting point, may also be enlisted to enable the building of bridges between incarnate and discarnate magical operatives. Such is the case with much "Faery magic" where sexual imaginative relationships are the preliminary step in building an energy interchange between a beautiful Faery being and the human magician. Celtic mythology frequently cites such practices, as this book indicates.

Polarity in its more general sense is, however, a relationship which involves an interaction of energies. Polarity may be said therefore to be apparent in a (non-sexual) mundane sense between, say, a teacher and a class of students, or an actor and his or her audience. In a more profound sense it may be used to describe the mystic's relationship with the divine. Such inner polarity is often called "vertical polarity".

Precession The "precession of the equinoxes" is an astronomical phenomenon which the Egyptians realised in noting that the orientation of the Earth and Sun were not quite the same at each Vernal Equinox. After observation over countless years it became apparent that the equinox point was moving backwards through the constellations of the zodiac, taking about 2,120 years to traverse each zodiacal constellation. The complete cycle takes therefore about 25,500 years and is often called the **Platonic Year**. The reason for this is that the Earth's axis *(cf)* 'wobbles'. In other words, the angled axis of the planet (23.5° from the vertical) itself scribes an arc as it moves through space/time. This means that what seem in our short lifetimes to be important positional constants in fact change over these considerable periods of time.

1) The rising Vernal Equinox sun, over periods of 2,210 years, appears to shift from one constellation to another.

2) Over the same period of time, the earth's tilted axis, projected into space, seems to move from one pole star to another. This of course means that the central star around which the night sky appears to revolve gradually changes.

At the present time the earth's axis, and thus our perceived centre of the heavens, is aligned to Polaris in Ursa Minor. At the time that the Great Pyramid was built however it was aligned to the star which we now call Alpha Draconis in the constellation Draco. Such things were important to ancient cultures and marked the turning of epochs. Something of this may be seen in the Arthuriad *(cf)* where the Pendragon epoch (relating to the Pole star in Draco) is succeeded by the new epoch of Arthur (Arth = bear in Welsh, relating to the "new" Pole Star in Ursa Minor ... the "Little Bear").

Preiddu Annwn *(pr. "Preth-awe Ah-noon")* Welsh, "The Spoils of the Deep". The poem written by one of the "Taliesin" bards describing a seven-fold journey into the Underworld of Annwn *(cf)*.

Pryderi *(pr. "Pree-derry")* A Welsh Mabinogi *(cf)* hero, son of Pwyll and Rhiannon (the Welsh Persephone). Also one of the seven (including Taliesin) companions of the Blessed head (of Bran) and central character of the *Manawydan son of Llŷr* story. He appears also at the beginning of *Math fab Mathonwy*. Here he is the keeper of the sacred swine of Annwn, but these are stolen from him by Gwydion. In the subsequent fight at Maentwrog, Gwydion slays Pryderi in single combat ... with the help of a little magic.

Qabalah/Kaballah Originally an oral teaching of mystical Judaism, finally written down by Jews in mediaeval Spain. Later developed by Renaissance gentile magi for magical (as distinct from mystical) use. It subsequently became the backbone of the Hermetic Order of the Golden Dawn's *(cf)* magical philosophy and practice and continues as such in many of the mystery schools of the present "western tradition". Its diagrammatic exegesis is Otz Chim – the Tree of Life – a representation of the emanation of creation from Godhead, through four "worlds".

Sacred king In the context of this work, 'kings' or tribal chieftains of the late Neolithic and Bronze Ages who, as fathers of their tribes, consummated their relationship with the land, the mother of the tribe, in voluntary sacrificial death, so that mother nature may be bountiful and the tribe might flourish. The concept became sophisticated to the extent that the 'king' would also, in entering the ancestral land, be able to mediate with the ancestral spirits within it and be allowed to merge and join them as part of an idealised pattern in the stars.

Shaman/Shamanic Fashionable and much misunderstood concept, particularly regarding the Celtic/Brythonic mysteries. Shamanism essentially describes the magico-religious practices of nomadic peoples rather than settled agrarian ones. The perceptions of the two groups, and thus their religious experience, are totally different. These differing perceptions shape differing approaches to natural religion and religious custom. The Celtic mysteries were not (the views of celebrated commentators notwithstanding) "shamanic". The Taliesin bards were not shamen (tribal seers/medicine men), nor did they, or their predecessors, embrace features of shamanism except in an incidental sense. The fact that they had a profound grasp of star lore and thus knowledge of the precession effect and the importance of the axial "tent pole" of the heavens does not mark them out as "shamen". Neither does the fact that they saw a seven-fold Annwn set between heaven and earth, or the fact that they were aware of changes in consciousness through the adoption of totem animal forms. If these things do mark them out as shamen then the same features also make most ancient cultures, not least the ancient Egyptians, "shamanic". Shamanic features like the concepts of "tent" mysticism and "ladders to heaven" may however be seen as much in originally nomadic peoples like the ancient Hebrews, as they may in native American tribes of Plains Indians.

Sidh/sidhe *(pr. "Shee")* Irish. The dwelling places of the *Tuatha dé Danann* *(cf)*, generally associated with Bronze Age and Neolithic sacred sites, which were seen as fortresses of, and entrances to, their underworld/ underground kingdom.

Single poetic theme According to Robert Graves, Alun Lewis and others, the only true theme for a poet worthy of the name. That is to mediate and celebrate the muse/goddess, personified in the beautiful beloved. As Alun Lewis put it *"the single poetic theme of life and death ... the question of what survives of the beloved."* Graves talks about *"the test of the poet's vision in the accuracy of his portrayal of the White Goddess."*

Son of the Morning Lucifer, but not in this sense (or indeed any undogmatic and true sense) analogous with Satan. The theme of Lucifer, the light bearing archangel, falling into the Earth was not originally one of deviation and consequent sin (had it been so, one of the early Christian fathers, Bishop Lucifer of Caligari and his adherents called "Luciferians" would hardly have had much credence in the fourth century Christian church!) The doctrine of Lucifer, the "son of the morning", in fact explained the light which is inherent in creation/matter.

Sovereignty The sacred relationship of a people to their land. The validation of such sovereignty arises from the validation and empowerment of the king's relationship to the land and tribe by the feminine power. In Neolithic and Bronze Age times this seems to have been secured through the voluntary sacrifice of sacred kings *(cf)* whose sacrificial death was seen to be a consummation of the sacred marriage between the king and the mother ... the land. Thus the phrase "the king and the land are one". Sovereignty seems to have been symbolised in the axis of the earth as it pointed to the appropriate Pole Star (*see* Axis and Precession) symbolising the king's alignment to the heavenly pattern in a very phallic/potent way, related, among other things, to the turning of the seasons.

Synchronicity Word coined by the psychologist C.G. Jung to describe the synchronisation of inner experience with outer events.

Taliesin *(pr. "Tal-ee-ess-in")* Welsh name given to mythological arch bard and probably to those who were, or hoped to be, initiated into his cult. First written usage of the name seems to be from 600 AD in the *Canu Aneirin (cf)*, but the title and its mythology may well have been in oral use from much earlier. The name means many things but its most popular translation is "radiant brow". Whilst a number of bards, over many hundreds of years, took the name, it appears to have been a magical or initiatory title or rank, rather than a personal name. The obtaining of the name through initiation at the hands of the goddess Ceridwen (*cf*) is set out in the cult mythological treatise known as the *Hanes Taliesin*.

Tantric Eastern yogic term. The use of sexual energies to make changes in consciousness (see also Polarity).

Templars The *Order of the Poor Knights of Christ and the Temple of Solomon*, founded during the Crusades in Jerusalem in 1118. The Knights Templar soon attained great power, wealth and prestige. They appear to have been an esoteric fraternity following a Gnostic, and thus heretical, philosophy under the thin guise of Christian piety ... whilst pursuing their aims through diplomatic intrigue and military force. In their early days they enjoyed the patronage of St Bernard of Clairvaux, head of the Cistercian monastic order, who called them the "militia of Christ". In 1139 they were sworn to papal allegiance, which set them to some extent beyond the authority of the kings of the various countries they were drawn from. Their popular romantic image seems to have shrouded their activities as shrewd and ruthless power brokers and fanatical warriors. Having said that, their esoteric influence and indeed their influence on many of the Grail mythographers (not least Wolfram von Eschenbach) and the Taliesin initiate bards of that time cannot be overstated. Their eventual snubbing of Phillipe IV of France and the installation of Louis's own 'tame' Pope, at the time when the holy land was all but lost to the Saracens, eventually sealed their fate. Accusations of heresy and sodomy attended their suppression in 1307. Their Grand Master Jacques de Molay was executed in France in 1314.

Torc *(pr. Tork)* Celtic neck ornament which, whilst offering some protection against sword and axe blows to the neck, probably had more spiritual than practical significance.

Totem As in totem animal. Animal forms which represent powers in nature to which the magician or warrior, or the dynasty that they represent, may relate. In magical terms, as in the *Hanes Taliesin*, they are creatures of, and thus a medium to meet with, the goddess.

Tree Alphabet According to Robert Graves's thesis, set out in *The White Goddess*, the trees mentioned in the Welsh *Cad Goddeu* represent sounds/letters with particular poetic associations and may thus be used as a code key to the mystery teachings concealed in poetry of Taliesin and others. My own subsequent researches appearing in later works confirm this. In less prosaic terms, "tree alphabets" were part of the Irish Ogham *(pronounced Oh-am)* system of notation, using notches or cuts, set along a central stemline. Examples survive on standing stones in Ireland and Wales, with two examples in England. The ancient authority for Ogham is the Irish *Book of Ballymote*. See Steve Blamires, *Celtic Tree Mysteries,* Llewellyn 1997.

Tuatha dé Danann Irish. The children of the goddess Danu who were the mythological pre-human inhabitants of Ireland. The Tuatha are distinguished by their beauty and their magic. The *Book of Invasions* describes how a deal was struck whereby humans had the surface of Ireland, whilst the Tuatha occupied the area under the earth. The **sidhe** *(cf)* were the dwelling places of the chiefs of the Tuatha (who are known elsewhere as "The Lords of Faery") and were identified with Neolithic and Bronze Age burial mounds. The Dagda, the head of the Tuatha (and father of Brighid), was said to have the impressive Newgrange tomb as his sidhe.

Tylwyth Teg *(pr. "Tul-uth-Teg")* Welsh, meaning "fair folk", the beings of Faery who may be considered to be the Welsh equivalent of the Tuatha dé Danann.

Underworld Distinctions made between the terms "Underworld", "Otherworld" and "Paradise" are arbitrary and misleading in terms of Celtic mythology. It is all one place and process, as the catalytic area between the natural and archetypal worlds. Ancient Celtic mythographers did not feel the need to invent nit-picking terms to label everything and place it in the neat boxes of modern academe. This catalytic area is therefore best described as an 'underworld', simply in the sense that it is symbolised as being 'below' the natural landscape. As such it is the formative area adjacent to the natural world and, by virtue of its underground darkness, adjacent also to the night sky of the archetypal 'starry' world. Certainly it has its divisions into various aspects of inner experience. Typically these are seven, but they are by no means separate, and overlap and interact readily.

This Welsh underworld is **Annwn** *(cf)*. the Irish is *Tír nan Óg* (the land of the Ever Young). These are areas of inner dynamic and evolution and should not be confused with the classical gloom of some static Hades of lost souls.

Ychen Bannog Welsh, "Long-horned Oxen", which appear in Welsh myth and legend – notably the two Ychen Bannog of Llandewi Brefi. This particular tale signifies the stellar associations of the oxen. The actual oxen cited were probably however the long horned *Bos primogenius* that existed in Wales in pre-Roman times.

Select Bibliography

Works cited

✓Berg, Wendy & Harris, Mike. *Polarity Magic*. Llewellyn, 2002.

De Santillana & Von Dechand. *Hamlet's Mill*. Godine, 1977.

Ellis, Peter Beresford. *The Druids*. Constable, 1994.

Graves, Robert. *The White Goddess*. Faber, 1961

Griffen, Toby D. *Names from the Dawn of British Legend*. Llanerch, 1994.

Jones, Gwyn and Thomas (trans.) *The Mabinogion*. Dragons Dream, 1982.

Matthews, John. *Taliesin*. Aquarian, 1991.

Monmouth, Geoffrey of. *The History of the Kings of Britain* (trans. Lewis Thorpe). Penguin, 1966.

Morganwg, Iolo. *The Triads of Britain*. Wildwood House, 1977.

Pennar, Meirion. *The Black Book of Carmarthen*. Llanerch, 1989.

Pennar, Meirion. *Taliesin Poems*. Llanerch, 1988.

Squire, Charles. *Celtic Myth and Legend*. Newcastle Publishing, 1975.

Stewart, R.J. *The Underworld Initiation*. Aquarian, 1985.

Stone, Brian (trans.) *Sir Gawain and the Green Knight*. Penguin, 1972.

Thom, Alexander; Thom, Archibald Stevenson; Burl, Aubrey. *Stone rows and standing stones: Britain, Ireland and Brittany*. B.A.R., 1990.

Velikovsky, Immanuel. *Worlds in Collision*. Macmillan, 1950.

Also recommended

Blamires, Steve. *The Irish Celtic Magical Tradition*. Aquarian, 1992.

Bord, Janet & Colin. *A Guide to Ancient Sites in Britain*. Paladin, 1976.

Duncan, Anthony. *Elements of Celtic Christianity*. Element, 1992.

✓Knight, Gareth. *The Secret Tradition in Arthurian Legend*. Weiser, 1996.

Merry, Eleanor C. *The Flaming Door*. Floris, 1992.

✓Stewart, R. J. *The Prophetic Vision of Merlin*. Arkana, 1986.

Index

Lightning Source UK Ltd.
Milton Keynes UK
UKOW051929100212

187067UK00001B/240/P